ܟܬܒܐ

ܕܬܘܪܵܨ ܡܡܠܠܐ ܘܡܦ̈ܩܢܐ

ܕܠܫܢܐ ܐܪܡܝܐ ܚܕܬܐ - ܟܠܕܝܐ

ܠܫܢܐ ܕܟܠܕ̈ܝܐ ܕܡܕܢܚܝܬܐ

ܘܡܦ̈ܩܢܐ ܕܢܣܘܐ ܒܒܝܬ ܢܗܪ̈ܝܢ

ܟܬܒܐ ܬܪܝܢܐ

ܒܝ ܡܫܝܚܐ ܡܝܟܐܝܠ ܒܙܝ

ܡܫܠܡܢܘܬܐ ܬܠܝܬܝܬܐ

ܫܢܬ ܒ̈ܝܛ

THE ADVANCED HANDBOOK OF THE MODERN ARAMAIC LANGUAGE CHALDEAN DIALECT

VOLUME III

BY

FR. MICHAEL J. BAZZI

Third Edition

2019

ISBN: 978-1-941464-00-7
Published by arrangement with Bazzi Publishing and Let in the Light Publishing

www.LetintheLightPublishing.com

Table of Contents

PREFACE

FLEXIBILITY IN USE OF CERTAIN VOWELS

Various traditions in Modern Aramaic use ܙܩܦܐ instead of ܦܬܚܐ and vice versa, and ܙܠܡܐ ܩܫܝܐ instead of ܙܠܡܐ ܦܫܝܩܐ and vice versa. To respect these various traditions, this book does not insist upon which of these vowels should be used. If the reader considers that ܙܩܦܐ should be used instead of ܦܬܚܐ or vice versa, or that ܙܠܡܐ ܩܫܝܐ should be used instead of ܙܠܡܐ ܦܫܝܩܐ or vice versa, he or she should feel free to use his or her preference; for example: of ܒܒܠ Babylon, or ܒܒܠ also ܓܚܟܠܗ to laugh or ܓܚܟܠܐ.

USE OF THE LETTERS ܗ OR ܐ FOR THE THIRD PERSON SINGULAR PAST TENSE VERBS

In Modern Aramaic, verbs indicating the third person singular, past tense can end with either ܐ or ܗ In this book ܗ is always used at the end of such verbs, for example: ܩܒܠܗ to receive. The letter preceding ܗ in such verbs will always have ܙܠܡܐ ܩܫܝܐ ܠ for example: ܦܠܛܠܗ to exit.

ADDITIONAL LETTER IN THE MIDDLE OF THE WORD

Some Modern Aramaic verbs in the past tense have the letter ܝ in the middle without a vowel. There is no rule to control which of the verbs need this addition. Example: to enter ܥܒܝܪܠܗ to catch ܕܒܝܩܠܗ to sing ܙܡܝܪܠܗ

ADDITIONAL LETTER ܐ IN THE MIDDLE OF THE WORD

Some Modern Aramaic words have the letter ܐ in the middle, without a vowel. There is no rule to control which of the words need this addition ܐ for example: fruit ܦܐܪܐ rock ܟܐܦܐ to commit sin ܚܛܐܠܗ .

THE OPTION OF WRITING THE LETTER ܬ OR ܛ IN MODERN ARAMIAC WORDS

In writing or speaking Modern Aramaic there is the option of using either of the two letters ܛ or ܬ

For example: bag ܓܢܛܐ or ܓܢܬܐ car ܛܘܡܒܝܠ or ܬܘܡܒܝܠ .

Introduction

In my first book, the "Aramaic Language-Chaldean Dialogue", I introduced the reader to reading and writing the twenty two letters of the Aramaic alphabet, the eleven sounds, the Estrangela letters, the seven vowels and the Aramaic numbers. Conversational phrases in modern Chaldean Aramaic, in the dialect of Chaldeans, were introduced in each lesson, providing a vocabulary of more than five hundred words that are used in modern Aramaic literature.

This second book will introduce the reader to the language spoken today by more than 800,000 Christians from the Middle East. A working knowledge of modern Chaldean Aramaic grammar will be developed. The reader will also become familiar with the essential vocabulary used in modern Chaldean Aramaic literature, and will learn modern Chaldean Aramaic words, with the emphasis placed on the roots of nouns and verbs. In addition, this book will enable theologians and scholars to read and understand the spiritual, liturgical and historical writings of Chaldean writers. Philologists who are interested in the modern form of Chaldean Aramaic will also find this book useful.

The modern Chaldean Aramaic dialect is currently used by Chaldean Catholics living in the region of Nineveh, especially in the following 10 villages: 1- Tilkepe, 2- Alqosh,3- Tesqopa,4- Biqopa,5- Botnayeh, 6- Karemlash, 7- Sharafiya, 8- Benydwaya, 9- Aynbaqra, 10- Dashqutan, and two Syriac cities 1- Qaraqosh(Baghdayda) 2- Bartilla.

According to the United Nations Educational Scientific and Cultural Organization (UNESCO), "a language spoken by fewer than 2,500 people is considered extinct. A language needs at least 100,000 speakers to pass from generation to generation. Society loses a rich source of history when a language dies."

Aramaic, a Semitic language, is more than 3,500 years old. Records indicate that it was used by the people of upper North region of Mesopotamia from the fourteenth century B.C. The records also show that Aramaic was used by most people of Mesopotamia from the eighth century B.C., to the sixth century B.C. By the sixth century B.C. Aramaic had become the lingua franca throughout the Middle East.

while the Jewish people were exiled to Nineveh 721B.C. and to Babylon 587 B.C., Aramaic became their language as well. When they returned to Palestine in the fifth century B.C., it remained their main language. When Christ was born, Aramaic was the spoken language in Palestine. This was the language used in schools and daily life. The early church also prayed and preached in Aramaic. Therefore, when the Chaldeans converted to Christianity and established the Church of the East in Mesopotamia, at the end of the first and beginning of the second century A.D., Aramaic was the liturgical language. Aramaic is still used in its scholastic form (Gushma or Leshana A̲ttiq̲a) by the Chaldean Catholic Church, the Assyrian Church of the East and the Syriac Churches in their liturgical prayers.

Aramaic was adopted by many nations and is still alive in different dialects. One of them is the modern Chaldean dialect, which is spoken by people who belong to the Chaldean Catholic Church.

Scholastic Aramaic utilizes a definite grammatical system. By utilizing specific rules, grammar determines how the words of a language relate to each other. Using grammar a person is able to read, write and speak a language correctly. Although this is true for Classical Aramaic, it is not as true for Modern Aramaic, especially the dialect used by Chaldeans of the cities and villages of Nineveh in Mesopotamia, modern day Iraq. In this case, it is not possible to discern an exact grammatical system for Modern Aramaic. This book will tackle this problem.

I hope to help all Chaldeans who have left their homeland and now live in other parts of the world, those who did not have the opportunity to learn the language, and the modern generation, to achieve a standard form of reading, writing and speaking Modern Aramaic-Chaldean. I also hope to help those Chaldeans who currently live in the cities and villages of Nineveh to achieve the same standard with the use of this book. Thus, I hope to help my fellow Chaldeans preserve our heritage and tradition by keeping the essence of the language spoken by Jesus Christ alive throughout the ages.

LESSON ONE ܦܘܫܩܐ ܩܕܡܝܐ

THE 22 LETTERS OF THE ARAMAIC ALPHABET ܐܬܘܬܐ ܕܠܫܢܐ ܐܪܡܝܐ

The alphabet of both Scholastic and Modern Aramaic-Chaldean is the same and has 22 letters.

1	ܐ	ܐܠܦ
2	ܒ	ܒܝܬ
3	ܓ	ܓܡܠ
4	ܕ	ܕܠܬ
5	ܗ	ܗܐ
6	ܘ	ܘܐܘ
7	ܙ	ܙܝܢ
8	ܚ	ܚܝܬ
9	ܛ	ܛܝܬ
10	ܝ	ܝܘܕ
11	ܟ	ܟܦ ܘܟܦ(ܟ) (ܟ)

12	ܠ	ܠܡܕ
13	ܡ	ܡܝܡ ܘܡܝܡ(ܡ)
14	ܢ	ܢܘܢ ܘܢܘܢ(ܢ) (ܢ)
15	ܣ	ܣܡܟܬ
16	ܥ	ܥܐ
17	ܦ	ܦܐ
18	ܨ	ܨܕܐ
19	ܩ	ܩܘܦ
20	ܪ	ܪܝܫ
21	ܫ	ܫܝܢ
22	ܬ	ܬܘ ܘܬܘ ܬܐ

Due to the influence of neighboring languages, six of the twenty two letters were modified in sound in classical Aramaic: (ܒ ܓ ܕ ܟ ܦ ܬ) and were added to the alphabet. However, only four of the six letters (ܒ ܓ ܕ ܬ) were given new sounds while two of them (ܒ : ܦ) for some unknown reason were pronounced like the letter (ܘ) **waw = w(ܒ: ܦ)**.

Of the six modified letters, five were modified simply by adding a dot underneath the letter, and one (ܦ) by merely adding a semi-circle attached below the letter (ܦ̮).

Letters		6 Sounds and their Pronounciation			Examples	
ܒ	b	ܒ݂	wa	ܒ݂ܵ	ܓܲܒ݂ܪܵܐ	man
ܓ	g	ܓ݂	gh	ܓ݂ܵ	ܦܲܓ݂ܪܵܐ	body
ܕ	d	ܕ݂	dh	ܕ݂ܵ	ܬܲܠܡܝܼܕ݂ܵܐ	student
ܟ	k	ܟ݂	kh	ܟ݂ܵ	ܐܘܼܟ݂ܠܵܐ	food
ܦ	p w	ܦ݂	wa	ܦ݂ܵ	ܢܲܦ݂ܫܵܐ	soul
ܬ	t	ܬ݂	th	ܬ݂ܵ	ܒܬܘܼܠܬ݂ܵܐ	virgin

These six sounds are expressed in one word **BG**

BGaDiKPaTh

ܒܓܲܕܟܦܲܬ (ܒ݂ ܓ݂ ܕ݂ ܟ݂ ܦ݂ ܬ݂)

An additional five sounds were also added to the Modern Aramaic alphabet:

Letters		5 extra Sounds and their pronounciation			Examples	
ܦ	p	ܦ̮	f	ܦ̮ܵ	ܦ̮ܝܼܠܵܐ	elephant
ܟ	k	ܟ̰	ch	ܟ̰ܵ	ܟ̰ܝܼܪܟ̰ܝܼܪܟ̰ܵܐ	cricket
ܨ	ss	ܨ̃	dh	ܨ̃ܵ	ܨ̃ܒܵܥ	hyena
ܓ	g	ܓ̰	j	ܓ̰ܵ	ܓ̰ܲܪܲܪܵܐ	grinding mill
ܦ	p	ܦ̃	v	ܦ̃ܵ	ܦ̃ܝܕܝܘ	video

These five sounds are expressed in one word **(FaCHDHaJaV)**.

(ܦ̮ ܟ̰ ܨ̃ ܓ̰ ܦ̃) ܦ̮ܲܟ̰ܨ̃ܲܓ̰ܦ̃

Note: Some writers use the sound **kh** for the letter ܫ with thick dot above ܫ݂ for example: ܡܸܫ݂ܚܵܐ **oil**

Thus, as mentioned above, Modern Aramaic alphabet consists of 22 letters and eleven sounds.

ܐܬܘܬܐ ܐܠܦܒܝܬܐ : ܙܘܥܐ ܘܢܘܩܙܐ

ܐܬܘܬܐ ܟܠܕܝܬܐ ܡܢ ܬܪܬܐ ܦܢܝܬܐ. ܐܬܦܠܓܘ ܠܙܘܥܐ ܘܢܘܩܙܐ. ܘܐܝܟ ܗܘܐ ܕܝܕܝܥ ܐܬܘܬܐ ܕܐܘܠܦܢܐ ܕܐܝܟܕܡܘܢܐ ܘܡܢ ܩܫܝܫܘܬܐ ܕܟܘܒܬܐ. ܘܡܫܟܠܠܐ ܕܦܘܫܐ ܡܢ ܡܫܡܥܢܐ ܘܡܬܚܝܢܐ ܘܡܢ ܚܘܪܐ (ܠܒܪܢܐ) ܘܕܥܬܐ(ܡܡܥܢܐ) ܗܘܠܝ ܐܝܬܝܗܝ ܗܝ ܚܕܬܐ ܘܟܠܝ ܦܠܚܐ ܒܫܩܠܬܐ ܐܝ ܕܡܬܩܢܝ ܐܬܘܬܐ ܒܠܗ. ܗܕ ܙܘܥܐ ܘܢܘܩܙܐ ܡܬܦܢܝܢܝ ܘܡܢܗ ܕܟܠܝܗܝ ܠܟܝܢܐ ܐܬܘܬܐ ܐܝܬܘ ܐܪܒܥܐ ܙܘܥܐ ܦܬܝܚܐ:

ܐ : ܙܘܥ (ܦܬܚܐ)

ܒ : ܐܚܝܐ

ܓ : ܛܘܦܐ (ܡܫܚܠܦܢܐ)

ܕ : ܣܝܡܐ

ܘܟܠ ܙܘܥܐ ܐܝܬܘܗܝ ܠܗܘܢ ܫܡܗܐ ܘܓܘܢܐ ܐܬܘܬܐ ܐܝܬܘ ܗܘܝܐܠܦ ܫܡܗܐ. ܡܬܚܙܝܢܝ ܐܝܟܢ

ܐ :	ܚܒܨ ܩܪܝܐ	ܙ :	ܙܩܦ
ܒ :	ܪܒܨܟ	ܚ :	ܐܒܢ(ܐܒ)
ܓ :	ܐܪܐ	ܛ :	ܐܝܠܘܢ(ܐܝܠܘܢ)
ܕ :	ܚܒܨ	ܝ :	ܪܒܨܐ ܐܪܝܟܐ (ܡܫܚܠܦ ܐ)
ܗ :	ܪܒܨ	ܝܐ :	ܪܒܨܐ ܩܪܝܐ (ܡܫܚܠܦ ܒ)
ܘ :	ܣܘܓܕܝ	ܝܒ :	ܚܒܨ ܐܪܝܟܐ

ܗܘܝ ܫܡܗܐ ܐܝܬܘ ܐܪܒܥ ܙܘܥܐ. ܘܗܘܝ ܙܘܥܐ ܐܝܬܘ ܙܘܥܐ ܬܦܩܬܐ ܡܬܚܙܝܢܝ ܐܝܟܢ ܐ : ܚܕܢܝܬܐ ܒ : ܬܪܝܢܝܬܐ ܓ : ܬܠܝܬܝܬܐ ܕ : ܐܪܒܥܝܬܐ ܗ : ܚܡܫܝܬܐ ܘ : ܫܬܝܬܐ. ܗܘܝ ܚܕܟܐ ܐܝܬܘ ܐܪܒܥ ܘܡܫܚܠܦ ܙܘܥܐ. ܘܗܘܝ ܙܘܥܐ ܐܝܬܘ ܡܬܩܪܝܢ ܡܫܬܢܝܢܐ (ܢܘܩܙܐ). ܘܟܠ ܡܫܬܢܝܢܐ ܐܝܬܘ ܡܬܩܪܝ ܕܦܘܩ (ܠܦܘܩܢܐ ܕܠܫܢܐ).

◆ ◆ ◆ ◆ ◆ ◆ ◆ ◆ ◆ ◆

VOCABULARY

English	Aramaic
field, farmland	ܚܩܠܐ
to harvest	ܚܨܕܠܗ (ܚܨܕܐ)
Thursday	ܚܡܫܒܫܒܐ
farmer	ܚܪܬܐ
mountain north	ܛܘܪܐ
August	ܛܒܚ (ܐܒ)
knowledge	ܝܕܥܬܐ
teaching	ܝܘܠܦܢܐ
day	ܝܘܡܐ
month	ܝܪܚܐ
each	ܟܠ
all	ܟܠܝ
star	ܟܘܟܒܐ (ܟܘܟܒܐ)
January	ܟܢܘܢ ܐܚܪܝ
December	ܟܢܘܢ ܩܕܡܝܐ
Sunday	ܚܕܒܫܒܐ
autumn	ܬܪܘܦܐ (ܡܥܪܒܢܬܐ)
October	ܬܫܪܝܢ ܩܕܡܝܐ
	ܬܫܪܝܢ ܐ
November	ܬܫܪܝܢ ܐܚܪܝ
	ܬܫܪܝܢ ܒ
west	ܡܥܪܒܐ
east	ܡܕܢܚܐ
April	ܢܝܣܢ

English	Aramaic
May	ܐܝܪ
September	ܐܝܠܘܠ (ܐܝܠܘܠ)
taking care	ܐܒܓܠܐ ܕܝܢܐ
these	ܐܢܝ
they	ܐܢܝ
astronomy	ܐܣܛܪܘܢܘܡܝܐ
Wednesday	ܐܪܒܥܒܫܒܐ
February	ܫܒܛ
March	ܐܕܪ
father	ܒܒܐ
spring	ܒܗܪ
north	ܓܪܒܝܐ
century	ܕܪܐ
to put	ܕܪܝܠܗ
land, south, field	ܕܫܬܐ
product, harvest, crops	ܕܓܠܐ
to give	ܗܘܠܗ
were	ܗܘܐ
season, time	ܙܒܢܐ
to cultivate	ܙܪܥܠܗ
to plant	
crop, plant	ܙܪܥܐ (ܡܙܪܥܢܘܬܐ)
grower, planter	ܙܪܘܥܐ
June	ܚܙܝܪܢ

VOCABULARY Cont.

English	Aramaic	English	Aramaic
Saturday, a week	ܫܒܬܐ	to wait	ܣܟܝܪܗ
season change	ܫܘܚܠܦܐ	winter	ܣܬܘܐ
		Friday	ܥܪܘܒܬܐ
name	ܫܡܐ	air	ܦܘܚܐ
year	ܫܢܬܐ	worker	ܦܠܚܐ
beginning	ܫܪܝܬܐ	special, chosen	ܦܪܝܫܐ
Monday	ܬܘܪܫܒܐ	designated	
south	ܬܝܡܢܐ	first, early	ܩܕܡܝܐ
Tuesday	ܬܠܝܘܫܒܐ	summer	ܩܝܛܐ
July	ܬܡܘܙ	reading	ܩܪܝܢܐ
		movement walking	ܪܚܫܬܐ

LESSON TWO ܦܣܘܩܐ ܕܬܪܝܢ

GENERAL INTRODUCTION

I. ESTRANGELA AND COMMON SCRIPT

There are two forms of script used by Eastern Aramaic writers: Estrangela and "common" script. The letters used in common script are smaller than those used in Estrangela. Estrangela has been in use since the second century BC. Only six of the 22 Aramaic letters have different shapes in Estrangela than in common script.

The Estrangela Letters ܐܣܛܪܢܓܝܠܐ

Out of the 22 alphabet letters, the following six letters have different shape when writing in Estrangela:

ܐ ܒ ܓ ܕ ܗ ܘ ܙ ܚ ܛ ܝ ܟ

ܠ ܡ ܢ ܣ ܥ ܦ ܨ ܩ ܪ ܫ ܬ

Letters					Examples	
1.	a	ܐ	ܐ	ܐ	ܐܒ	August
2.	d	ܕ	ܕ	ܕ	ܕܪܐ	century
3.	h	ܗ	ܗ	ܗ	ܐܠܗܐ	God
4.	m	ܡ	ܡ	ܡ	ܡܪܝܡ	Mary
5.	r	ܪ	ܪ	ܪ	ܪܒܐ	great
6.	t	ܬ	ܬ	ܬ	ܬܪܒܝܬܐ	education

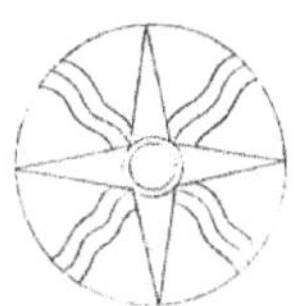

Note: • **No vowels are used when writing in Estrangela**

• **The final m is the same** writing in both normal or Estrangela

The "common script" of the Aramaic letters is 22:

ܐ ܒ ܓ ܕ   ܗ ܘ ܙ   ܚ ܛ ܝ   ܟ (ܟ ܟ)

ܠ ܡ (ܡ)   ܢ (ܢ ܢ)   ܣ ܥ ܦ ܨ   ܩ ܪ ܫ ܬ

II. JOINING AND ENJOINING LETTERS

Of the 22 Aramaic letters, 14 are joined with both a preceding and following letter (the joining letters), while the remaining eight (the enjoining letters) are joined with proceeding letters only. These eight letters are not joined at their left to the letters, which follow them. Each of these eight letters standalone (are not attached) when preceded by one of the eight enjoining letters. The eight enjoining letters

Letters	Examples			
ܐ	ܐܝܕܐ	hand	ܩܒܪܐ	tomb
ܕ	ܥܒܕܐ	slave	ܩܪܕܐ	monkey
ܗ	ܥܗܐ	time	ܢܘܗܪܐ	light
ܘ	ܚܘܐ	Eve	ܙܘܙܐ	money
ܙ	ܚܙܘܐ	Vision	ܘܙܐ	goose
ܨ	ܩܨܪܐ	Palace	ܨܨܪܐ	cockroach
ܪ	ܡܪܝܐ	Lord	ܢܗܪܐ	river
ܬ	ܒܬܘܠܬܐ	virgin	ܒܨܪܬܐ	examination, demand

III. THE SUPPRESSOR ܡܒܛܠܢܐ

Sometimes a letter appears in a word but is not pronounced, it is silent. This is indicated by use of the suppressor (ܡܒܛܠܢܐ – ̄) a slanted line placed above a letter. It is placed above only the following eight letters: ܐ ܗ ܘ ܠ ܢ ܡ ܬ ܪ

Example: human being ܒܪܢܫܐ

Note: the suppressor is used with small and Estrangela letters.

IV. DOUBLING ܡܫܢܝܘܬܐ 1

The pronunciation of a letter is sometimes doubled when it is:

a) Modified by a vowel like ܚܘܒܐ love

b) follows either of two vowels

ܛܒܚܐ	ܛܰܒܳܚܳܐ	cook
ܘܠܒܐ ܥܒܕܐ	ܠܶܒܳܐ	heart

V. THE PLURAL POINTS ܣܝܡܐ

A plural noun is indicated by placing two small horizontal dashes (ܣܝܡܐ ̈–) above one of its letters. These dashes are called the plural point.

Example: ܡܰܠܟܳܐ king = ܡܰܠܟܳܐ̈ kings

The two dashes are usually placed over a non- vocalized letter at the end of the word. However, when the letter ܪ is in the word, the short horizontal line over the letter ܪ does not appear, and is instead replaced by the plural points ܪ̈ . When a plural ܪ̈ has a ̈– the usual two points for the ̈– are not used and the ̈– is instead indicated by placing only one point over the left dash of the plural points, for example ܫܰܦܺܝܪܬܳܐ beautiful, becomes ܫܰܦܺܝܪ̈ܬܳܐ

If there is more than one ܪ in a word, the plural points will be placed on the final ܪ for example:

ܙܰܠܺܝܩܳܐ ray or glow becomes ܙܰܠܺܝܩܶ̈ܐ

Note: the plural sign is used with small and Estrangela letters.

VI. VOWELS ܙܰܘ̈ܥܶܐ

The Aramaic language has seven vowels. These are listed below with their names and examples.

The Seven Aramaic Vowels ܙܰܘ̈ܥܶܐ : ܡܫܰܚܠܦܶ̈ܐ : ܦܫܝܛܐ

	Vowel Name		Sound			Example	
1	ܙܩܦܐ	ܳ	long a	aa	ܡܳ	ܡܳܪܳܐ	Lord
2	ܦܬܚܐ	ܰ	short a	ah	ܡܰ	ܡܰܠܟܳܐ	King
3	ܙܠܡܐ ܦܫܝܩܐ	ܶ	short i	i	ܡܶ	ܡܶܫܚܳܐ	Oil
4	ܙܠܡܐ ܩܫܝܐ	ܹ	long e	ay	ܪܹ	ܪܹܫܳܐ	Head
5	ܪܘܚܐ	ܘܿ	long o	oh	ܘܿ	ܢܚܝܪܐ	Nose
6	ܪܒܨܐ	ܘܼ	long oo	oo	ܘܼ	ܙܘܼܙܳܐ	Money
7	ܚܒܨܐ	ܝܼ	long y	ee	ܝܼ	ܡܫܝܼܚܳܐ	Christ

Note : Some grammarians add an eight vowel named **Assaqa (ܥܨܳܨܳܐ)** When a vocalized letter with zlama psheeqa precedes the uvocalized letter ܝ **e** : Example The house of El (Beth ayl) ܒܶܝܬ ܐܝܠ

We may find the seven vowels composed in the following sentences:

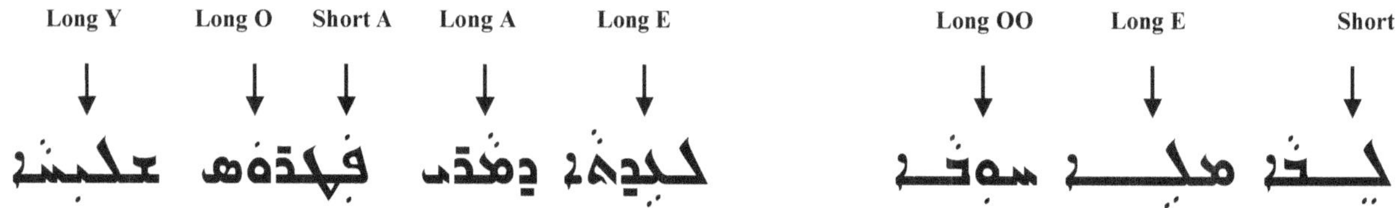

(A heart filled with love for the church of St. Peter the apostle)

Note that the first four vowels are designated by dots which can be applied to all the letters of the Aramaic alphabet. The last three vowels are formed with either the letter ܘ or ܝ and a dot placed above or below them. ܘ can have a dot placed either above ܘܿ or below it ܘܼ The letter ܝ has a dot placed below it ܝܼ only. Once either of these letters has such dots it is no longer a consonant but a vowel. When the first four vowels end a word a slient Alap is added but not pronounced.

	Vowels		Examples	
1	ܦܵ	ܙܩܵܦܵܐ	ܦܵܦܵܐ	Pope
2	ܦܲ	ܦܬܵܚܵܐ	ܦܲܠܵܚܵܐ	worker
3	ܦܸ	ܙܠܵܡܵܐ ܦܫܝܼܩܵܐ	ܦܸܩܵܐ	frog
4	ܦܹ	ܙܠܵܡܵܐ ܩܫܝܵܐ	ܦܹܐܪܵܐ	fruit
5	ܘܿ	ܪܘܵܚܵܐ	ܦܘܿܩܵܐ	nose
6	ܘܼ	ܪܒܵܨܵܐ	ܦܘܼܫܵܩܵܐ	translation
7	ܝܼ	ܚܒܵܨܵܐ	ܦܝܼܠܵܐ	elephant

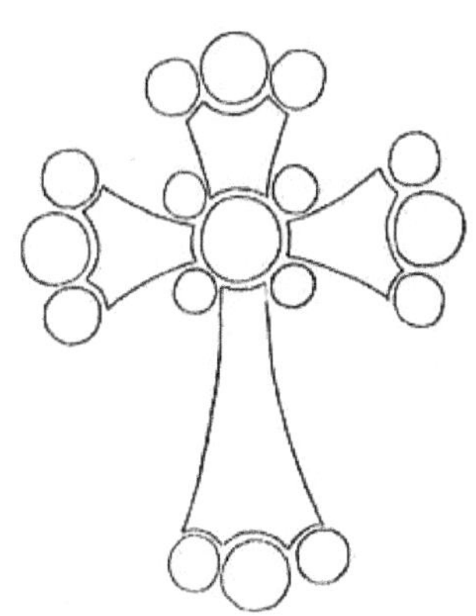

ܝܘܕܝܐ ܘܐܪܡܝܐ : ܫܠܝܡܘܢ ܘܚܝܪܡ

ܡܢ ܒܬܪܗ ܕܕܘܝܕ. ܡܬܡܠܟܠܗ ܫܠܝܡܘܢ. ܐܝܟ ܡܠܟܐ ܚܕܐ. ܘܡܠܟܘܬܗ ܗܘܬ ܡܠܟܘܬܐ. ܕܡܫܝܢܐ ܐܝܟ ܫܢܝܐ ܕܝܢ. ܒܗܘ ܙܒܢܐ ܐܢܫܐ ܒܢܝܢܐ ܒܝܬܘܬܐ. ܘܒܢܝܢ ܡܕܝܢܬܐ ܕܪܒܝܬܐ. ܕܡܬܩܪܝܢ ܒܫܘܠܛܢܐ ܐܢܫܐ ܕܗܘܐ ܘܒܢܝܢܐ ܕܐܝܟ. ܗܘ ܡܢܝܐ ܠܫܢܐ ܟܠܕܝܐ. ܕܐܝܬܘܗ ܕܘܡܝܐ ܡܢ ܠܫܢܐ ܐܪܡܝܐ. ܠܫܢܐ ܕܡܬܦܫܩܠܗ ܒܝܬܗ. ܗܪܟܐ ܐܝܟ ܡܠܟܐ. ܘܐܝܬܘܗ ܗܪܟܐ ܗܘܝܐ ܘܡܠܟܐ ܡܕܝܢܬܐ. ܘܒܝܬܗ ܡܬܦܫܩܠܗ ܘܡܬܘܠܝܠܗ. ܘܗܘܠܗ ܘܡܝܬܠܗ ܟܬܒܐ ܟܠܕܝܐ. ܡܢ ܙܒܢܐ ܕܡܠܟܐ ܘܐܪܡܝܐ. ܗܘܠ ܕܪܐ ܐܢܫܝܐ ܕܐܬܠܐ ܕܗܘܐ. ܟܠܕܝܐ ܡܬܚܫܒܐ ܘܡܬܩܪܒܐ ܒܠܫܢܐ ܐܪܡܝܐ ܝܗܢܐ. ܠܟܢ ܐܝܟ ܙܒܢܐ. ܘܡܢ ܒܬܪ ܕܐܬܐ ܕܐܘܡܬܐ ܐܝܟ ܒܡܠܟܐ ܐܢܫܝܐ. ܐܚܪܢܐ ܗܢܘܢ ܗܘܝܢ ܐܝܟ ܠܘܬܢ ܐܪܡܝܐ ܟܠܕܝܐ. ܡܬܝܕܥܬܐ ܟܠܕܝܬܐ ܕܐܝܬ ܗܘܝܢ ܕܫܪܝܠܗ ܒܗܘܝܐ. ܒܝܬܠܗ ܐܝܟ ܠܘܬܢܘܬܗ ܗܢܘܢ ܕܠܫܢܐ ܕܡܘܕܥܝܢ. ܘܐܝܟ ܕܫܪܝܠܗ ܒܕܥܬܐ. ܠܫܢܐ ܕܟܬܒܝܐ ܐܚܪܢܐ ܐܝܬܘܗ. ܘܐܝܟ ܕܫܪܝܠܗ ܒܗܘܕܝܐ ܠܫܢܐ ܗܘܕܝܐ ܒܝܬܠܗ ܒܠܘܬܢܘܬܗ. ܘܐܝܟ ܕܗܘܝܐ ܒܒܝܬ ܗܢܘܢ ܦܘܠܚܢܐ ܐܚܪܢܐ ܠܡܫܝܚܝܘܬܗ

ܘܡܢ ܗܪܟܐ ܠܫܢܐ ܐܪܡܝܐ ܟܠܕܝܐ ܫܪܝܐ ܒܝܠܗ ܐܪܡܝܐ ܝܗܢܐ. ܡܬܝܕܥܐ ܠܫܢܐ ܝܗܘܕܐ. ܘܗܘ ܒܝܠܗ ܗܢܝܐ ܫܪܫܐ ܕܗܘܐ ܟܠܕܝܐ ܕܝܗܘܕܐ ܕܦܘܠܚ ܠܟܠܕܝܐ ܕܝܥܩܘܒ. ܫܠܝܡܘܢ ܚܕ ܡܠܟܐ ܕܫܪܝܠܗ ܒܝܫܘܥܐ. ܘܡܢܝܐ ܗܘܠܗ ܒܠܫܢܐ ܕܝܗܘܕܝܐ ܒܠܫܢܐ ܒܝܬܝܐ ܘܐܝܟ ܒܟܠ ܟܠܕܝܐ. ܐܚܪܢܐ ܘܥܒܪܝܐ ܝܘܢܝܐ ܘܫܡܝܐ. ܕܡܬܩܪܝܢ ܠܫܢܐ ܐܪܡܝܐ ܫܪܫܐ ܟܠܕܝܐ.ܡܬܡܠܟܐ ܒܫܡܐ ܕܡܠܟܐ. ܗܘ ܐܢܫܐ ܘܫܢܝܐ ܘܫܒܝܐ

◆ ◆ ◆ ◆ ◆ ◆ ◆ ◆ ◆ ◆

VOCABULARY

English	Aramaic	English	Aramaic
dialogue,	ܗܲܒܵܠܵܐ ܘܫܩܵܠܵܐ	to enter	ܥܒܵܪܹܗ
conversation		nation	ܐܘܼܡܬܵܐ
give and take		child	ܝܲܠܵܐ
also	ܗܲܡ	Iran, Persia	ܐܝܼܪܵܢ
he was	ܗܘܵܐ	thousand	ܐܲܠܦܵܐ
we were	ܗܘܝܼܬܵܐ	God	ܐܲܠܵܗܵܐ
small, young	ܙܥܘܿܪܵܐ	with	ܐܡܝܼܕ
future	ܙܲܒܢܵܐ ܕܐܵܬܹܐ	people	ܐܢܵܫܹܐ
to live	ܚܝܵܝܹܗ	women	ܐܢܸܫܹܐ
friend	ܚܲܒܪܵܐ	to want	ܒܥܵܝܠܹܗ
some	ܚܲܕܟܡܵܐ	woman, wife	ܒܲܟܬܵܐ
life	ܚܲܝܹܐ	together	ܒܲܗܕܵܕܹܐ
young woman	ܚܡܬܵܐ	in	ܒܓܵܘ
another	ܐܚܪܹܢܵܐ (ܚܝܼܢܵܐ)	between two rivers	ܒܹܝܬ ܢܲܗܪܝܢ
last, final	ܚܪܵܝܵܐ (ܐܚܪܵܝܵܐ)	Mesopotamia	
new	ܚܕܼܬܵܐ	home	ܒܲܝܬܵܐ
to him	ܛܵܠܹܗ	child , boy, son	ܒܪܘܿܢܵܐ
mother	ܝܡܵܐ	once , one time	ܓܵܗܵܐ
when	ܟܘܼܕ	husband, man	ܓܲܒܪܵܐ
mouth	ܦܸܡܵܐ	similar to	ܓܒܝܼܕ
to mix	ܟܘܼܓܠܹܗ	look alike	
to write	ܟܬܵܒܘܼܠܹܗ	terrace, balcony	ܓܲܪܒܝܼܬܵܐ
language, tongue	ܠܸܫܵܢܵܐ	young man	ܓܘܿܢܡܵܐ
it is not	ܠܲܝܬܹܗ	now	ܕܗܵܐ
but	ܠܟܹܢ	branch	ܕܘܼܡܟܵܐ

VOCABULARY

Cont.

English	Aramaic	English	Aramaic
people	ܐܢܫܐ	to teach	ܡܘܠܦܠܗ
Arabic	ܥܪܒܝܐ	to talk, to speak	ܡܘܚܟܠܗ
old	ܥܬܝܩܐ	to let walk	ܡܘܪܫܠܗ
to work	ܦܠܚܠܗ	to let use	
joy, happiness	ܦܨܝܚܘܬܐ	to tell, to say	ܡܪܝܗ (ܐܡܪܝܗ)
Persian	ܦܪܣܝܐ	therefore	ܡܢ ܗܕܐ
clear	ܨܦܝܐ	that is why	
Holy, Saint	ܩܕܝܫܐ	to call, to shout	ܡܥܘܝܛܠܗ
Kurdish	ܟܘܪܕܝܐ	to pray	ܡܨܘܠܝܠܗ
Apostle	ܫܠܝܚܐ	Lord	ܡܪܝܐ (ܡܪܐ)
to hear	ܫܡܝܥܠܗ	to begin	ܡܫܘܪܝܠܗ
to receive	ܫܩܠܗ	village	ܡܬܐ
neighbor	ܫܒܒܐ	stranger	ܢܘܟܪܝܐ
	ܫܒܒܬܐ	relatives	ܢܫܘܬܐ
for	ܩܐ	modern Aramaic	ܣܘܪܝܐ (ܣܘܪܬ)
Turkish	ܬܘܪܟܝܐ	Popular dialect	
word	ܚܒܪܐ	to stop talking,	ܣܟܝܗ
to come	ܬܐܠܗ	to reside	
to understand	ܦܗܡܠܗ	easy	ܣܢܝܐ
		to help	ܥܕܪܗ

The Ziggural of Ur as now restored. Build by the kings of the Third Dynasty of Ur (2112-2004 B.C.). It was rebuild or repaired by successive Babylonian rulers down to Nabonidus (556-539 B.C.)

LESSON THREE ܦܣܘܩܐ ܕܬܠܬܐ

THE NOUNS (ܫܡܗ̈ܐ) ܫܡܗ̈ܐ

Although in English, nouns and adjectives are separate classes of words, Aramaic treats adjectives as a type of noun, and referring to them as "adjective nouns" thus Chaldean philologists divide the Chaldean Aramaic language into three parts:

1- nouns (ܫܡܗ̈ܐ : ܫܡܐ) which contain pronouns and adjectives

2- verbs (ܡܠܐ : ܡܠܬܐ) (ܗܡܟܠܢ̈ܐ : ܗܡܟܠܢܐ)

3- particles (ܐܙܓ̈ܐ : ܐܙܓܐ)

NOUNS ܫܡܗ̈ܐ

Modern Aramaic nouns are either primitive or derivative.
Primitive nouns cannot be traced to any other words, for example, mouth (ܦܘܡܐ : ܦܡܐ)
Derivative nouns are derived from other root words, which are verbs, for example, walking (ܗܠܟܐ) is derived from the verb to walk (ܗܠܟܠܗ)
In Aramaic, nouns are classified as being either.

Nouns	Translation	Examples	
Substantive noun	ܡܫܬܡܗܢܐ: ܐܘ ܕܩܝܡ ܡܢ ܩܢܘܡܗ	honey	ܕܒܫܐ

Substantive nouns indicate:

person	ܦܪܨܘܦܐ : ܡܕܡ ܩܢܘܡܝܐ	Simon	ܫܡܥܘܢ
place	ܕܘܟܬܐ	Babylon	ܒܒܠ
thing	ܨܒܘܬܐ : ܡܕܡ	rock	ܟܐܦܐ
quality	ܕܝܠܝܘܬܐ : ܫܡܐ	educator	ܡܠܦܢܐ
events	ܓܕܫ̈ܐ	war/fighting	ܩܪܒܐ

An adjective nouns	ܫܘܡܗܐ	sweet	ܚܠܝܐ

Modifies another noun	ܫܡܠܐ	good	ܛܒܐ

Substantive nouns and adjective nouns agree in both gender ܓܢܣܐ for example, special nature ܟܝܢܐ ܦܪܝܫܐ and number ܡܢܝܢܐ for example, three nights. ܬܠܬܐ ܠܠܝܘܬܐ

1-AGREEMENT OF NOUNS IN GENDER ܓܢܣܐ

In Modern Aramaic all nouns are classified as either masculine ܕܟܪܢܐ or feminine ܢܩܒܢܬܐ. (there is no neuter un Aramaic).
King ܡܠܟܐ.is an example of a masculine word. Queen ܡܠܟܬܐ is an example of a feminine word.

Proper nouns ܫܡܗܐ ܕܝܠܝܐ specifying a man's occupation or status are masculine for example a man ܓܒܪܐ who is a teacher is ܡܠܦܢܐ.
The following are also examples of masculine proper nouns:

The Names of	Examples	
rivers	Tigris and Euphrates	ܦܪܬ ܘܕܩܠܬ
mountains	the mountain of olives	ܛܘܪܐ ܕܙܝܬܐ
hills	Tilkepe	ܬܠܟܐܦܐ
people	Chaldeans	ܟܠܕܝܐ
months of the year	April	ܢܝܣܢ

Masculine nouns and adjectives usually end in a ܙܩܦܐ and ܐ when they are singular and in the definite state.
For example: the good boy ܒܪܘܢܐ ܛܒܐ .

Proper nouns specifying a woman's occupation or status are feminine, for example: a female teacher is ܡܲܠܦܵܢܝܼܬ݂ܵܐ

The following are also examples of feminine proper nouns:

The Names of	**Examples**	
countries	Mesopotamia	ܒܹܝܬ ܢܲܗܪܝܼܢ
towns	Ur of the Chaldeans	ܐܘܼܪ ܕܟܲܠܕܵܝܹܐ
cities	Alkosh	ܐܲܠܩܘܿܫ
islands	Ireland	ܐܝܼܪܠܲܢܕܵܐ
letters of the alphabet	A	ܐܵܠܲܦ
parts of the body usually referred to in pairs	eye	ܥܲܝܢܵܐ

Feminine nouns and adjectives usually end in ܬܵܐ with a ܙܩܵܦܵܐ above ܬܵܐ ܬ when they are singular and in the definite state, for example, the good girl ܒܪܵܬܵܐ ܛܵܒ݂ܬܵܐ

2 -AGREEMENT OF NOUNS IN NUMBER ܡܸܢܝܵܢܵܐ

In Modern Aramaic both substantive and adjective nouns are either singular ܚܲܕ݂ (ܚܲܕ݂ܢܵܝܵܐ)، or plural ܣܲܓܝܼܐܹܐ (ܣܲܓܝܼܐܢܵܝܵܐ) to make nouns plural the following rule applies: When a word ends with ܐ and the preceding letter has a ܙܩܵܦܵܐ the ܐ remains but the ܙܩܵܦܵܐ changes to ܙܠܵܡܵܐ ܦܫܝܼܩܵܐ Example: one king: ܡܲܠܟܵܐ kings: ܡܲܠܟܹ̈ܐ

❖ ❖ ❖ ❖ ❖ ❖ ❖ ❖ ❖ ❖

ܝܕܥܬܐ ܡܠܝܬܐ : ܬܫܥܝܬܐ ܟܪܝܟܬܐ ܕܥܕܬܐ ܟܠܕܝܬܐ

ܟܠ ܐܢܫܐ ܒܥܠܡܐ. ܒܡܫܟܢ ܕܝܢ ܕܫܢܬܐ ܫܢܝܐ ܒܐܪܥܐ ܕܐܬܘܪܝܐ ܕܡܕܝ. ܒܥܠܡܐ ܡܕܡܢܐ ܕܟܝܘܢ ܕܗܘܐ. ܠܟܢ ܬܫܥܝܬܐ ܕܡܕܝܢܬܐ. ܘܡܢ ܒܝܬܢܝܘܬ ܥܕܬܐ ܟܠܕܝܬܐ. ܒܡܫܟܢ ܬܫܥܝܬܐ ܟܪܝܟܬܐ ܒܬܫܥܝܬܐ ܕܝܠܗ ܕܟܝܘܢ ܡܕܡܢܐ܀

ܡܥܠܝܬܐ ܟܠܕܝܐ. ܒܡܕܝܢܬܐ ܒܘܪ ܢܝܢܘܐ. ܕܗ ܕܒܝܬܢܝܐ ܡܢܝ ܬܠܟܦܐ ܕܡܕܝܢܬܐ (ܕܡܘܨܠ). ܘܕܝܠܗ (ܕܝܠܢܐ). ܘܡܫܘܚܬܐ (ܕܢܝܢܘܐ). ܡܢܗ ܐܬܪܐ ܒܐܘܪܚܐ ܕܡܕܢܚܐ (ܡܢ: ܠܗ) ܥܠܘܗܝ ܡܫܝܕ ܠܐ ܒܢܝܚܘܬܐ ܒܫܢܐ ܝܕܥܐ ܒܢܘܗ ܡܕܡܢ. ܟܠܗܘܢ ܒܡܕܝܢܬܐ ܒܝ ܒܦܠܓܐ ܕܝܠܗ ܒܝ ܒܡܕܢܚܐ܀

ܒܡܥܠܝܬܐ (ܬܠܟܦܐ) ܕܡܕܝܢܬܐ: ܡܥܠܝܬܐ ܒܥܠܡܐ ܐܬܪܐ ܠܒܘܪܟܬܗ ܐܬܘܪܝܐ ܒܗ ܫܢܐ. ܘܬܠܟܦܐ ܕܝܠܗ: ܒܪܒܥ ܠܡܢܝܢܐ ܕܐܪܥܐ ܡܫܘܚܬܐ 119.62 ܒܦܠܓܐ ܕܝܠܗ ܝܡܝܢ. ܕܥܒܕܝܢ ܐܝܟ ܕܒܝܬܐ ܕܒܝܬ ܐܢ ܘܕܝܢܐ. ܘܬܠܟܦܐ ܕܡܫܘܚܬܐ: ܒܥܠܡܐ ܡܥܠܝܬܐ ܐܬܪܐ. ܕܡܫܝܡܢܝܢ ܡܢ ܥܝܢܐ ܕܝܠܗ. ܕܐܬܪܐ ܕܡܝܐ ܕܫܢܬܐ. ܠܟܘܪܐ ܕܫܢܐ܀

ܟܠ ܬܠܟܦܐ ܕܐܝ ܝܠܗ ܟܠܕܝܐ. ܕܬܫܥܝܬܐ ܘܡܕܒܚܢܐ ܘܕܝܪܐ ܘܥܘܡܪܐ (ܥܒܕܘܬܐ ܕܫܢܬܐ ܕܡܕܝܢܬܐ ܒܝ ܡܢܟܠ ܕܥܘܪܐ). ܐܝ ܬܠܟܦܐ ܐܝܬ ܕܪܝܐ ܒܥܘܡܪܐ ܕܒܫܢܬܗ ܣܘܪܝܐ. ܕܐܝܬܗ ܬܠܟܦܐ ܡܢ ܫܢܐ ܡܕܡܢ ܕܥܒܕܐ ܕܥܘܡܪܐ (ܥܕܬܐ). ܗܘܠ ܡܕܒܚܢܐ ܐܚܪܢܐ ܕܥܒܕܐ ܕܒܠܠܐ ܕܝܕܐ܀

ܬܠܟܦܐ ܕܥܕܬܐ ܕܝܕܐ ܟܠܕܝܬܐ. ܦܝܫ ܡܬܩܪܝܐ ܡܢ ܥܠܝܬܐ ܘܡܠܟܝܬܐ ܕܡܕܝ. ܘܡܢ ܒܬܪ ܡܕܝܢܬܐ ܐܬܪܐ ܘܣܝܡܐ. ܘܡܢ ܡܕܒܚܢܐ ܕܥܕܬܐ ܡܕܝܢܬܐ ܟܠܕܝܐ. ܘܡܕܒܚܢܐ ܒܫܢܬܐ 410 ܠܡܪܝ. ܒܥܘܗܕܢܐ (ܡܫܝܚܐ) ܕܡܪܝ ܐܝܫܘܥ ܘܡܪܝ ܡܕܝܢܬܐ. ܡܬܩܪܝܢܐ ܬܠܟܦܐ ܕܡܪܝ ܐܕܝ ܘܡܪܝ ܡܪܝ. ܘܡܪܝ ܝܫܘܥ ܒܪ ܢܘܢܐ. ܘܡܪܝ ܝܘܚܢܢ ܕܢܝܢܘܐ. ܘܡܪܝ ܐܦܪܝܡ ܒܢܝܐ ܕܥܘܡܪܐ. ܘܐܚܪܢܐ ܡܠܟܐ ܟܠܕܝܐ ܕܐܪܒܥܐ ܕܪܐ ܡܕܡܢܐ ܕܡܥܠܝܐ. ܘܒܡܫܟܢ ܬܠܟܦܐ ܕܥܕܬܐ. ܡܢ ܝܕܥܐ ܘܬܫܥܝܬܐ ܕܥܕܬܐ ܕܡܕܝܢܬܐ ܕܟܠܗ ܘܬܫܒܘܚܬܐ܀

◆ ◆ ◆ ◆ ◆ ◆ ◆ ◆ ◆ ◆ ◆ ◆

VOCABULARY

English	Aramaic	English	Aramaic
daily	ܟܘܕܝܘܡ	Gospel	ܐܘܢܓܠܝܘܢ
bride	ܟܠܘ	Which one?	ܐܝܡܐ
salvation	ܓܠܝ	be able, contain	ܐܒܕܗ
end, final	ܓܠܝܬܐ	to know, to understand	ܐܒܝܫܟܠܗ
to complete	ܟܡܠܗ	the last	ܐܚܪܢܐ
to finish		light	ܒܗܪܐ
a harp lyre	ܟܢܪܐ	blessing	ܒܘܪܟܬܐ
to dress, to wear	ܠܘܫܠܗ	may be	ܒܠܟܝ
to put on		especially	ܒܦܪܝܫܘܬܐ
night	ܠܠܝܐ (ܠܠܝܢܐ)	will be	ܒܦܝܫ
instead	ܡܚܕܠ	the world, the universe	ܒܪܝܬܐ
because	ܡܚܒܕ	announcement	ܒܫܪܐ
east	ܡܕܢܚܐ	butterfly	
city	ܡܕܝܢܬܐ (ܡܕ̈ܝܢܬܐ)	to gather, to collect	ܓܡܠܠܗ
to believe	ܡܗܝܡܢܗ	Memorial	ܕܘܟܪܢܐ
death	ܡܘܬܐ	remembrance	ܬܟܪܘܢܐ
to show	ܡܘܚܘܝܠܗ	judgment , rules	ܕܝܢܐ
to sing, to chant	ܡܘܙܡܪܗ	upright, righteous	ܙܕܝܩܐ
psalm, song	ܡܙܡܘܪܐ	Prayer Book, circle	ܚܘܕܪܐ
writings, fables	ܡܬܠܢܝܬܐ	New Testament	ܚܕܬܐ
morning	ܡܨܒܚܐ	suffering, sadness	ܚܫܐ
to gather	ܡܓܘܡܠܠܗ	rite , liturgy, order	ܛܟܣܐ
to collect		or	ܝܢ

VOCABULARY

Cont.

English	Aramaic	English	Aramaic
to admit	ܩܪܪܗ	to descend	ܢܚܬܠܗ
to become cold		to come down	
to rise, to wake up	ܩܡܠܗ	martyr	ܣܗܕܐ
to stand up		local council	ܣܘܢܗܕܘܣ
to call, to read	ܩܪܝܠܗ	feast, holiday	ܥܐܕܐ
Catholic, universal	ܩܬܘܠܝܩܝܐ	manner, custom	ܥܕܐ
big, great, adult	ܪܒܐ	time	ܥܕܢܐ
Holy Spirit	ܪܘܚܐ ܕܩܘܕܫܐ	the world	ܥܠܡܐ
symbol	ܪܡܙܐ	evening	ܥܪܘܒܬܐ
evening	ܪܡܫܐ	Old Testament	ܥܬܝܩܬܐ
prayer		commandment, order	ܦܘܩܕܢܐ
to walk , to follow	ܪܚܫܠܗ	half, middle, center	ܦܠܓܐ
head , beginning	ܪܫܐ	Pentecost, fifty days	ܦܢܛܩܘܣܛܐ
Liturgical season	ܫܒܘܥܐ	to order	ܦܩܕܠܗ
of seven weeks		lent	ܨܘܡܐ ܪܒܐ
to watch	ܫܗܪܗ	to fast	ܨܡܠܗ
to keep vigil to		Morning, next day	ܨܦܪܐ
become famous		tomorrow	
Saturday, week	ܫܒܬܐ	early morning, dawn	ܩܕܡܬܐ
sleep	ܫܢܬܐ	consecration	ܩܘܕܫܐ
to thank	ܫܟܪܗ	sanctifying	
disciple	ܬܠܡܝܕܐ	to kill	ܩܛܠܗ
service	ܬܫܡܫܬܐ		

LESSON FOUR ܩܘܼܪܵܝܵܐ ܕܐܲܪܒܥܵܐ

PRONOUNS (ܚܠܘܼܦ ܫܡܵܗܵܐ) ܫܡܵܗܹ̈ܐ ܚܠܘܼܦܵܝܹ̈ܐ

A pronoun is a word which takes the place of a noun. They can be classified as follows:

Classification	Examples			
1- **Personal** ܦܲܪܨܘܿܦܵܝܵܐ	you	ܐܲܢ̱ܬ	I	ܐܵܢܵܐ
2- **Demonstrative** ܡܚܲܘܝܵܢܵܐ	this	ܐܵܗܵܐ	that	ܐܵܘܵܐ
3- **Interrogative** ܡܫܲܐܠܵܢܵܐ	who	ܡܲܢ	which	ܐܲܝܢܵܐ
4- **Possessive** ܡܕܝܼܠܵܐ	mine	ܝ	my book	ܟܬܵܒܝܼ

Note: in the following charts which set out the various pronouns, the following abbreviations apply: **M** refers to masculine; **F** refers to feminine; **S** refers to singular and **P** refers to plural.

1- Personal pronouns ܚܠܘܼܦ ܫܡܵܗܵܐ ܦܲܪܨܘܿܦܵܝܵܐ

Pronouns	Masculine			Plural		
1st Person	m/f	I	ܐܵܢܵܐ	m/f	we	ܐܲܚܢܲܢ
2nd Person	male	you	ܐܲܢ̱ܬ	female	you	ܐܲܢ̱ܬܝ
				m/f	you	ܐܲܚܬܘܿܢ(ܝ)
3rd Person	male	he	ܐܵܗܘܼ	female	she	ܐܵܗܝܼ
				m/f	they	ܐܵܢܝܼ

2-Possessive Suffix Pronouns ܚܠܦ ܫܡܗܐ ܡܩܢܝܢܐ

The possessive case is indicated in eight ways by adding one of the following suffixes letters to a noun:

1	2	3	4	5	6	7	8
ܝ	ܢ	ܐܘܟ	ܐܝܟ	ܐܘܟܘܢ	ܝܗ	ܐܗ̇	ܗܘܢ

Example: Rose ܘܪܕܐ , My Rose ܘܪܕܝ

1st Person	m/f:	my (Rose	ܝ	ܘܪܕܝ
	pl m/f:	our (Rose)	ܢ	ܘܪܕܢ
2nd Person	m:	your	ܘܟ	ܘܪܕܘܟ
	f:	your (Rose)	ܟܝ	ܘܪܕܟܝ
	pl m/f:	your (Rose)	(ܘܟܘܢ)(ܢ)	ܘܪܕܘܟܘܢ(ܢ)
3rd person	m:	his (Rose)	ܗ	ܘܪܕܗ
	f:	her (Rose)	ܗ̇	ܘܪܕܗ̇
	pl, m/f:	their (Rose)	ܗܘܢ	ܘܪܕܗܘܢ

When a possessive noun is in the plural form the word ܕܝܝ follows it. Example: my pencils ܩܠܡܐ ܕܝܝ

3-Demonstrative pronouns ܚܠܦ ܫܡܗܐ ܡܚܘܝܢܐ

Persons	Pronouns	
M/F	this	ܗܕܝ or ܗܕ
M/F	these	ܗܢ
MS	that	ܐܘܐ

Persons	Pronouns	
FS	that	ܐܝܐ
MP	those	ܐܢܝ
FP	those	ܐܢܝ

4-Interrogative pronouns ܚܠܦ ܫܡܗ̈ܐ ܡܫܐܠܢ̈ܝܐ

Here, no distinction is made between the masculine and feminine:

Who	ܐܝܡܢܐ
How	ܐܝܟ
What	ܡܘܢܐ
who is it	ܡܢܝܠܗ
which is it	ܐܝܡܠܗ

what is it	ܡܝܠܗ
how much it cost	ܒܟܡܝܠܗ
Where	ܐܝܟܐ
how many	ܐܟܡܐ
from where is it	ܡܢ ܐܝܟܐ ܝܠܗ

ܦܪܢܣܐ ܕܝܠܦܢܐ : ܥܐܕܐ ܕܫܢܬܐ ܚܕܬܐ ܕܝܘܡܐ ܩܕܡܝܐ

ܥܐܕܐ ܕܫܢܬܐ ܕܥܡ̈ܡܐ ܒܙܒܢ̈ܐ ܠܐܬܪ̈ܘܬܐ ܫܢ̈ܝܐ ܘܐܝܟܢܐ ܗܘܐ ܥܐܕܐ

ܐ — ܣܘܪ̈ܝܐ: ܐܝܬܗ ܒܐܕܪ ܫܢܝܥܣܪܐ

ܒ — ܐܠܕ̈ܝܐ: ܐܝܬܗ ܒܐܕܪ ܫܢܝܥܣܪܐ

ܓ — ܕܝܢܐ: ܐܝܬܗ ܒܐܡܪܐ ܫܢܝܥܣܪܐ

ܕ — ܝܘܡܐ: ܐܝܬܗ ܥܣܪܐ ܫܢܝܥܣܪܐ

ܗ — ܦܪܣܝܐ ܘܡܘܠܕܐ: ܐܝܬܗ ܥܣܪܐ ܫܢܝܥܣܪܐ

ܘ — ܦܪܘܛܘܩܝܐ ܘܥܠܝ̈ܡܐ: ܐܝܬܗ ܥܣܪܐ ܫܢܝܥܣܪܐ

ܙ — ܡܨܪܝܐ (ܩܒܛܐ): ܐܝܬܗ ܥܣܪܐ ܫܢܝܥܣܪܐ

ܚ — ܝܘܢܝܐ (ܐܬܢܐ ܘܪܘܡܐ): ܐܝܬܗ ܥܣܪܐ ܫܢܝܥܣܪܐ

ܛ — ܒܒܠ (ܣܘܪܝܐ) ܐܬܘܪܐ: ܐܝܬܗ ܐܕܪ ܫܢܝܥܣܪܐ ܘܒܐܕܪܐ ܕܥܐܕܐ ܐܫܬܝܬܐ

ܕܐܝܬ ܥܐܕܐ ܒܟܠܗ ܥܡܐ ܐܬܘܪܝܐ܀

ܒܘܪ ܡܕܝܢܬܐ ܐܬܘܪ. ܟܠܕܝܐ ܡܬܘܪܬܐ. ܒܫܘܬܐܣܣܘ ܒܐܕܪ ܥܐܕܐ ܕܐܫܬܝܬܐ ܡܥܝܢܬܐ. ܡܢ ܩܕܡ ܕܐܬܐ ܡܥܘܕܝܬܗ ܒܪܝܫܗ ܡܢ ܐܬܪܐ ܡܥܝܢܐ ܠܟܠܗܘܢ. ܗܘܝܠܗ ܘܡܬܝܠܗ.ܘܡܬܒܪܟܠܗ ܘܐܝܬܝܗ ܫܢܐ. ܦܬܚܠܗ ܐܠܝܬܐ ܘܡܝܬܠܗ ܘܢܦܩܠܗ. ܘܡܥܘܕܝܬܗ ܒܘܫܐ ܕܡܘܕܥܐ ܐܠܗܐ ܥܠܝܬܐ. ܘܐܝܟ ܐܡܪ ܐܠܗܝܐ ܘܡܥܝܢܬܐ ܡܕܝܢܬܐ. ܦܬܚܠܗ ܡܥܝܢܬܐ ܡܥܝܢܬܐ ܡܬܦܠܚܬܐ ܒܟܘܠܗ ܒܕܝܢܬܐ. ܟܢܫܐ ܡܢ ܐܬܪܐ ܘܐܬܘܪܐ ܡܬܘܠܐ ܘܡܬܝܠܐ. ܘܥܐܕܐ ܐܫܬܝܬ ܬܠܬܐ ܒܫܢܬܐ. ܕܡܢ ܒܟܠܗܘܢ ܕܟܠܗܘܢ ܒܦܬܚ ܫܢܬܐ ܐܠܝܬܐ ܡܕܝܢܬܐ. ܕܡܢܬܐ ܒܟܠ ܐܬܪܐ ܕܥܐܕܐ ܐܫܬܝܬܐ ܡܥܝܢܐ ܕܐܝܬܝܗ ܗܘ ܟܠܗ ܕܟܠܗܘܢ. ܘܒܝܘܡܐ ܒܟܠ ܒܘܠ ܒܬܪܐ ܕܫܢܬܐ ܕܐܬܘܪܝܐ. ܘܐܢܐ ܡܢܗ ܠܗ

ܢܒܝܐ ܐܫܥܝܐ ܕܐܡܪܗ. ܘܚܙܘܝܐ ܐܫܥܝܐ ܒܓܠܝܬܐ ܕܚܠܡܐ. ܒܕܪܗ ܡܫܝܚܐ ܠܗܐ ܕܗܘܐ ܗܕ
ܕܝܡ ܒܝܫܬܐ ܘܡܒܥܬܐ. ܘܐܒܥܡ ܕܐܡܪܗ. ܒܦܠܛܐ ܥܡܗ ܒܝܬܐ ܥܒܪܬܐ. ܘܐܡܘܒ ܠܟܒܪܬܐ
ܓܘܠܐ ܕܚܠܘ. ܘܡܠܟܢܐܠܗ ܐܡܪ ܐܢܬܐ ܒܡܘܬܦܪܐ ܘܡܥܬܦܣܢܬܐ. ܘܟܠܗ ܒܫܢܐ ܐܡܝܗ
ܒܡܠܟܘܬܐ ܕܫܡܝܐ ܗܘܠ ܐܒܪ ܐܒܪܝܢ܀

❖ ❖ ❖ ❖ ❖ ❖ ❖ ❖ ❖ ❖

VOCABULARY

English	Aramaic	English	Aramaic
to encounter	ܡܠܘܩܝܠܗ	to give birth	ܐܒܠܓܠܗ
to give birth	ܡܘܗܘܝܠܗ	(in modern	
in modern Aramaic refers to a woman		Aramaic refers to animal female)	
to send	ܡܫܘܕܪܗ	mystery, Mass	ܐܪܙܐ
to think	ܡܚܘܫܒܠܗ	sacrament	
prophet	ܢܒܝܐ	between	ܒܝܢܝ
law	ܢܡܘܣܐ	Christmas	ܥܐܕ ܝܠܕܐ
The Annunciation	ܣܘܒܪܐ	to see, to find	ܚܙܝܠܗ
to be baptized	ܥܡܝܕܠܗ	clothes	ܓܘܠܐ
to emerge	ܦܠܛܠܗ	The Epiphany	ܕܢܚܐ
to come out		to be born	ܗܘܝܠܗ
to spread	ܦܪܫܠܗ	to carry	ܛܥܝܢܗ
to stay, to become	ܦܝܫܠܗ	to suffer	ܛܥܝܢܗ
Lent, fast	ܨܘܡܐ		ܚܫܐ
cross	ܨܠܝܒܐ	to preach	ܡܘܟܪܙܠܗ
Resurrection, Easter	ܩܝܡܬܐ	to show	ܡܘܚܙܝܠܗ
to repent	ܬܝܒܠܗ	to die	ܡܝܬܠܗ
glory	ܬܫܒܘܚܬܐ	to welcome	ܡܩܘܒܠܠܗ

LESSON FIVE ܦܣܘܩܐ ܕܚܡܫܐ

THE NUMBERS (ܚܘܫܒܐ ܡܢܝܢܝܐ) (ܫܥܒܘܦܐ) ܡܢܝܢܐ

In the Aramaic language, the 22 letters are also used to form the numbers, so that each letter stands for one number. Thus, the numbers one (1) to four hundred (400) correspond to the 22 letters of the Aramaic alphabet

A- The Aramaic single numbers (1-9) ܡܢܝܢܐ ܦܫܝܛܐ

Letter	ܐ	ܒ	ܓ	ܕ	ܗ	ܘ	ܙ	ܚ	ܛ
Number	1	2	3	4	5	6	7	8	9

B-THE TENS (10-90) ܥܣܪ̈ܝܬܐ

After (10) ܝ each succeeding letter is ten more than the last until ܩ (100)

Letter	ܝ	ܟ	ܠ	ܡ	ܢ	ܣ	ܥ	ܦ	ܨ
Number	10	20	30	40	50	60	70	80	90

C -HUNDREDS ܡܐܘ̈ܬܐ

After 100 ܩ each succeeding letter is 100 more than the last until400ܬ

Letter	ܩ	ܪ	ܫ	ܬ
Number	100	200	300	400

D -COMPOUND NUMBERS ܚܘܫܒܐ ܡܢܝܢܝܐ ܡܪܟܒܐ

Aramaic numbers are divided into simple ܚܘܫܒܐ ܦܫܝܛܐ and compound numbers ܚܘܫܒܐ ܡܪܟܒܐ. The simple numbers are the singles from section **A** above, the tens from section **B** and the hundreds from section **C**. The compound numbers are formed by joining together simple numbers. Example:

11 = ܝܐ   12 = ܝܒ   37 = ܠܙ   99 = ܨܛ   480 = ܬܦ

Note: The rules concerning joining and enjoining letters should be applied .Rules for forming the compound numbers:

1. Always begin with the larger number to the right, followed by the smaller. Example:

11=ܝܐ 12=ܝܒ 37=ܠܙ 88= ܦܚ 498=ܬܨܚ 123=ܩܟܓ

2. There are two methods employed to count from **500 to 999**:
    a- The following method is used by some Aramaic grammarians and in the majority of liturgical books, and it is the most common method:

Method	ܬ+ܩ	ܬ+ܬ+ܩ				
	ܬܩ	ܬܬܩ	ܬܩܟܐ	ܬܪܗ	ܬܬܨܛ	ܬܬܩܨܛ
Number	500	900	521	605	899	999

    b- The second method, which is employed by other grammarians, is as follows: beginning at 100 and up to 999 each letter from ܝ to ܨ represents 100 when a dot is placed over the letter as follows:

ܝ̇ = 100 ܢ̇ܡܗ = 545
ܟ̇ܒ = 202 ܨ̇ܛ = 909

3- Alap is the cardinal numeral 1 (one), but when Alap stands alone and a slanted line is placed beneath it ܐ̗ it equals one thousand (1,000). When a small horizontal line is placed beneath it ܐ̱ it equals ten thousand (10,000). But when two slanted lines joined at the top are placed beneath the alap, ܐ̭ it equals one hundred thousand (100,000)

4- In a four digit number indicating a year, as in ܐ̗ܨ̇ܦܛ - 1989
The following method is employed:

a. When the numerals ܐ through ܛ are the first number of a four digit number, each one counts as a thousand, that is ܐ is 1،000 ܒ is 2,000, etc. until ܛ which is 9,000.

b. When the numerals ܩ through ܨ are the second number of a four digit number, each one counts as a hundred, that is ܩ is 100 ܪ is 200 etc. until ܨ which is 900

c. The third number of a four digit number follows the basic method of tens of section B.

d. For the final digit, the basic method of singles of section A is followed, for example: 1988 ܐܨ̈ܦܚ notice that three dots are placed over the second letter to indicate that it is in the hundreds .

5- Chaldeans decided upon another method for representing years: the three dots used in rule 4 d (see above) are in this new rule placed above one of the nine single numbers (ܐ–ܛ) to represent thousands.

Thus years can be represented as follows:

ܒ̈	=	2000	ܓ̈	=	3000	ܓ̈ܒ	=	3002
ܒ̈ܐ	=	2001	ܓ̈ܐ	=	3001	ܓ̈ܓ	=	3003
ܒ̈ܝܕ	=	2014						

6- Dates in Modern Aramaic first (day) second (month) third (year) are written as follows:

Example: 25/12/2014 ܟܗ : ܝܒ : ܒ̈ܝܕ

ܡܕܝܢܬܐ ܣܡܝܟܬܐ : ܚܕܬܐ ܘܥܬܝܩܬܐ ܒܠܕܝܬܐ

ܒܢܝܢܐ ܕܟܠܗܘܢ ܡܕܝܢܬܐ. ܡܫܚܠܦܐ ܘܡܕܡܝܐ ܘܡܬܬܚܡܢܝܬܐ ܒܩܣܡ ܚܘܪ̈ܐ ܘܡܥܡܪܢܝܬܐ ܒܟܠ ܕܘܟܬܐ. ܦܫܛܐ ܡܕܝܢܬܐ ܘܡܬܠܦܬܐ ܢܟܝܦܐ ܘܒܝܬܝ̈ܐ. ܒܦܘܪܣܐ ܗܝ ܐܢ̈ܫܐ ܕܐܦܘܗܝ ܘܩܫܝ̈ܐ ܒܒܝܬܘܬܗܘܢ. ܒܟܝܢܐ ܡܢ ܚܕܬܐ ܘܥܬܝܩܬܐ. ܐܢ ܕܟܠ ܗܘܠܝܟܐ ܕܥܬܝܩ ܒܘܟܢܐ ܕܡܠܟܐ. ܩܝܢܐ ܡܢܐ ܕܦܪܣܐ ܦܪܢܣܐ. ܐܝܟ ܕܒܛܝܒܘܬܐ ܬܠܝܠܘܬܐ. ܕܡܢ ܩܕܡ ܕܐܬܩܢ ܐܠܝܢ ܬܠܝܠܘܬܐ ܕܐܕܝܗ ܕܒܥܘܡܪܐ ܕܐܬܩܢ. ܘܥܬܝܩ ܠܘܝܬܠܗ ܕܘܟܝ ܡܢܐ ܕܠܣܒܠܗ ܗܕܐ. ܚܕܬܐ ܒܥܡܘܪܐ ܕܝܢܘܬܐ. ܒܐܝܕ ܡܢ ܡܕܝܢܬܐ. ܘܚܒܪܐ ܕܒܝܬܐ ܐܝ ܝܘܡܐ ܐܝ ܫܢܬܐ. ܒܡܣܝܪܬܐ ܬܠܝܗ ܒܘܬܟܐ ܥܫܝܢܐ. ܕܒܥܬܐ ܘܕܒܥܬܐ. ܐܢ ܬܠܘܬܝ̈ܐ ܢܘ ܥܘܦܩܬܐ. ܘܚܕܬܐ ܒܒܝܬܐ ܝܡܝܘ. ܘܦܕܐ ܗܝ ܦܩܐ ܒܠܝܘ ܠܫܢܐ ܘܠܘܩܒܐ ܘܩܝܪܐ ܐܢ ܓܓܝܓ ܘܗܒܠܝ. ܐܢ ܕܘܟܬ ܘܡܝܪ̈ܐ ܐܢ ܐܒܝܬܐ

ܡܢܐ ܕܡܥܒܕܐ ܒܐܝܠܐ. ܘܕܟܐ ܒܝܬܘ ܬܠܝܡ ܗܝ ܡܝܢܝܘ. ܗܘܢܐ ܘܡܬܩܪܐ. ܘܡܫܦܠܝܓ ܚܕܐ ܕܝܘ ܠܕܘܟܐ. ܒܣܝܪ ܠܥܡܪܐ ܘܒܗܓܪ ܣܓܡܬܐ ܕܬܚܘܦܬܐ ܕܒܐܡܪܬܗ: ܬܪܝܢ ܗܡܦܢܐ ܕܒܘܪܡܝܐ ܡܣܝܟܝ ܚܕܬܐ ܕܡܠܟܝܘ. ܠܟܝ ܬܪܝܢ ܗܡܦܢܐ ܕܡܕܝܢܬܐ. ܗܣܘܗܘܢ ܚܕܬܐ ܡܕܝܢܬܐ. ܐܝ ܬܪܝܢ ܒܡܣܘܥܪܐ ܠܐ ܗܘܐ ܗܡܦܢܐ. ܥܡܪܐ ܒܗܦܢܐ ܝܫܢܐ ܝܩܝܪܐ ܘܠܝܡ ܕܕܟܝ ܕܡܬܝܩܪܐ.

ܡܢ ܟܐܕ ܓܕܐ ܐܒܠܗܐ ܗܘܝܐ ܒܡܣܘܥܪܐ. ܒܠܘܥ ܚܕܬܐ ܓܕܘܦܐ ܒܐܬܠܝܗ. ܘܚܕܬܐ ܓܡܝܫܐ ܠܕܘܟܝܗ. ܒܐܝܪ ܦܥܡܝܗ. ܘܒܓܕܐ ܗܘܗܡܢܝܬܗ ܠܐܒܢܝܗ. ܒܦܠܝܓ ܠܕܘܟܐ ܘܚܕܬܐ ܡܝܢܝܗ. ܣܥܪܝܗ ܘܫܥܪܢܝܗ. ܐܢ ܟܘܕܝܗ ܘܒܘܕܝܢܝܗ. ܐܘ ܒܬܚܒܠܝܗ ܘܒܬܓܠܢܝܗ ܒܡܕܥܡܝ ܣܦܪܝܗ. ܘܚܕܬܐ ܠܓܢܐ ܗܦܟܐ ܘܡܚܒܐ ܘܒܝܬܐ. ܘܠܓܢܐ ܐܡܡܝܐ ܕܝܕܥܐ. ܘܠܓܘܗܪܐ ܡܠܟܝ̈ܐ ܗܘܢܐ. ܘܠܓܐ ܓܢܐ ܚܕܬܐ ܒܬܘܪܟܐ. ܘܒܥܝܡܠ ܝܡܝܘ ܟܘܡܐ ܠܒܚܬܐ ܡܢܘܪ ܕܝܘ. ܒܦܠܠܓܝ ܚܕܬܐ ܘܒܘܡܐ ܘܐܡܣܘܣܝ ܣܦܪ̈ܐ ܕܢܫܘܣܝ. ܡܢܐ ܕܒܗܘܕܐ ܕܘܒܝ. ܘܒܢܘܗܝ ܬܠܒܘܗܝ ܝܘܡ ܕܥܡܐ. ܘܐܒܣܘܗܝ ܒܝܠܦܢܝ. ܘܕܝܢܝ ܡܦܣܘܗܝ ܒܐܒܝܐ ܕܡܕܝܢܬܐ ܐܠܗܐ܀

◆ ◆ ◆ ◆ ◆ ◆ ◆ ◆ ◆ ◆ ◆ ◆ ◆

VOCABULARY

English	Aramaic	English	Aramaic
Cheese	ܓܘܒܬܐ	To make, to do	ܥܒܕܠܗ
Thunder	ܓܪܓܡܬܐ	to accomplish	
To draw, to pull	ܓܪܫܠܗ	Earth, dust	ܥܦܪܐ
Place	ܕܘܟܬܐ	Raisins	ܐܒܝܫܐ
Grape syrup	ܕܘܫܐ (ܡܝܘܬܐ)	To say	ܐܡܝܪܗ (ܡܝܪܗ)
The world	ܕܘܢܝܐ	To eat	ܐܟܝܠܗ (ܟܠܗ)
the weather, sky		Meal	ܐܟܠܬܐ
Yard, courtyard	ܕܪܬܐ	To tie	ܐܣܝܪܗ (ܝܣܪܗ)
Danger	ܕܪܟ	Hand	ܐܝܕܐ
To be able	ܗܘܠܝܗ	When	ܐܝܡܢ
Plow	ܗܘܦܟܪ	Foot	ܐܩܠܐ
to direct toward	ܗܘܠܗ ܬܠܗ	Ground	ܐܪܥܐ
To turn		Meal	ܒܘܫܠܐ
Food supply	ܙܘܕܐ (ܡܘܢܐ)	cooked food	
Animal	ܚܝܘܐ	Dusk, sunset	ܒܘܪܡܫܐ
Wisdom	ܚܟܡܬܐ	twilight	
Donkey	ܚܡܪܐ	To seed, to	ܒܘܙܠܗ
To be ready,	ܚܙܕܪܗ	spread	
to arrive to attend		Onion	ܒܨܠܐ
Lentils	ܛܠܘܦܚܐ	Mule	ܒܪܓܠ
Long, tall	ܝܪܝܟܐ	Seeds	ܒܪܘܙܐ
Abundance	ܟܒܪܐ	Lightning	ܒܪܩܐ
plenty		After wards	ܒܬܪ
It can be	ܟܘܗܐ	Plow or Acre	ܒܪܬܐ

VOCABULARY

Cont.

English	Aramaic	English	Aramaic
Date syrup	ܣܝܠܢ	Mule	ܟܘܕܢܐ
Plowshare,	ܣܟܬܐ	Bag	ܟܝܣܐ (ܓܘܢܐ)
cutting blade		Bread	ܠܚܡܐ
of plow		Obligated	ܠܘܙܡܐ ܠܗ
Red	ܣܘܡܩܐ	There is not	ܠܝܬ
To wait for, until	ܣܟܝܪܗ	To catch up	ܠܚܩܠܗ
To keep, safe	ܣܡܝܪܗ	,to reach	
Tools, equipment	ܟܝܪܐ	Coverall, apron	ܡܙܘܪ
Depth	ܥܘܡܩܐ	To prepare	ܡܘܬܩܢܪܗ
Animal food	ܥܠܝܦ	Rain	ܡܛܪܐ
supply		To arrive	ܡܛܠܗ
Face	ܦܬܐ	to become ripe	
The moistened	ܦܪܝܠܗ ܦܪܪܐ	Filled up with	ܡܠܐ
soil was enough		To dine	ܡܘܚܫܡܠܗ
Long homemade	ܦܫܡܐ	to have supper	
trousers		To pull out	ܡܘܦܠܛܠܗ
To stay	ܦܝܫܠܗ	to release	
to become		Until, how much	ܡܩܐ
Toward	ܨܘܒ	Before, ahead	ܡܩܡ
Clear	ܨܦܝܬܐ	Open sleeve	ܣܦܣܟܬܐ
Barley	ܣܥܪܐ	To send away	ܣܚܠܗ
Strong	ܩܘܝܐ	to kick	
Dates	ܩܝܪܐ		

VOCABULARY **Cont.**

English	Aramaic	English	Aramaic
Moist, wet	ܬܠܝܠܐ	Animals used	ܡܥܢܬܐ
The rest	ܬܦܣܝܬܐ	in the farm	
To remember	ܬܟܪܗ	Cold	ܩܪܝܪܐ
One	ܚܕܐ	Soil	ܪܟܡ
To roll	ܓܢܠܗ	Shoulder	ܪܘܫܐ
to fold up		Saddle	ܪܫܘܢܐ
Some	ܚܕܟܡܐ	Noodles,	ܪܝܫܬܐ ܘܪܝܫܬܐ
Wheat	ܚܛܐ	sliced pasta	
To look	ܚܝܪܗ	Cooked lentils	ܫܘܦܬܐ
Thick wool coat	ܓܡܫܝܐ	with meat	
Darkness	ܚܫܟܐ	Sky, heaven	ܫܡܝܐ
Sister, new	ܚܬܐ	Sunrise	ܫܪܩ
Lady's bag, purse	ܓ̰ܢܬܐ	Hot	ܫܚܝܢܐ
Blue cheese	ܓ̰ܝܓ̰ܠ		(ܚܡܝܡܐ)
Animal feeding bag	ܓ̰ܘܗܪܐ	Hay, straw	ܬܘܢܐ

Tilkepe - 1972

Vocabulary

English	Aramaic	English	Aramaic
Grape syrup	ܕܒܫܐ	Raisins	ܐܚܒܝܫܐ
The world, sky	ܕܘܢܝܐ	To say	ܐܡܝܪܗ
the weather			ܡܝܪܗ
Yard, courtyard	ܕܪܬܐ	To eat	ܐܟܝܠܗ. ܟܠܝܗ
Danger	ܕܪܕ	Meal	ܐܟܠܬܐ
To be able	ܗܘܠܝܒܗ	To tie	ܐܣܝܪܗ (ܝܣܪܗ)
Plow	ܗܘܦܟܪܐ	Hand	ܐܝܕܐ
To turn ,to direct	ܗܘܠܝܗ ܬܠܝܗ	When	ܐܝܡܢ
toward		Foot	ܐܩܠܐ
Food supply	ܙܘܕܐ	Ground	ܐܪܥܐ
One	ܚܕܐ	cooked food	ܒܫܠܐ
Some	ܚܕܟܡܐ	Meal	
Wheat	ܚܛܐ	Dusk, sunset,	ܒܪܡܫܐ
Animal	ܚܝܘܢ	twilight	
To look	ܚܝܪܗ	To seed	ܒܕܪܠܗ
Wisdom	ܚܟܡܬܐ	to spread	
Long, tall	ܝܪܝܟܐ	Onion	ܒܨܠܐ
Abundance, plenty	ܟܒܝܪܬܐ	Mule	ܒܓܠܐ
It can be	ܟܘܝܐ	Seeds	ܒܙܪܥܐ
Mule	ܟܘܕܢܐ	Lightning	ܒܪܩܐ
Bag	ܟܝܣܐ	After wards	ܒܬܪ
Bread	ܠܚܡܐ	Yoke	ܒܝܪܐ
Obligated	ܠܘܒܫܠܗ	Cheese	ܓܒܬܐ
There is not	ܠܝܬ	Thunder	ܓܪܓܡܬܐ
To catch up	ܠܚܝܩܠܗ	To draw, to pull	ܓܪܫܠܗ
,to reach		Place	ܕܘܟܬܐ

VOCABULARY

Cont.

English	Aramaic	English	Aramaic
To make, to do	ܥܒܝܕܠܗ	Coverall, apron	ܡܐܙܪ
to accomplish		To prepare	ܡܘܚܕܪܗ
Earth, dust	ܥܘܦܪܐ	Rain	ܡܛܪܐ
Donkey	ܚܡܪܐ	To arrive	ܡܛܠܗ
To be ready	ܚܕܝܪܗ	to become ripe	
to arrive		Filled up with	ܡܠܝܐ
to attend		to have supper	ܡܘܥܫܠܗ
Darkness	ܚܫܘܟܐ	To dine	
Sister, new	ܚܬܐ	To pull out	ܡܘܦܠܛܠܗ
Lady's bag, purse	ܓܢܛܐ	to release	
Blue cheese	ܓܓܟ	Until, how much	ܟܡܐ
Animal feeding bag	ܓܘܗܪܐ	Before, ahead	ܩܡ
To roll, to fold up	ܓܒܝܠܗ	Open sleeve	ܣܦܣܟܐ
Lentils	ܛܠܘܦܐ	To send away	ܣܛܠܗ
Thick wool coat	ܓܡܗܢܝܐ	to kick , to out fire	
Toward	ܨܘܒ	Date syrup	ܣܝܠܢ
Clear	ܨܦܝܐ	Plowshare, cutting	ܣܟܬܐ
Barley	ܣܥܪܐ	blade of plow	
Animals used in	ܒܥܝܪܐ	Red	ܣܡܘܩܐ
the farm		To wait for, until	ܣܒܝܪܗ
Dates	ܬܡܪܐ	To keep, safe	ܣܡܕܪܗ
Cold	ܩܪܝܪܐ	Tools, equipment	ܟܝܪܐ
Strong	ܩܘܝܐ	Depth	ܥܘܡܩܐ
Hoisted sail	ܪܟܫ	Animal food	ܥܠܝܦ
Shoulder	ܪܘܫܐ	supply	

VOCABULARY

Cont.

English	Aramaic	English	Aramaic
Hay, straw	ܬܒܢܐ	Saddle	ܪܫܘܢܐ
Humid, wet	ܬܠܝܠܐ	Noodles	ܪܝܫܬܐ
The rest	ܬܡܫܝܬܐ	sliced pasta	
To remember	ܬܓܒܪܗ	Cooked lentils	ܫܘܦܬܐ
The moistened	ܦܪܝܠܗ	with meat	
soil was enough	ܦܪܢܐ	Sky, heaven	ܫܡܝܐ
Long homemade trousers	ܦܫܡܐ	Sunrise	ܡܕܢܚ
To stay, to become	ܦܫܠܗ	Hot	ܚܫܝܢܐ
Face	ܦܬܐ		ܫܚܝܢܐ

❖❖❖❖❖❖❖❖❖❖

LESSON SIX ܦܘܫܩܐ ܕܫܬܐ

THE NUMBERS–CONTINUED ܡܢܝܢܐ

(ܫܘܡܠܝܐ ܡܢܝܢܐ)

Modern Aramaic numbers are divided into cardinal and ordinal numbers.

THE CARDINAL NUMBERS (ܫܘܡܠܝܐ ܡܢܝܢܐ ܦܫܝܛܐ) ܡܢܝܢܐ ܐܝܟܝܐ

The single cardinal numbers from 1–10 (ܥܣܪܐ ܡܘܢܝܐ) ܚܕܢܐ ܡܘܢܝܐ

Numbers	Feminine	Masculine
One	ܚܕܐ	ܚܕ
Two	ܬܪܬܐ	ܬܪܐ
Three	ܬܠܬ	ܬܠܬܐ
Four	ܐܪܒܥ	ܐܪܒܥܐ
Five	ܚܡܫ	ܚܡܫܐ
Six	ܐܫܬ	ܐܫܬܐ
Seven	ܐܫܒܥ	ܫܒܥܐ
Eight	ܬܡܢܐ	ܬܡܢܝܐ
Nine	ܬܫܥ	ܬܫܥܐ
Ten	ܥܣܪ	ܥܣܪܐ

The compound cardinal number : ܫܘܡܠܝܐ ܡܢܝܢܐ ܡܪܟܒܐ : ܥܣܪܐ ܡܪܟܒܐ

From 11 –19 the same word is used for both the masculine and feminine .

Eleven	ܚܕܥܣܪ	Sixteen	ܐܫܬܥܣܪ
Twelve	ܬܪܥܣܪ	Seventeen	ܐܫܒܥܣܪ
Thirteen	ܬܠܬܥܣܪ	Eighteen	ܬܡܢܥܣܪ
Fourteen	ܐܪܒܥܣܪ	Nineteen	ܐܬܫܥܣܪ (ܐܥܣܪ)
Fifteen	ܚܡܫܥܣܪ		

Tens: the simple tens from 20 to 100 (for example 20, 30, 40 etc.) use the same word for both the masculine and the feminine: ܚܘܫܒܬܐ ܡܠܝܬܝܬܐ ܘܗܘܝܢ ܕܝܒܝܕܗ

Twenty	ܥܣܪܝܢ	Fifty	ܚܡܫܝܢ	Eighty	ܬܡܢܐ
Thirty	ܬܠܬܝܢ	Sixty	ܐܫܬܝܢ	Ninety	ܬܫܥܝܢ
Forty	ܐܪܒܥܝܢ	Seventy	ܫܒܥܝܢ	One hundred	ܐܡܐ

- From 100 onwards, the same word is used for both masculine and feminine simple numbers. The hundreds are formed by using the masculine single numbers plus one hundred ܐܡܐ for example:

  200 men or women: ܬܪܐ ܐܡܐ

  500 men or women: ܚܡܫܐ ܐܡܐ
- One thousand: ܐܠܦܐ when forming the thousands in spoken and written Aramaic, the same rule is applied as for the hundreds but using the word ܐܠܦܐ one thousand for example:

  5,000 men or women: ܚܡܫܐ ܐܠܦܐ ܓܒܪ̈ܐ ܘܐܢ̈ܫܐ

  70,000 men or women: ܫܒܥܝܢ ܐܠܦܐ ܓܒܪ̈ܐ ܘܐܢ̈ܫܐ

The following are specific rules concerning numbers applied only in the Modern Aramaic of the people of Nineveh.

- **Numbers 21-99 in the compound form:** When writing a number as a numeral (as mentioned above in lesson 5, Section D, Rule 1) the larger number is written first, followed by the smaller. For example 45 is ܡܗ However, when this number is pronounced, or written as it is pronounced, then the smaller number is used first and then the larger, for example 45 men ܚܡܫܐ ܘܐܪܒܥܝܢ ܓܒܪ̈ܐ
- **Numbers 21-99:** When using the number one (1) in forming compound numbers in spoken Chaldean (for example 21, 31, 41,…,91) instead of using ܚܕ for the masculine or ܚܕܐ for the

feminine, the word ܚܕ is used instead for the masculine, for example:

21 men or women ܚܕ ܘܥܣܪܝܢ ܓܒܪ̈ܐ ܘܢܫ̈ܐ

31 men or women ܚܕ ܘܬܠܬܝܢ ܓܒܪ̈ܐ ܘܢܫ̈ܐ

THE ORDINAL NUMBERS ܡܢܝܢ̈ܐ ܡܣܕܪ̈ܐ

(ܥܣܩܘܬܐ ܡܢܝܢ̈ܐ ܡܫܚܠܦܢ̈ܐ) ܥܣܩܘܬܐ ܡܢܝܢ̈ܐ ܓܢܣܢ̈ܐ

	Feminine	Masculine
First	ܩܕܡܝܬܐ	ܩܕܡܝܐ
Second	ܕܬܪܬܝܢ	ܕܬܪܝܢ

The ordinal numbers are formed in the same way as the cardinal numbers but with the addition of the letter ܕ at the beginning.
Simple ordinal numbers differ in gender for example:

Third:	masculine	ܕܬܠܬܐ
	feminine	ܕܬܠܬ

Numbers do not change in gender, for example. ܕܚܕܥܣܪܐ however, from 21 –99 the ordinal numbers do differ in gender. For example:

Twenty first:	masculine	ܕܚܕ ܘܥܣܪܝܢ
	feminine	ܕܚܕܐ ܘܥܣܪܝܢ

From the hundreds, the ordinal numbers do not differ in gender for both masculine and feminine. For example:

One hundredth is ܕܡܐܐ

Two hundredth is ܕܬܪܝܢ ܡܐܐ

Thousandth is ܕܐܠܦܐ

Two thousandth ܕܬܪܝܢ ܐܠܦܝܢ and so on

ܝܘܢܝܐ ܥܬܝܩܐ : ܢܡܘܣܐ ܕܟܣܦܝ ܐܘܡܢܐ ܒܡܬܘܡܝܘܬܐ ܕܓܠܝܢܐ ܕܫܡܫܐ

ܗܘ ܢܡܘܣܐ ܒܚܫܒܢܐ ܕܫܥܬܐ. ܢܡܘܣܐ ܠܗ ܕܡܬܩܪܐ. ܒܘܠܝ ܓܠܝܢܐ ܡܫܩܠܝܬܐ ܒܡܫܟܚܬܐ ܚܕܬܐ. ܗܝ ܕܐܝܬܝܗ ܕܡܫܬܡܫ ܡܢܗ. ܫܥܬܐ ܕܐܝܬܝ ܕܗܘܝ ܠܫܥܬܐ ܟܠܗ ܝܘܡܐ ܕܣܡܟܐ. ܒܡܫܟܚܬܐ ܚܕܬܐ ܒܫܢܬܐ ܗܝ ܕܗܘܐ ܒܡܫܚܬܐ ܒܐܝܕܝܬܐ ܕܗܘܝ ܠܫܥܬܐ. ܒܡܫܚܬܐ ܕܛܠܠܐ. ܡܢ ܟܠ ܢܩܠܐ ܒܥܠܡܐ ܕܫܡܫܐ ܡܢ ܢܩܦܐ. ܠܡܕܝ ܟܕ ܘܝܩܕ. ܐܢ ܕܐܣܦܪ ܠܗ ܕܫܡܫܐ. ܘܟܦܪܐ ܘܩܕܡ ܒܡܫܚܬܐ ܕܦܘܪܫܢܐ ܕܡܚܡܠ ܩܕܡ. ܡܠܬܐ ܡܢ ܡܬܚܝܐ ܐܢ ܩܢܡ. ܕܡܫܬܡܠܝܐ ܡܫܚܠܦܐ ܡܢ ܛܘܪܐ. ܟܠ ܝܘܡܐ ܕܡܫܟܚܬܐ ܒܡܫܚܐ ܡܬܕܢܚܐ ܘܡܬܥܪܒܐ ܘܡܬܚܠܦ. ܘܒܡܬܚܠܦ ܒܠܘܩܒܠ. ܘܒܫܡܝ ܓܘ ܒܘܪܟ ܐܢ ܒܕܘܒܪܢ. ܕܒܫܡܫܐ ܒܫܡܫܐ ܕܐܢܫܘܬ ܒܚܠܝܗ ܟܠܗ܀

ܡܢ ܙܒܢܐ ܩܕܡܝܐ. ܗܘܠ ܫܢܬܐ ܕܐܠܦܐ ܕܩܕܡ. ܐܢܫܐ ܡܬܚܘܝܢܐ ܟܠܗܘܢ. ܒܗܘܢܐ ܕܫܥܬܐ ܕܒܝܘܡܐ. ܐܢ ܡܫܟܢܐ ܕܫܡܫܐ. ܠܗܢ ܟܠ ܐܘܪܚܐ ܢܡܘܣܐ ܕܐܠܦܐ ܕܩܕܡ. ܡܫܘܚܬܐ ܒܡܫܚܠܦܢ ܫܥܬܐ ܘܦܢܝܬܐ. ܘܐܠܦܐ ܒܚܘܫܒܢ ܠܗ ܘܡܫܠܡܠܝ܀

ܒܢܝܫܝܢܐ ܗܝ ܒܚܘܠܝ ܒܦܢܝܐ ܡܫܬܘܐ ܦܬܘܚܐ ܘܡܬܚܬܝ. ܘܗܝ ܐܝܬܝܗ ܕܠܫܡܫܐ ܒܐܝܕܐ. ܡܫܬܘܐ ܗܘܝܐ ܘܝܕܥܐ. ܠܗܢ ܡܢ ܦܠܓܘܬܐ ܕܐܝܬܝܗ ܕܫܥܬܐ ܕܡܬܚܙܝ. ܟܠܗܘܢ ܒܝܕܥܬܐ ܠܟܠܝ ܟܠܝܐ ܘܗܘܝܐ ܒܗܘܢܐ ܘܝܕܥܐ. ܗܝ ܒܫܥܬܐ ܘܡܫܚܠܦܝ. ܘܐܠܦܐ ܗܘ ܟܠܗ ܡܕܝܢܬܐ ܘܡܘܦܠܝܢܬܐ ܕܝܢ ܘܦܠܦܝ ܘܡܫܬܥܝܢܘܬܐ.

❖ ❖ ❖ ❖ ❖ ❖ ❖ ❖ ❖ ❖

VOCABULARY

English	Aramaic	English	Aramaic
merchant	ܡܲܟ݂ܕܵܢܵܐ	baking	ܐܲܦܝܵܐ
clay grill, brazier	ܡܲܢܩܲܠ	respect, in honor	ܐܝܼܩܵܪܵܐ
grease, fat, oil	ܡܶܫܚܵܐ	brother	ܐܲܚܘܿܢܵܐ
my lady	ܡܵܪܬܝܼ	linseed	ܒܙܪܟܬܢ
parable	ܡܲܬ݂ܠܵܐ	oak nut, acorn	ܒܲܠܘܼܛܵܐ
to exude	ܡܬܘܡܝܚܠܗ	in the beginning	ܒܪܵܫܝܼܬ
fire	ܢܘܼܪܵܐ	cooking	ܒܫܵܠܵܐ
Nineveh city	ܢܝܼܢܘܹܐ	around	ܕܘܵܪ ܡܕܵܪ
supper	ܚܲܫܵܡܵܐ	cinnamon	ܕܵܪܨܝܼܢ (ܕܵܪܓ̰ܝܼܢ)
twenty	ܥܸܣܪܝܼ	until	ܗܘܼܠ
small mud oven	ܬܲܢܵܐ	cardamom	ܗܹܝܠ
story	ܬܲܫܥܝܼܬܵܐ	olives	ܙܲܝܬܹܐ
wood	ܩܲܝܣܵܐ	to leave, to go	ܙܸܠܹܗ
chaff, straw	ܬܸܒ݂ܢܵܐ	fable	ܚܟܘܼܬܵܐ
quarter	ܪܘܼܒ݂ܥܵܐ (ܪܘܼܒ݂ܥܹܐ)	sheep dry manure	ܛܝܦܬܐ
aroma, smell	ܪܹܝܚܵܐ	dung	
oil lamp	ܫܪܵܓ݂ܵܐ	electricity	ܟܲܗܪܲܒܵܐ
to drink	ܫܬ݂ܹܝܠܹܗ	to set in motion	ܡܘܼܬܲܠܓܸܠܹܗ
Advent prayers	ܣܘܼܒܵܪܵܐ	to heat, to warm	ܡܘܼܫܚܸܢܹܗ
snow, ice	ܬܲܠܓܵܐ	to bring	ܡܘܼܬܹܝܠܹܗ
furnace, clay oven	ܬܲܢܘܼܪܵܐ	to illuminate	ܡܘܼܢܗܸܪܹܗ
second	ܬܪܲܝܢܝܼܬܵܐ	to light, to burn	ܡܘܼܠܗܸܠܹܗ
tea	ܓ̰ܵܝ	to be capable	ܡܨܹܐܠܹܗ ܒܥܒܵܕܹܗ
coal, charcoal	ܦܸܚܡ	to grill	ܡܫܘܼܝܠܹܗ
gas lamp	ܦܵܢܘܿܣ	water	ܡܝܼܵܐ (ܡܲܝܵܐ)

LESSON SEVEN ܦܣܘܩܐ ܕܫܒܥܐ

VERB (ܗܘܡܟܪܢܐ)(ܦܥܠܐ) ܡܠܬܐ

A verb is a word that, by itself, expresses an action or a state of being without the use of another word. The majority of Modern Aramaic verbs are derived from root words which generally consists of two, three, or four letters, referred to here as bilateral, trilateral, etc.

A- Bilateral verbs (most of which originated in Classical Aramaic):

Examples		
to sew	ܚܝܛܠܗ	ܚܛ
to suck	ܡܝܨܠܗ	ܡܨ
to sleep	ܢܝܡܠܗ	ܢܡ

B- Trilateral verbs, for example:

Examples		
to want	ܒܥܐܠܗ	ܒܥܐ
to come	ܐܬܠܗ	ܐܬܐ
to go	ܙܠܗ	ܐܙܠ

C- Quadrilateral verbs:

Examples		
make disciple	ܡܬܘܬܠܡܕܠܗ	ܬܠܡܕ
conjugate	ܡܨܘܪܦܠܗ (ܠܡܠܬܐ)	ܨܪܦ
change	ܡܫܘܚܠܦܠܗ	ܫܚܠܦ

There are four main tenses in Modern Aramaic:

1. Perfect (past tense)
2. Active participle serving as the present tense
3. Imperfect future
4. Imperative or order. These tenses differ according to gender, number and person

PAST TENSE (ܙܲܒܼܢܵܐ ܥܒܼܝܼܪܵܐ) ܙܲܒܼܢܵܐ ܕܦܝܼܫܠܹܗ

The verb to rest ܢܝܼܚܠܹܗ (ܢܵܚ)

		Masculine			Feminine		
First Person	Singular	I rested	ܝܼ	ܢܝܼܚܠܝܼ	I rested	ܝ	ܢܝܼܚܠܝ
	Plural	we rested	ܢ	ܢܝܼܚܠܲܢ	we rested	ܢ	ܢܝܼܚܠܲܢ
Second Person	Singular	you rested	ܘܼܟ݂	ܢܝܼܚܠܘܼܟ݂	you rested	ܟ݂	ܢܝܼܚܠܵܟ݂
	Plural	you rested	ܵܘܟ݂ܘܿܢ	ܢܝܼܚܠܵܘܟ݂ܘܿܢ	you rested	ܵܘܟ݂ܘܿܢ	ܢܝܼܚܠܵܘܟ݂ܘܿܢ
Third Person	Singular	he rested	ܗ	ܢܝܼܚܠܹܗ	she rested	ܗ̇	ܢܝܼܚܠܵܗ̇
	Plural	they rested	ܗܘܿܢ	ܢܝܼܚܠܗܘܿܢ	they rested	ܗܘܿܢ	ܢܝܼܚܠܗܘܿܢ

Note: the dot placed over the letter ܗ in the third person singular feminine ܗ̇ ← this dot indicates that the word is feminine.

◆ ◆ ◆ ◆ ◆ ◆ ◆ ◆ ◆ ◆

ܥܹܐܕܵܐ ܡܫܝܼܚܵܝܵܐ : ܥܹܐܕܥܹܐܕܵܐ ܕܪܹܫܵܐ ܕܫܢܬܵܐ ܚܕܲܬܵܐ ܘܥܹܐܕܵܐ ܕܒܹܝܬ ܝܲܠܕܵܐ

ܒܝܘܡ ܥܹܐܕܥܹܐܕܵܐ ܕܪܹܫܵܐ ܕܫܢܬܵܐ ܚܕܲܬܵܐ. ܟܠܚܕ ܟܠܒܢܝܼܢܵܫܵܐ ܡܚܲܠܦܝܼܢ ܫܠܵܡܵܐ. ܚܕܵܐ ܡܢ ܥܵܕܵܬܵܐ ܕܥܹܐܕܵܐ ܕܒܝܼܬܵܝܹܐ. ܕܡܥܲܕܥܕܝܼ ܟܢܘܼܫܝܵܐ ܡܟܲܢܫܵܐ ܒܥܲܕܬܵܐ. ܒܲܪ ܕܥܕܵܐ ܥܲܡ ܚܲܒܼܪܵܐ ܒܒܲܝܬܵܐ ܒܦܘܼܪܦܵܐ ܕܡܢܵܬܵܐ ❖

ܒܥܹܐܕܥܹܐܕܵܐ ܕܒܹܝܬ ܝܲܠܕܵܐ. ܟܠܚܕ ܟܲܢܝܫܵܐ ܟܠܕܝܼܵܐ. ܡܪܲܘܲܚܵܐ ܕܡܘܼܠܕܹܗ ܡܫܝܼܚܵܐ. ܗܵܐ ܘܟܠܵܐ ܘܡܫܝܼܚܵܐ ܐܠܵܗܵܐ. ܒܝܘܡ ܕܥܹܐܕܵܐ. ܕܝܼܠܹܗ ܡܘܼܠܕܵܐ ܒܡܲܥܪܬܵܐ ܕܒܹܝܬܠܚܡ❖

ܘܒܦܘܡܐ ܕܗܝܡܢܐ ܡܢ ܐܗ ܝܘܡܢܐ. ܒܢܘܟ ܐܝܕܐ ܕܡܫܝܚܐ ܡܕܝܢܬ ܒܚܒܝܒܘܬܐ ܕܟܠ ܡܘܡܐ ܒܢܝܢܐ. ܘܒܢܝܕܒܚܬܐ ܕܗܕܐ ܒܗܒܕܐ ܐܝܕܗܐ. ܒܢܝܐ ܕܡܫܝܚܐ ܡܕܝܢܬ ܒܚܘܠܗܬܐ. ܒܗܕ ܡܠܐܟܐ ܡܝܬܝܗ ܐܠܗܐ: ܒܝܕ ܐܚܝܢܗܝ. ܘܒܡܘܗܘܢܝܗܝ ܒܕܦܢܐ. ܘܒܡܕܢܝܗܝ ܥܡܝܗ ܐܬܦܬ. ܘܒܢܝܕܒܚܬܐ ܕܗܠܝܐ. ܒܗܒܕܐ ܐܝܕܗܐ ܦܝܫܘܗܐ ܕܘܒܕܢܐ ܘܐܠܝܒܚܬ. ܒܗܦܢܐ ܕܢܦܫܝ ܡܝܡܝܢܐ. ܘܒܢܝܕܒܚܬܐ ܕܐܕܒܚܐ ܐܒܓܗܐ ܒܡܣܓܠܡ ܠܡܕܝ ܢܘܗܟ ܒܢܐ. ܒܘܕ ܒܡܚܒܝܕܝܗ ܡܠܐܟܐ ܘܡܝܬܝܗ ܐܠܝܗ: ܕܡܫܝܚܐ ܡܕܝܢܬ ܐܝܠܗ ܒܚܘܠܗܬܐ. ܘܐܝܠܗ ܒܚܒܝܒܘܬܐ ܒܢܝܠܐ ܕܐܘܢܐ ܕܡܘܕܥܐ. ܒܘܕ ܘܠܝܗ ܡܠܐܟܐ. ܒܡܚܝܡܠܗ ܡܕܝ ܢܘܗܟ ܗܐ ܡܫܝܚܐ ܡܕܝܢܬ ܠܒܝܗ. ܦܥܠܝܗ ܐܒܕܗ ܡܢ ܢܡܘܫܐ. ܠܒܢ ܒܡܚܘܡܠܗ ܕܢܝܬܕܐ ܒܚܘܠܗܬܗ ܗܘܠ ܡܘܦܗ. ܘܒܗܕ ܡܘܗܐ ܕܡܕܝ ܢܘܗܟ. ܡܫܝܚܐ ܡܕܝܢܬ ܢܝܬܕܗ ܒܚܘܠܗܬܗ ܘܟܠ ܐܝܕܝܥܠܗ ܐܒܕܐ. ܗܘܠ ܕܝܡܚܝܐܠܗ ܐܠܗܐ ܡܢ ܐܗ ܐܕܒܐ ܠܥܡܢܐ ܕܝܢܢܐ ܘܦܓܕܐ܀

ܒܐܗ ܝܘܡܢܐ ܐܝܬ ܫܒܥܐ ܡܥܝܢܬܐ. ܒܝܗܡܝ ܡܢ ܘܡܐ ܘܦܝܪܐ. ܐܕܒܗ ܘܝܗܒܝ ܬܦܫܬܐ. ܘܐܝܬ ܕܒܝܗܡܝ ܥܒܕܐ ܬܦܫܬܐ. ܘܐܝܬ ܗܠܟܬܐ. ܘܐܝܬ ܫܝ ܡܦܫ ܡܢܡ ܐܝܕܐ ܕܒܝ ܐܠܕܐ. ܒܥܒܕܬܐ ܡܢܡ ܐܝܕܐ ܕܗܦܢܐ ܕܡܕܝ. ܚܠܕܝܬܐ ܒܐܦܕܝ ܗܓܒܬܐ ܘܒܘܠܬܓܝ. ܘܒܢܝܗܒ ܐܢ ܒܘܦܒ ܓܒܠܐ ܫܢܬܐ. ܘܒܡܝܣܪܒ ܓܕܘܐ ܘܦܘܪܩܢܐ ܘܠܒܡܦܬܐ ܫܠܘܬܐ܀

ܘܒܝܪܬܐ ܕܐܝܕܐ ܘܚܦܕܐ. ܒܥܡܠܒ ܐܢܫܐ ܕܡܥܐ ܕܚܐ. ܘܒܗܦܕܒ ܠܐܕܘܐ ܕܦܠܓܐ ܕܠܝܠܝܐ. ܐܠܦܠܬܐ ܕܡܫܬܐ ܒܐܥܒ ܡܢܠܐ ܕܡܒܝܕܬܐ. ܕܒܡܝܗܒ ܒܦܝܫܘܬܐ ܘܒܐܡܕܒ: ܗܘܝܠܗ ܡܕܝ. ܘܡܓܦܚܬܐ ܒܐܡܕܒ ܥܘܓܫܐ ܠܥܡܝܗ. ܡܢܡܐ ܕܒܡܥܕܝܐ ܐܕܘܐ ܒܡܠܗܝ ܒܝܕܬܐ ܕܐܝܕܬܐ ܐܝܗܕܐ. ܢܡܝܕ ܡܓܕܐ ܕܐܒܥܦܬ ܗܦܠܐ. ܘܒܗܕ ܐܕܘܐ. ܒܝܐܕܒ ܒܡܠܘܟܐ ܠܒܝܬܐ. ܘܝܡܐ ܒܡܦܠܓܐ ܡܢ ܗܒܘܕܐ. ܒܘܕܡܐ ܕܒܕܒܐ.ܘܒܠܝ ܐܢܫܐ ܕܒܝܬܐ ܒܐܗܘܒܬܐ ܘܒܐܓܠܒܬܐ ܒܦܝܫܘܬܐ. ܒܗܕ ܦܠܓܐ ܕܠܝܠܝܐ ܘܒܡܘܓܒܐ. ܡܦܠܒܬܐ ܐܝܕܝܬܗ: ܓܕܘܐ ܘܦܘܪܩܢܐ ܘܦܕܝܐ ܗܐ ܐܢܫܐ ܘܚܦܕܐ܀

ܒܦܘܡܐ ܕܒܗܕ ܒܝ ܐܠܕܐ. ܡܠܦܬܐ ܐܠܦܠܬܐ ܕܡܫܬܐ ܡܢ ܟܠܗܬܐ. ܕܐܡܓܒܬܐ ܒܐܝܕܐ ܓܒܕ ܕܟܝ ܒܒܢܬܗܝ. ܘܒܘܕ ܕܐܕܒܬܐ ܠܒܝܬܐ ܕܠܗܕܝܫܗܝ. ܘܐܒ ܗܒܝܬܐ ܒܘܡܬܓܗܫܝܗܝ. ܘܡܕܒܬܐ ܘܐܡܕܒܬܐ: ܘܠܝܗ ܐܝܕܐ ܘܡܝܕܝܬܐ ܘܐܠܘܗܝ ܚܠܘܗܝ ܒܚܒ ܫܡܢܬܐ܀

❖ ❖

VOCABULARY

English	Aramaic	English	Aramaic
natural	ܟܝܢܝܐ	torch, fire	ܫܪܓܐ
to fall	ܢܦܠܗ	alley, street	ܫܘܩܐ
beef tripe	ܟܪܒܐ. ܦܟ̰ܐ	in, with	ܓܘ
lemon	ܠܝܡܘܢܐ ܢܝܡܘܦܝ	jar	ܓܘܪܢܐ
filth, dirt	ܡܘܣܐ	clothes bundle	ܒܘܩܟ̰ܐ
to observe a feast,	ܡܘܥܕܠܗ	pregnant	ܒܛܝܢܬܐ
to celebrate		to torment , to afflict	ܒܠܠܗ
Angel	ܡܠܐܟܐ	virgin	ܒܬܘܠܬܐ
to fill	ܡܠܠܗ	soul, spirit	ܢܦܫܐ
seeds and nuts,	ܡܝܕܬܐ	to return	ܕܥܪܗ
things		to sleep	ܕܡܟܠܗ
to distribute	ܡܦܠܓܠܗ	courtyard	ܕܪܬܐ
to divide		to buy	ܙܒܢܗ
to ascend, to move	ܡܣܘܩܠܗ	fat, lard	ܙܗܡܐ
Christ	ܡܫܝܚܐ	to be ready	ܙܒܠܗ
the anointed one		to sing	ܙܡܪܗ
nativity, cavern	ܡܥܪܐ	power	ܚܝܠܐ
crib		sweet	ܚܠܘܝܐ
to respond	ܡܥܘܢܠܗ	baby	ܛܦܠܐ
		sweet Chaldean pastry	ܟܘܠܝܟ̰ܐ

VOCABULARY

Cont.

English	Aramaic	English	Aramaic
to shake	ܢܙܥܠܗ	to guard, to keep	ܢܛܪܗ
spirit	ܪܘܚܐ	to observe	
odor	ܪܝܚܐ	old age	ܣܒܘܬܐ
to sit down	ܬܘܠܗ	orange	ܦܘܪܬܩܠ
flat loaves	ܬܟܪܬܐ	meat	ܒܣܪܐ
remember	ܬܟܪܗ	money	ܦܪܐ
to stitch , to sew	ܚܛܠܗ	body	ܦܓܪܐ
to eat	ܟܠܗ	to fast	ܨܡܠܗ
in laws	ܒܝ ܚܡܝܢܬܐ	strength, power	ܚܘܝܠܐ
mixed roasted nuts	ܟܪܘܐ	voice	ܩܠܐ
		fast	ܩܠܘܠܐ
		to permit, to leave	ܫܒܩܠܗ

❖ ❖ ❖ ❖ ❖ ❖ ❖ ❖ ❖ ❖

LESSON EIGHT ܩܪܝܢܐ ܕܬܡܢܝܐ

VERB (CONTINUED) ܡܠܬܐ

PRESENT TENSE (ܙܒܢܐ ܕܩܝܡܐ) ܙܒܢܐ ܕܗܘܐ

In Modern Aramaic the present tense is formed by adding either one letter (ܟ) or two letters (ܟܝ) to the beginning of a verb.

For example, to leave (ܙܠܝܗ) becomes, (ܟܐܙܠ) while to ascend or to climb (ܣܠܩܗ) becomes .(ܟܝܣܠܩ) Different verbs have different endings:

Notice that in the preceding examples both ܟ and ܟܝ were used

Conjugation of the verb to leave (ܙܠܝܗ)

		Masculine		Feminine	
First Person	**Singular**	I am leaving	ܟܐܙܠ	I am leaving	ܟܐܙܠ
	Plural	we are leaving	ܟܐܙܠܚ	we are leaving	ܟܐܙܠܚ

		Masculine		Feminine	
Second Person	**Singular**	you are leaving	ܟܐܙܠܬ	you are leaving	ܟܐܙܠܬܝ
	Plural	you are leaving	ܟܐܙܠܝܬܘܢ	you are leaving	ܟܐܙܠܝܬܘܢ

		Masculine		Feminine	
Third Person	**Singular**	he is leaving	ܟܐܙܠܗ	she is leaving	ܟܐܙܠܐ
	Plural	they are leaving	ܟܐܙܠܝ	they are leaving	ܟܐܙܠܝ

Conjugation of the verb to ascend to climb (ܣܠܩܗ)

		Masculine		Feminine	
First Person	Singular	I am ascending	ܒܣܩܢ	I am ascending	ܒܣܩܢ
	Plural	we are ascending	ܒܣܩܚ	we are ascending	ܒܣܩܚ

		Masculine		Feminine	
Second Person	Singular	you are ascending	ܒܣܩܬ	you are ascending	ܒܣܩܬ
	Plural	you are ascending	ܒܣܩܘܬܘܢ	you are ascending	ܒܣܩܘܬܘܢ

		Masculine		Feminine	
Third Person	Singular	he is ascending	ܒܣܩ	she is ascending	ܒܣܩܐ
	Plural	they are ascending	ܒܣܩܝ	they are ascending	ܒܣܩܝ

FUTURE TENSE (ܙܒܢܐ ܡܥܬܝܕܐ) ܙܒܢܐ ܕܐܬܐ

In Modern Aramaic there is no specific rule governing the future tense. The tradition is that in some cases the present tense is used with the addition of the word ܒܶܕ for example ܘܠܶܒ becomes ܒܶܕܘܳܠܶܒ. Generally speaking, when the future tense is formed with the verb ܘܠܶܗ the following words are used either:

Separately ܘܒܠܶܝܡ ܒܶܕܘܳܠܶܒ or

Together ܐܢܐ ܘܒܠܶܝܡ ܘܳܠܶܒ / ܐܢܐ ܘܒܠܶܝܡ ܒܶܕܘܳܠܶܒ

When spoken, the present tense is also used for the future tense, for example ܕܘܳܠܶܒ,could be understood as "I will go" or "I am going"

Conjugation of the verb to ascend (ܗܣܠܶܝܗ)

		Masculine		Feminine	
First Person	**Singular**	I will ascend	ܘܒܠܶܝܡ ܪܗܣܶܝܡ	I will ascend	ܘܒܠܳܡ ܪܗܣܳܡ
	Plural	we will ascend	ܘܒܠܘܢ ܪܗܣܒܘܢ	we will ascend	ܘܒܠܘܢ ܪܗܣܒܘܢ

		Masculine		Feminine	
Second Person	**Singular**	you will ascend	ܘܒܠܶܝܟ ܪܗܣܶܝܟ	you will ascend	ܘܒܠܶܟ ܪܗܣܒܶܟ
	Plural	you will ascend	ܘܒܠܦܬܘܢ ܪܗܣܒܬܘܢ	you will ascend	ܘܒܠܦܬܘܢ ܪܗܣܒܬܘܢ

		Masculine		Feminine	
Third Person	**Singular**	he will ascend	ܘܒܠܶܝܗ ܪܗܣܶܝܣ	she will ascend	ܘܒܠܳܗ ܪܗܣܳܐ
	Plural	they will ascend	ܘܒܠܒ ܪܗܣܒ	they will ascend	ܘܒܠܒ ܪܗܣܒ

ܝܘܢܢ ܗܡܝܟܢܐ : ܢܘܗܪܐ ܕܫܡܫܐ ܕܗܘܐ ܒܡܬܩܦܢܘܬܐ ܕܡܠܟܘܬܐ ܕܢܝܢܘܐ

ܒܥܕܢܐ ܝܘܢܢܐ ܕܢܘܗܪܐ ܕܫܡܫܐ ܕܗܘܐ. ܕܡܬܩܪܝܢܐ ܥܢܢܐ ܫܘܠܐ ܡܥܝܢܐ. ܘܩܐܡ ܗܘܐ ܒܡܠܝܘܬ ܡܠܟܘܬܐ ܡܥܝܢܐ. ܟܕ ܕܫܘܒܩܐ (ܫܘܒܩܐ) ܕܡܢܐ. ܗܡܢܢ ܬܘܡܟܬܐ ܚܕ ܗܘܝܐ. ܡܢܝ ܦܥܠܗ ܝܘܢܢ ܥܡܗ ܐܬܘܪ. ܕܝܠܗ ܦܘܩܕܢܗ ܡܠܟܐ܀

ܬܡܐ ܬܘܡܟܬܐ. ܚܕ ܫܪܪܐ ܕܩܕܡ ܕܡܠܬܐ. ܒܢܘܢ ܫܪܪܐ ܕܟܠ ܕܐܢܫܐ. ܟܠܗ ܡܢܝ ܘܗܘܐ ܠܘܩܒܠ ܗܠܝܢ ܥܬܝܩܐ. ܒܝܕܥܬܗ ܡܢ ܐܝܕܐ ܕܡܢܝ ܗܘܢܐ ܡܠܟܘܬܐ. ܒܢܘܗܪܐ ܕܗܘܕܝܐ. ܘܚܕ ܐܢ ܗܘܐ ܡܥܘܪܠܗ ܐܬܘܪ. ܟܠܗ ܥܬܝܩܐ ܐܢܫܝܐ ܕܫܢܝܐ ܕܝܗ. ܒܡܕܥܘܪܐ ܘܡܦܠܚܢܐ. ܗܘܠ ܗܘܐ ܕܦܥܠܗ ܠܠܒܐ. ܘܡܝܬܠܗ ܘܡܣܠܗ ܠܫܡܝܐ܀

ܡܢ ܫܪܪܐ ܕܟܠܐ. ܒܠܝ ܒܬܘܗܢܐ. ܒܢܘܢ ܕܐܬܘܪܝܐ ܕܘܟܪܢܐ ܕܫܢܐ ܐܢ ܒܥܠܡܐ ܡܢ ܗܘܕܐ ܘܡܕܝܢܬܐ ܒܬܘܪܥܐ ܕܐܬܘܪܝܐ. ܒܬܘܟܬܐ ܡܕܝܢܬܐ ܗܘܐ ܦܬܚܬܐ ܗܘ ܕܘܟܪܢܐ ܕܡܠܟܐ ܕܡܢܝ ܗܘܢܐ ܡܠܟܘܬܐ.. ܒܬܘܟܬܐ ܕܗܘܐ ܒܢܘܢ ܒܐܬܘܪ ܕܘܟܪܢܐ ܕܫܘܕܥܬܐ ܕܡܢܝ ܦܫܬܘܗ ܘܦܘܠܚܗ. ܘܒܬܘܟܬܐ ܕܫܠܡ ܒܢܘܢ ܕܘܟܪܢܐ ܕܐܬܘܪ ܐܘܪܫܠܡ. ܒܥܕܢܐ ܐܝܠܝܢ: ܡܢܝ ܘܡܕܘܗ ܘܠܘܩܒܠ ܘܗܘܢܐ. ܘܕܘܟܪܢܐ ܕܡܠܟܐ ܕܡܢܝ ܐܬܦܩܘܗ ܒܢܘܢܘܐ ܒܬܘܟܬܐ ܕܐܬܘܪ. ܘܒܬܘܟܬܐ ܕܫܡܥ ܒܢܘܢ ܕܘܟܪܢܐ ܕܡܠܟܐ ܗܢܝܢ܀ ܡܢܝ ܦܠܚܘܗ. ܘܡܢܝ ܠܒܝܬܘܪܗ. ܘܡܢܝ ܗܘܢܗ. ܘܫܒܘܩܝ. ܘܒܬܘܟܬܐ ܕܐܬܘܪ. ܒܡܕܝܢܬܐ ܚܕܐ ܡܠܟܘܬܐ. ܕܘܟܪܢܐ ܕܡܢܝ ܐܦܩܘܗ ܘܡܢܝ ܢܟܣܘܗ ܕܢܝܢܘܐ܀ ܘܗܘ ܒܐܬܘܪ ܒܬܘܟܬܐ. ܒܡܕܝܢܬܐ ܚܕܐ ܡܠܟܘܬܐ. ܕܘܟܪܢܐ ܕܡܢܝ ܐܬܦܩܘܗ. ܘܡܢܝ ܐܬܦܫܛܘܗ. ܘܡܢܝ ܦܘܩܕܢܗ. ܘܒܬܘܟܬܐ ܕܐܬܘܪ. ܒܐܬܘܪ ܕܘܟܪܢܐ ܕܦܩܕ ܕܟܠ ܚܕܐ ܡܠܟܘܬܐ. ܢܟܣ ܕܘܟܪܢܐ ܕܫܢܐ ܦܪܘܩܐ. ܘܒܬܘܟܬܐ ܐܢܫܝܬܐ ܕܗܡܢ. ܒܡܕܝܢܬܐ ܚܕܐ ܡܠܟܘܬܐ. ܠܡܕܝܢܬܐ ܡܢܝܐ. ܒܐܬܘܪ ܗܘܐ ܡܠܟܘܬܐ ܒܡܠܟ ܫܡܫܘܫܐ ܕܫܢܐ ܐܢ ܕܗܘܝܢܐ. ܘܚܕ ܐܬܘܪ ܚܘܠܐ ܡܗܘܝܡܢܐ ܠܟܠܗ ܡܠܟܐ ܕܗܘܝܢ ܡܢܝܐ ܕܫܢܐ. ܘܕܡܝܟܠ ܠܟܢܫܘܢ ܐܠܗܐ ܕܡܠܟܘܬܐ ❖

❖ ❖ ❖ ❖ ❖ ❖ ❖ ❖ ❖ ❖ ❖ ❖

VOCABULARY

English	Aramaic	English	Aramaic
Christian	ܡܫܝܚܝܐ	the Gospel	ܐܘܢܓܠܝܘܢ
	ܟܪܣܛܝܢܐ	writer of	ܐܘܢܓܠܝܣܛܐ
strange name given	ܣܘܪܝܐ	The Gospel.	
for Christians of		evangelist	
Mesopotamia		six	ܐܫܬܐ
Fried Chaldean	ܣܡܒܘܣܟܐ	cemetery	ܒܝܬ ܩܒܪܐ
turnover		cemeteries	ܩܘܪܝܬܐ
to climb	ܣܠܩܐ	more	ܒܝܬܝܪ
to ascend		circumcision	ܓܘܙܪܬܐ
age	ܥܘܡܪܐ		ܓܙܘܪܬܐ
funeral rite	ܥܢܝܕܐ	to visit	ܙܝܪܐ
deceased	ܥܢܝܕܐ	patron	ܡܪܝ ܦܛܪܘܢܐ
meaning, translation	ܦܘܫܩܐ	Greek	ܝܘܢܝܐ
tomb	ܩܒܪܐ	it means	ܝܥܢܝ
patron	ܫܦܝܪ	Savior	ܡܚܠܨܢܐ
rice	ܪܘܙܐ	to teach	ܡܘܠܦܐ
dates	ܬܘܡܪܐ	to die	ܡܝܬܐ
thirty	ܬܠܬܝܢ	dead	ܡܝܬܐ
eight	ܬܡܢܝܐ		

LESSON NINE ܦܣܘܩܐ ܕܬܫܥܐ

VERBS – CONTINUED (ܡܫܘܟܢܐ)ܡܠܐ̈

THE IMPERATIVE ܡܠܬܐ ܦܘܩܕܢܝܬܐ

The imperative case is used to express a command. It exists only in the second person singular or plural. The second person singular has no rule governing its formation. The second person plural, both masculine and feminine; ends with the letter ܘ for example, to wait ܣܟܪܗ becomes, in the imperative ܣܟܘܪܘ or with the addition of (ܘܢ) ܣܟܘܪܘܢ

The following is the list of verbs taken from the twenty Readings ܩܪ̈ܝܢܐ in this book, conjugated in four tenses.

Verb	Past	Present	Future	M. Singular	F Singular	Plural
to eat	ܟܠܝܗ	ܟܐܟܠ	ܘܒܝܠܗ ܐܟܠ	ܐܟܘܠ	ܐܟܘܠܝ	ܐܟܘܠܘ
to go	ܙܠܝܗ	ܟܐܙܠܗ	ܘܒܝܠܗ ܐܙܠܗ	ܣܝ	ܣܝܐ	ܣܘ
to put	ܕܪܝܠܝܗ	ܟܐܕܪܗ	ܘܒܝܠܗ ܕܪܗ	ܕܪܝ	ܕܪܝܐ	ܕܪܘ
to walk	ܡܫܠܝܗ	ܟܡܫܐ	ܘܒܝܠܗ ܡܫܐ	ܡܫܘܐ	ܡܫܘܐܝ	ܡܫܘܐܘ
to change	ܡܫܘܚܠܦܠܝܗ	ܟܡܫܚܠܦ	ܘܒܝܠܗ ܡܫܚܠܦ	ܡܫܚܠܦ	ܡܫܚܠܦܝ	ܡܫܚܠܦܘ
to give	ܗܒܠܝܗ	ܟܝܗܒܠ	ܘܒܝܠܗ ܝܗܒܠ	ܗܒܠ	ܗܒܠܝ	ܗܒܠܘ
to wait	ܣܟܪܗ	ܟܝ ܣܟܪ	ܘܒܝܠܗ ܣܟܪ	ܣܟܘܪ	ܣܟܘܪܝ	ܣܟܘܪܘ
to plant	ܙܪܥܠܝܗ	ܟܙܪܥ	ܘܒܝܠܗ ܙܪܥ	ܙܪܘܥ	ܙܪܘܥܝ	ܙܪܘܥܘ
to harvest	ܚܨܕܠܝܗ	ܟܚܨܕ	ܘܒܝܠܗ ܚܨܕ	ܚܨܘܕ	ܚܨܘܕܝ	ܚܨܘܕܘ
to enter	ܥܒܪܗ	ܟܝܥܒܪ	ܘܒܝܠܗ ܥܒܪ	ܥܒܘܪ	ܥܒܘܪܝ	ܥܒܘܪܘ
to want	ܒܥܠܝܗ	ܟܝܒܥܐ	ܘܒܝܠܗ ܒܥܐ	ܒܥܝ	ܒܥܝ	ܒܥܘ
to come	ܬܐܠܝܗ	ܟܐܬܐ	ܘܒܝܠܗ ܐܬܐ	ܬܝܐ	ܬܝܐ	ܬܝܘ
to carry	ܫܩܠܝܗ	ܟܫܩܠ	ܘܒܝܠܗ ܫܩܠ	ܫܩܘܠ	ܫܩܘܠܝ	ܫܩܘܠܘ

Verb	Past	Present	Future	Singular	Plural
to stay	ܦܝܼܫܠܹܗ	ܒܦܵܝܫ	ܘܒܠܹܗ ܦܵܝܫ	ܦܘܼܫ	ܦܘܼܫܘܼ
to gather	ܟܢܝܼܫܠܹܗ	ܒܟܵܢܹܫ	ܘܒܠܹܗ ܟܵܢܹܫ	ܟܢܘܿܫ	ܟܢܘܼܫܘܼ
to understand	ܐܒܝܼܢܵܠܹܗ	ܒܢܵܝܢܵ	ܘܒܠܹܗ ܢܵܝܢܵ	ܐܒܝܼܢܘܿܢ	ܐܒܝܼܢܘܼܢܘܼ
to find	ܫܟܝܼܚܠܹܗ	ܒܫܵܟܹܚ	ܘܒܠܹܗ ܫܵܟܹܚ	ܫܟܘܿܚ	ܫܟܘܿܚܘܼ
to put on	ܠܒܝܼܫܠܹܗ	ܒܠܵܒܹܫ	ܘܒܠܹܗ ܠܵܒܹܫ	ܠܒܘܿܫ	ܠܒܘܼܫܘܼ
to pray	ܨܠܘܼܠܹܐܠܹܗ	ܒܨܲܠܘܹܐ	ܘܒܠܹܗ ܨܲܠܘܹܐ	ܨܲܠܝ	ܨܲܠܘܼ
to admit	ܡܘܼܕܝܹܗ	ܒܡܵܘܕܹܐ	ܘܒܠܹܗ ܡܵܘܕܹܐ	ܡܘܿܕܝ	ܡܘܼܕܘܼ
to be vigilant	ܥܝܼܪܝܹܗ	ܒܥܵܝܪܹܐ	ܘܒܠܹܗ ܥܵܝܪܹܐ	ܥܝܼܪܝ	ܥܝܼܪܘܼ
to be born	ܗܘܝܼܠܹܗ	ܒܗܵܘܹܐ	ܘܒܠܹܗ ܗܵܘܹܐ	ܗܘܝ	ܗܘܘܼ
to help	ܚܝܼܪܹܗ	ܒܚܵܝܪ	ܘܒܠܹܗ ܚܵܝܪ	ܚܘܿܪ	ܚܘܼܪܘܼ
to do	ܥܒܝܼܕܠܹܗ	ܒܥܵܒܹܕ	ܘܒܠܹܗ ܥܵܒܹܕ	ܥܒܘܿܕ	ܥܒܘܼܕܘܼ
to get out	ܦܠܝܼܛܠܹܗ	ܒܦܵܠܹܛ	ܘܒܠܹܗ ܦܵܠܹܛ	ܦܠܘܿܛ	ܦܠܘܼܛܘܼ

ܡܕܝܢ̈ܬܐ ܡܫܡܗ̈ܬܐ : ܢܝܢܘܐ ܕܐܬܘܪ ܘܪܘܡܐ ܕܐܬܘܪ̈ܝܐ

ܗܘܐ ܒܫܘܪܝܐ ܕܒܢܝܢܐ. ܒܡܫܬܪܐ ܡܢ ܢܝܢܘܐ ܕܒܢܝ ܐܬܘܪܝܐ ܘܐܪܡܝܐ. ܠܘܬ ܫܘܪܝܗ ܒܫܘܒܐ. ܐܝܟܢܐ ܒܗܘܐ ܕܐܬܘܪܝܐ ܒܥܘܒܕܐ ܐܬܘܪܝܐ. ܡܢ ܐܝܟܢܐ ܡܫܪܝܬܐ ܒܘܟܪܐ ܒܢܝܢܐ. ܘܡܠܟ̈ܐ ܕܝܠܗ ܡܫܘܬܐ ܒܕܘܟ ܠܫܘܪܝ ܘܡܠܟܐ ܡܢ ܟܘܫܝܬܐ. ܘܒܬܪܗ ܒܢܝܢܐ. ܘܡܠܟܘܬܐ ܘܥܬܝܩܬܐ ܘܡܕܝܢܬܐ ܘܒܢܝܢܐ ܒܡܠܟ ܗܢܐ. ܘܗܘܐ ܐܢܬܐ ܒܡܕܝܢܬܐ ܡܫܪܝܐ ܘܡܫܡܗܐ ܡܢ ܐܬܪ̈ܘܬܐ. ܘܫܘܪ̈ܐ ܢܝܢܘܐ ܪܡܢܐ ܒܫܘܪܝ. ܠܘܬ ܒܐܘܪܚܐ ܕܡܕܝ ܕܪܕܐ ܕܫܘܪܝ. ܗܢܐ ܪܘܫܐ ܫܘܪܝ ܠܡܫܘܬܐ. ܘܟܪܐ ܡܫܒܝܐ ܒܫܪܝ. ܘܟܠܗܐ ܡܢ ܒܢܝܢܐ ܦܠܓ ܡܕܝܢ. ܘܡܠܟܘܬܐ ܒܡܠܟܝ ܫܘܪܐ. ܘܡܢ ܬܫܥܝܢ ܕܫܘܪܝ ܗܢܐ ܠܒܢܝܢܘܬܐ. ܢܝܢܘܐ ܦܬܝܚܐ ܒܚܘܠ ܕܘܟܬܐ. ܘܒܠܝܠܝ ܐܪܒܥ ܡܢ ܥܕܢܐ. ܘܒܦܬܝܚܘܬܐ ܝܬܝܪ ܡܫܠܡܐ ܘܦܬܝܚܬܐ ܘܒܘܪ̈ܓܐ ܕܫܘܪܝ ܐܬܪܢܐ. ܘܗܘܘ ܒܬܐ ܕܒܘܪܓܐ❖

ܒܗܢܐ ܕܫܘܪܝ ܡܢ ܐܝܟ ܢܝܢܘܐ ܕܐܬܘܪ ܒܝܬܐ ܟܠܕܝܐ ܒܡܫܒܚܘ ܒܪܬܐ ܕܐܬܘܪܝܐ ܗܢܐ ܒܕܘܟܬܐ ܡܫܡܗܐ. ܠܘܬ ܕܗܘܐ ܒܗܘܦܟܠܗ ܒܫܪܒܬܐ ܒܗܕ ܐܟܪܐ.. ܒܠܚܘܕ ܒܡܕܝܢܬ ܗܢܝ ܒܘܕ ܘܡܠܐ ܒܘܪܓܐ ܐܪܒܥ ܬܫܥܝܢ. ܒܡܫܬܘܕܥܐ ܗܢܝ ܡܠܟܐ ܘܡܕܝܢܬܐ ܡܫܝܚ ܠܡܠܟܐ ܒܐܘܪܫܠܡ. ܘܐܬܪܘܬܐ ܗܢܐ ܒܡܫܟܢܗ ܠܐܬܪܗ ܘܡܫܘܕܥܠܗ ܠܡܠܟܐ❖

ܫܪܒܬܐ ܬܫܥܝܢ ܡܢܗ ܢܝܢܘܐ ܕܐ. ܒܐܬܪܘܬܐ ܕܒܢܝܢܐ ܒܗܕ ܫܪܒܬܐ ܕܡܠܟܐ ܕܐܬܘܪ. ܒܝܬܐ ܟܠܕܝܐ ܒܕܪܐ ܗܠܝܢ ܬܫܥܝܢ ܢܝܢܘܐ ܕܐܬܘܪܝܐ. ܘܒܬܪ ܕܡܠܟܐ ܟܘܫܝܐ ܡܢ ܐܬܪܐ ܒܡܫܒܚܐ ܘܡܠܟܐ. ܟܠ ܟܠܕܝܐ ܡܫܒܚܝܢ ܒܫܡܝ ܗܠܝܢ ܬܫܥܝܢ ܡܢ ܟܘܪܐ ܘܥܕܢܐ. ܘܐܦ ܫܪܒܬܐ ܟܠ ܒܟܠܝ ܡܢܝܢ ܗܠܝܢ ܬܫܥܝܢ. ܘܒܗܢܐ ܕܫܡܘܥܐ ܒܗܕ ܐܬܘܪܐ. ܒܟܠܝ ܐܟܪܐ ܕܒܢܝ ܐܝܟܢܐ. ܘܐܦ ܗܢܐ ܒܡܠܟܘ ܫܡܘܥܐ ܕܒܢܝܢ ܐܬܘܪܝܐ. ܗܢܐ ܕܡܫܠܡ ܡܢܝܢ ܡܢ ܐܬܪܐ❖

❖ ❖ ❖ ❖ ❖ ❖ ❖ ❖ ❖ ❖ ❖ ❖ ❖

VOCABULARY

English	Aramaic	English	Aramaic
debt, favor	ܡܸܢܬܵܐ	then	ܐܸܢܓܵܗܵܐ
old man	ܣܵܒ݂ܵܐ	to learn	ܐܝܼܠܸܦܠܹܗ
to close	ܣܟ݂ܸܪܠܹܗ	forty	ܐܲܪܒܥܝܼ
flea	ܦܸܪܛܵܢܵܐ	faucet, pipe	ܒܘܼܪܝܼ
prayer	ܨܠܘܿܬ݂ܵܐ	truly	ܒܟܹܐܢܘܼܬ݂ܵܐ
reservoir, marsh	ܨܲܗܪܝܼܓ݂	well	ܒܹܪܵܐ
swimming	ܨܚܵܝܵܐ	atonement	ܟܲܦܘܼܬܵܐ
thanksgiving in scolastic Aramaic	ܡܵܘܕܝܵܢܘܼܬ݂ܵܐ	three days fasting	
lice	ܩܲܠܡܹܐ	ditch	ܓܘܼܡܨܵܐ
pencil	ܩܲܠܡܵܐ	arm	ܕܪܵܥܵܐ
to thank, favor	ܥܒ݂ܸܕܠܹܗ (ܛܒ݂ܵܝܹܗ) ܡܸܢܬܵܐ	swamp	ܓܲܡܵܐ
		young man	ܓܲܘܢܡܵܐ
		temple	ܗܲܝܟܠܵܐ
to rejoice	ܦܨܸܚܠܹܗ	halva sweet delight	ܚܲܠܘܵܐ
forgiveness	ܫܘܼܒܩܵܢܵܐ	to request	ܛܠܸܒ݂ܠܹܗ
dirt	ܥܲܦܪܵܐ	sickness, disease	ܟܘܼܪܗܵܢܵܐ
repentance	ܬܝܵܒ݂ܘܼܬ݂ܵܐ	to bless	ܡܘܼܒܵܪܸܟ݂ܠܹܗ
variety	ܬܲܪܘܵܐ	to offer	ܡܘܼܩܪܸܒ݂ܠܹܗ
glaucoma trachoma	ܬܪܲܟ݂ܘܿܡܵܐ	to fill	ܡܠܹܐܠܹܗ

LESSON TEN ܩܪܝܢܐ ܕܥܣܪܐ

CONJUGATION OF THE VERB TO BE ܐܝܠܝܗ

1. PAST TENSE ܘܝܘܐ

		Masculine		Feminine	
First Person	Singular	I was	ܐܢܐ ܘܝܘܐ	I was	ܐܢܐ ܘܝܘܐ
	Plural	we were	ܐܚܢܢ ܘܝܚܘܐ	we were	ܐܚܢܢ ܘܝܚܘܐ
Second Person	Singular	you were	ܐܢܬ ܘܝܬܘܐ	you were	ܐܢܬܝ ܘܝܬܘܐ
	Plural	you were	ܐܚܬܘܢ ܘܬܘܢܘܐ	you were	ܐܚܬܘܢ ܘܬܘܢܘܐ
Third Person	Singular	he was	ܗܘ ܘܝܘܐ	she was	ܗܝ ܗܘܐ
	Plural	They were	ܐܢܝ ܗܘܐ	they were	ܐܢܝ ܗܘܐ

2. PRESENT TENSE ܐܝܘܢ

		Masculine		Feminine	
First Person	Singular	I am	ܐܢܐ ܐܝܘܢ	I am	ܐܢܐ ܐܝܘܢ
	Plural	we are	ܐܚܢܢ ܐܝܘܚ	we are	ܐܚܢܢ ܐܝܘܚ
Second Person	Singular	you are	ܐܢܬ ܐܝܘܬ	you are	ܐܢܬܝ ܐܝܘܬ
	Plural	you are	ܐܚܬܘܢ ܘܬܘܢ	you are	ܐܚܬܘܢ ܘܬܘܢ
Third Person	Singular	he is	ܗܘ ܐܝܠܝܗ	she is	ܗܝ ܐܝܠܗ
	Plural	they are	ܐܢܝ ܐܝܠܢ	they are	ܐܢܝ ܐܝܠܢ

3. FUTURE TENSE ܒܸܕܗܵܘܹܐ OR ܘܝܼܠܹܗ ܗܵܘܹܐ

		Masculine		Feminine	
First Person	**Singular**	I will be	ܐܵܢܵܐ ܒܸܕܗܵܘܹܢ	I will be	ܐܵܢܵܐ ܒܸܕܗܵܘܝܵܢ
	Plural	we will be	ܐܲܚܢܲܢ ܒܸܕܗܵܘܲܚ	we will be	ܐܲܚܢܲܢ ܒܸܕܗܵܘܲܚ
Second Person	**Singular**	you will be	ܐܲܢ݇ܬ ܒܸܕܗܵܘܹܬ	you will be	ܐܲܢ݇ܬܝ ܒܸܕܗܵܘܝܵܬܝ
	Plural	you will be	ܐܲܚܬܘܿܢ ܒܸܕܗܵܘܝܼܬܘܿܢ	you will be	ܐܲܚܬܘܿܢ ܒܸܕܗܵܘܝܼܬܘܿܢ
Third Person	**Singular**	he will be	ܗܵܘ ܒܸܕܗܵܘܹܐ	she will be	ܗܵܝ ܒܸܕܗܵܘܝܵܐ
	Plural	theywill be	ܐܵܢܝܼ ܒܸܕܗܵܘܝܼ	They will be	ܐܵܢܝܼ ܒܸܕܗܵܘܝܼ

4. IMPERATIVE TENSE ܦܸܥܠܵܐ ܕܦܘܼܩܕܵܢܵܐ

	Masculine		Feminine	
Singular	you become	ܗܘܝ	you become	ܗܘܝ
Plural	you become	ܗܘܵܘ	you become	ܗܘܵܘ

ܝܘܡܢܐ ܠܡܠܦܢܐ : ܢܝܣܢ ܕܫܢ̈ܬܐ ܘܡܪܕܘܬܐ ܕܕܪܐ

ܒܢܝܼܣܵܢ ܕܫܢ̈ܬܐ ܕܪܸܫܵܐ. ܥܠܡܵܐ ܟܠܵܗ ܡܚܘܼܕܬܵܐ. ܘܟܠܝܼܠܵܐ ܕܚܲܕܬܸܐ ܘܡܫܲܘܚܲܪܬܐ ܕܡܲܪܕܘܼܬ̈ܐ ܕܒܪܝܼܬܵܐ. ܘܟܠܗ ܒܘܼܪܟܬܵܐ ܘܚܲܕܘܼܬܵܐ ܕܥܠܡܵܐ ܡܢ ܚܲܕܬܘܼܬܵܐ. ܘܡܘܼܬܒ̈ܐ ܡܢ ܟܠܗ ܕܪ̈ܓܝܼܐ ܫܡܝܵܢ̈ܐ ܘܐܪ̈ܥܐ ܘܡܲܠܟܘܼܬܵܐ ܐܬܘܼܪܝܵܐ ܘܒܵܒܠܝܵܐ ܘܐܟܲܕܝܵܐ. ܕܝܵܗܒܝܼ ܕܘܼܟܬܵܐ ܒܡܫܝܼܚܘܼܬܗ ܠܟܠܵܐ. ܘܟܠܗ ܒܕܝܼܬܐ ܒܡܲܠܟܵܐ ܚܕ ܐܠܗܐ. ܘܡܫܡܫܝܼܢ ܠܐܠܗܵܐ ܘܒܪܝܼܟܵܐ : ܗܘ ܡܫܘܚܠܦܢܐ ܕܥܠܡܐ ܕܐܝܬܘܗܝ ܐܝܟ ܡܪܝܐ. ܐܢܐ ܕܝܗܒ ܚܝܘܬܐ ܒܛܘܗܡܐ ܕܐܝܟ ܘܡܠܟܘܬܐ ܕܒܝܬܐ. ܘܟܠܗܝܢ ܒܢ̈ܝܢܐ ܘܡܕܝܢ̈ܬܐ ܘܚܘܪ̈ܐ. ܡܢܗ ܒܟܬܒܐ ܕܢܝܐ. ܘܗܕܐ ܗܝ ܒܘܪܟܬܐ ܘܡܠܟܘܬܐ ܟܠܗ ܐܝܟ ܒܡܫܝܚܝ ܥܘܡܪ̈ܐ ܕܒܪܝܬܐ ܘܫܠܝܡܘܬܗ܀

ܗܕܐ ܥܘܕ ܒܡܫܬܐ ܚܕܘܬܐ ܕܝܠܗ ܢܝܣܢ. ܐܝܟ ܒܡܫܘܚܬܐ ܕܒܝܬܐ ܗܕܐ ܒܡܕܝܢ ܒܫܠܝܡܘܬܐ ܕܐܬܘܪ. ܒܪܫ ܫܢܬܐ ܕܐܬܘܪ ܕܪܐ ܫܡܫܐ ܬܘܡܬܐ. ܒܡܫܬܐ ܐܬܚܕ ܚܕܬܐ . ܚܕܬܐ ܡܢ ܡܥܒܕܢܐ ܥܠܡܐ. ܐܝܟ ܒܪܝܟ ܦܪܘܩܐ ܒܟܠ ܐ̄ ܢܝܣܢ. ܚܕܬܘܬܐ ܒܪܝܫܐ ܒܚܝܘܬܐ ܘܐܫܬܘܝܢ. ܘܗܝ ܒܥܠܡܐ ܗܘܐ ܦܠܚܐ ܕܢܝܣܢ. ܡܢ ܚܘܬܡܐ ܕܐ̄ ܬܘܡܬܐ ܕܐܝܟ ܚܝܐ ܘܫܠܡܐ. ܘܟܢܫܐ ܘܒܝܬܐ ܘܒܪܝܬܐ ܘܡܠܟܘܬܐ ܘܡܕܒܪܢܘܬܐ. ܘܡܬܒܪܟܘܢ ܒܢ ܦܘܪܩܢܐ ܡܚܘܕܬܐ ܒܒܝܬܐ. ܘܥܡܗ ܕܐܬܡܠܟ ܕܝܠܗ ܒܝܬܐ ܡܛܝܒ ܒܫܡܫܐ. ܘܡܢ ܕܫܡܫܐ ܐܬܐ ܕܕܝܢܐ ܘܐܪܥܐ܀

ܡܢ ܚܕܬܘܬܐ ܕܫܢܬܐ ܗܘܐ ܐܬܚܕܬܘ. ܥܠܡܐ ܦܠܚܘܬܐ ܒܢܝܣܢ ܗܕܐ ܐܬܘܪ ܠܒܪܝܬܐ. ܥܠ ܗܕܐ ܐܝܟ ܡܪܝܐ ܕܒܪܝܬܐ ܡܫܘܚܬܐ. ܡܢܗ ܘܡܬܚܕܬܐ ܘܚܕܬܐ ܒܥܠܡܐ. ܐܢܐ ܚܕܬܐ ܕܡܬܚܕܬܐ ܡܥܒܕܢܐ ܘܚܕܘܬܐ ܕܫܢܬܐ. ܘܗܕܐ ܕܝܢ ܚܝܐ ܘܐܪ̈ܥܐ. ܘܡܬܚܕܬܝܢ ܕܡܕܝܢܬܐ ܘܚܕܘܬܐ ܒܚܕܬܘܬ ܕܐܬܡܠܟܘܬܐ. ܘܚܕܬܐ ܡܢ ܥܡܡܐ ܒܕܘܟܬܐ ܐܬܘܪ ܒܗܝܟܠܐ ܒܡܠܟܘܬܐ ܡܢ ܒܒܝܬܐ. ܘܡܢ ܗܕܐ ܗܘܐ ܕܒܪܝܬܐ ܕܝܘܡܐ (ܚܕܬܐ). ܐܬܪܐ ܒܚܕܬܘܬ ܘܐܝܟ ܠܡܠܟܐ ܚܕܬܐ ܗܘ ܟܠܗ ܕܐܬܪܐ. ܡܬܚܕܬܐ ܒܗܕܐ ܕܒܪܝܬܐ ܒܚܕܘܬܐ. ܗܕܐ ܐܬܪܐ ܒܒܝܬ ܕܐܬܪܐ ܘܒܝܬܐ. ܕܝܢ ܕܚܕܬܐ ܒܫܢܬܐ ܘܐܝܟ ܕܒܪܝܬ ܠܡܠܟܘܬܐ. ܒܟܠ ܦܘܪܩܢܐ ܥܠܡ ܒܚܕܬܐ ܥܠܡ ܒܡܠܟܘܬܐ. ܘܡܠܟܘܬܐ ܘܐܬܪܐ ܡܬܚܕܬܐ ܒܡܕܒܪܢܘܬܐ ܕܝܢܐ ܕܡܠܟܘܬܗ ܘܡܫܘܚܬܐ. ܢܝܣܢ ܥܠܗ ܐܬܪܐ ܒܡܫܘܚܬܗ ܚܕܬܐ. ܥܠܡܐ ܒܚܕܬܐ ܕܝܠܗ ܐܬܚܕܬܘ. ܚܕܬܐ ܘܡܠܟܘܬܐ ܡܢ ܡܫܘܚܬܐ. ܘܐܢ ܕܝܠܗ ܡܠܟܘܬܐ ܚܕܬܐ ܐܝܟ ܡܠܟܘܬܐ ܕܒܪܝܬܐ. ܥܠܡܐ ܕܝܠܗ ܕܫܡܫܐ ܕܫܢܬܐ ܚܕܬܘܬܐ ܗܘ ܐܬܪܐ ܒܚܕܬܘܬܐ. ܘܚܕܬܘܬܐ ܕܢܝܣܢ ܒܥܠܡܐ ܒܚܕܬܐ ܠܒܝܬܗ. ܘܠܒܝܬܗ ܒܚܕܬܐ ܘܒܚܕܬܐ ܘܡܠܟܘܬܐ ܡܢ ܥܠܡܐ ܘܡܫܘܚܬܐ. ܘܡܢ ܗܕܐ ܘܚܕܬܐ ܒܫܢܬܐ ܕܐܬܪܐ : ܒܢܝܣܢ܀

VOCABULARY

English	Aramaic	English	Aramaic
chick	ܙܪܪܐ	female sheep	ܐܘܢܐ
to purchase	ܙܒܢܗ	Palm Sunday	ܐܘܫܥܢܢܐ
to buy		to give birth to	ܐܝܠܝܕܠܗ
blue	ܙܪܩܐ	to produce	
sweetness	ܚܠܝܘܬܐ	dandelion	ܐܩܠܐ ܕܕܝܒܐ
crushed	ܛܚܝܢܐ	leg	ܐܩܠܐ
Sesame butter	ܛܚܝܢ	malva	ܐܪܥܐ
fiancée	ܛܠܝܬܐ	widow	ܐܪܡܠܬܐ
green	ܝܘܪܩܐ	Threshing floor	ܒܝܕܪܐ
greens, vegetables	ܝܪܩܐ	ground	ܒܝܕܪܐ
black	ܟܘܡܐ	bird	ܒܘܫܒܚܐ
onion leek	ܟܪܬܐ ܟܪܕܐܒ	suit	ܒܕܠܐ
to laugh	ܓܚܟܠܗ	uniform	
homily	ܟܪܘܙܘܬܐ	sprout	ܒܪܛܘܦܐ
preaching		blossom	ܒܪܛܘܦܐ
to spend time	ܡܘܦܝܬܠܗ	grove garden	ܒܣܬܢܐ
to add	ܡܘܙܝܕܠܗ	delicious	ܒܣܝܡܐ
shrine	ܡܙܪ	pleasant	
to play	ܡܛܘܝܠܠܗ	outdoors	ܒܪܝܐ
venerable, reverend	ܡܝܩܪܐ	sunset	ܓܢܢܐ
honorable		sunset	ܓܢܝܬܐ ܕܫܡܫܐ
to converse, to chat	ܡܫܘܥܠܠܗ	cracked wheat	ܓܘܪܓܘܪ
amazing, miraculous	ܡܬܡܗܐ	rooster	ܕܝܟܐ
		park yard	ܕܪܬܐ

VOCABULARY

Cont.

English	**Aramaic**	**English**	**Aramaic**
spring	ܪܒܝܥܐ ܒܗܪ	to raise, to nurture	ܡܪܘܒܪܗ
dance	ܪܩܕܐ	to start	ܡܫܘܪܐ
yellow	ܙܥܘܦܬܐ	Hide and seek	ܡܛܘܫܝܐ
Iris	ܣܦܣܢܐ	river	ܢܗܪܐ
beauty	ܫܘܦܪܐ	mare	ܣܘܣܬܐ
festival, feast	ܥܐܕܐ	red	ܣܡܘܩܐ
Sesame oil	ܫܝܪܓ	sumacs	ܣܡܘܩܐ
deacon	ܫܡܫܐ	deed	ܥܒܕܐ
intercession	ܫܦܥܬܐ	lily	ܥܦܪܢܐ
cow	ܬܘܪܬܐ	children, kids	ܥܝܢܬܐ
Chaldean folklore	ܚܓܐ	wheat	ܚܛܬܐ
dance		nice person, generous	ܠܒܗ ܦܬܝܚܐ
white	ܚܘܪܐ	to open	ܦܬܚܠܗ
donkey female	ܚܡܪܬܐ	brown	ܩܗܘܐܝ
garbanzo beans	ܚܪܛܡܨܐ	eggs hen lying on	ܩܒܦܘ
to eat breakfast	ܦܛܪܗ	priest	ܩܫܐ
To incubate	ܦܩܣܠܗ	horse racing	ܪܗܛܘ
outdoor park	ܓܪܐ	to ride	ܪܟܘܠܗ
To flow, to run	ܓܪܠܗ	kind of color	ܪܢܓܐ

LESSON ELEVEN ܩܪܝܢܐ ܕܚܕܥܣܪ

CONJUGATION OF THE VERB TO HAVE ܐܝܬܗ

1- PAST TENSE ܐܝܬܗ

		Masculine		Feminine	
First Person	Singular	I had	ܐܝܬܘܠܝ	I had	ܐܝܬܘܠܝ
	Plural	we had	ܐܝܬܘܠܢ	we had	ܐܝܬܘܠܢ
Second Person	Singular	you had	ܐܝܬܘܠܘܟ	you had	ܐܝܬܘܠܟܝ
	Plural	you had	ܐܝܬܘܠܟܘܢ	you had	ܐܝܬܘܠܟܘܢ
Third Person	Singular	he had	ܐܝܬܘܠܗ	she had	ܐܝܬܘܠܗ̇
	Plural	they had	ܐܝܬܘܠܗܘܢ	they had	ܐܝܬܘܠܗܘܢ

2- PRESENT TENSE ܐܝܬܝ

		Masculine		Feminine	
First Person	Singular	I have	ܐܝܬܝ	I have	ܐܝܬܝ
	Plural	we have	ܐܝܬܢ	we have	ܐܝܬܢ
Second Person	Singular	you have	ܐܝܬܘܟ	you have	ܐܝܬܟܝ
	Plural	you have	ܐܝܬܘܟܘܢ	you have	ܐܝܬܘܟܘܢ
Third Person	Singular	he has	ܐܝܬܗ	she has	ܐܝܬܗ̇
	Plural	they have	ܐܝܬܗܘܢ	they have	ܐܝܬܗܘܢ

3- FUTURE TENSE ܒܹܕܗܵܘܹܝܠܝ

or ܒܹܕܗܵܘܹܝܠܝ or ܘܒܸܝܢ ܗܵܘܹܝܠܝ

		Masculine		Feminine	
First Person	**Singular**	I will have	ܒܹܕܗܵܘܹܝܠܝ	I will have	ܒܹܕܗܵܘܹܝܠܝ
	Plural	we will have	ܒܹܕܗܵܘܹܝܠܢ	we will have	ܒܹܕܗܵܘܹܝܠܢ

Second Person	**Singular**	you will have	ܒܹܕܗܵܘܹܝܠܘܼܟ݂	you will have	ܒܹܕܗܵܘܹܝܠܵܟ݂ܝ
	Plural	you will have	ܒܹܕܗܵܘܹܝܠܵܘܟ݂ܘܿܢ	you will have	ܒܹܕܗܵܘܹܝܠܵܘܟ݂ܘܿܢ

Third Person	**Singular**	he will have	ܒܹܕܗܵܘܹܝܠܹܗ	she will have	ܒܹܕܗܵܘܹܝܠܵܗ̇
	Plural	they will have	ܒܹܕܗܵܘܹܝܠܢ	they will have	ܒܹܕܗܵܘܹܝܠܝ

4- IMPERATIVE ܗܵܘܹܝܠܘܼܟ݂ ܣܘܼܕ or ܗܵܘܹܝܠܘܼܟ݂

		Masculine		Feminine	
First Person	**Singular**	have	ܣܘܼܕ ܗܵܘܹܝܠܘܼܟ݂	have	ܣܘܼܕ ܗܵܘܹܝܠܵܟ݂ܝ
	Plural	have	ܣܘܼܕ ܗܵܘܹܝܠܵܘܟ݂ܘܿܢ	have	ܣܘܼܕ ܗܵܘܹܝܠܵܘܟ݂ܘܿܢ

ܡܲܕܢܚܵܐ ܣܘܼܪܚܵܝܹܐ: ܢܘܼܗܪܵܐ ܕܝܵܘܡܵܐ ܘܚܘܼܕܵܪܵܐ ܕܫܲܢ̱ܬܵܐ

ܢܘܼܗܪܵܐ ܕܝܵܘܡܵܐ ܘܦܘܼܢܵܝܵܐ ܕܝܵܘܡܵܐ. ܒܡܲܦܩܵܢ ܐܲܠܵܗܵܐ ܟܠܝܵܬܵܐ ܕܡܲܬܡܲܢܝܵܬܵܐ ܕܝܵܘܡܵܐ. ܝܵܘܡܵܐ ܗ̄ܘ ܒܪܹܐ ܒܡܲܠܟܘܼܬܵܐ. ܘܐܲܢ̈ܫܹܐ ܒܡܲܦܩܝܼܢ ܟܸܬܒܘܼܢܵܐ ܕܝܘܼܩܵܪܵܐ ܒܕܲܥܬܵܐ. ܫܸܡܫܵܐ ܒܝܵܘܡܵܐ ܠܲܒܵܪܵܐ ܕܐܲܪܥܵܐ. ܡܢ ܒܵܬ݂ܪ ܡܲܢܘܼܬܵܐ ܘܦܘܼܫܵܐ. ܘܐܲܢܵܫܹܐ ܒܟܠܝܠ ܠܡܘܼܦܩܵܢܹܐ ܕܡܘܼܕܥܵܢܵܐ ܘܡܲܬܟܠܝܵܬܵܐ ܒܫܸܡܫܵܐ. ܘܒܲܒܝܼܬܵܐ ܐܲܢ̈ܫܹܐ ܘܚܲܝܘܵܬܵܐ ܒܝܼܬܵܐ ܒܡܲܫܟܠܝܼܢ ܥܒܵܕܹܐ ܘܟܠܝܵܬܹܐ ܘܗܲܒܝܼ ܒܫܝܢܐ. ܘܒܲܐܝܟܵܢܵܝܘܼܬܵܐ ܒܡܲܗܟܝ ܟܠܵܦܵܢܘܼܬܵܐ ܕܠܝܠܝܐ ܘܐܲܝܟܵܐ ܕܕܲܝܪܵܐ. ܘܒܲܒܵܗܵܐ ܗܘܵܐ ܘܐܲܪܒܥܵܐ ܘܟܘܼܪܟܵܫܵܐ܀ ܝܘܼܡܵܐ ܕܫܲܢܬܵܐ. ܒܲܬܲܪ ܒܢܲܝܢܵܐ ܗܵܘܐ ܕܐܝܬ ܘܲܡܲܬܒܲܥ ܒܲܝܬܵܐ ܘܗܘܵܐ ܕܫܲܡܥܵܐ ܒܡܲܫܟܢܵܐ ܒܢܲܝܫܵܐ. ܟܠ ܕܦܲܢܝܵܐ ܟܘܼܠܵܗܵܐ ܕܗܘܼܢܵܝܘܼܬܵܐ ܕܝܘܡܢܐ ܥܵܡܵܐ ܕܐܲܠܵܗܵܐ ܐܲܝܟ ܘܫܲܡܥܵܐ ܐܲܡܲܪ ܠܡܵܪܝ܀

ܒܟܠ ܚܕܵܐ ܡܢ ܫܥܵܬܵܐ ܕܝܵܘܡܵܐ. ܒܡܲܢܝܵܢ ܟܲܠܝܼܬܵܐ ܥܠܵܡܵܐ ܕܚܕܵܐ ܡܢ ܡܕܝܼܢ̈ܬܵܐ. ܟܠܗ ܫܥܵܬܵܐ ܕܥܒܵܕܵܐ. ܒܲܬܲܪ ܒܠܝܠܘܵܬܵܐ ܝܘܼܡܵܐ ܕܐܘܼܡܵܢܵܘܵܬܵܐ. ܒܥܵܡܵܐ ܕܐܘܼܡܵܢܘܵܬܵܐ ܡܲܚܙܝܼܬܵܐ ܦܲܪܨܘܼܦܵܐ ܥܡܘܼܪܵܐ ܕܥܒܵܕܘܼܗ. ܘܒܟܠ ܐܲܢ̈ܫܹܐ ܘܚܲܝܘܵܬܵܐ ܘܟܠ ܠܥܵܠܡܵܐ. ܘܗܵܘܐ ܡܲܫܟܠܝܘܼܬܵܐ ܩܵܐ ܒܠ ܫܥܵܬܵܐ ܐܲܢܵܫܹܐ ܐܝܬ ܚܕܵܐ ܡܢ ܩܵܢܵܐ ܒܪ ܥܵܡܵܐ. ܐܲܝܟܵܐ ܚܕܵܐ ܐܲܠܦܵܐ ܡܢ ܐܲܠܦܹ̈ܐ ܕܡܲܢܵܐ. ܘܐܲܪܒܥ ܒܡܲܢܝܵܢܵܐ ܩܠܵܐ ܕܐܘܼܡܵܢܘܵܬܵܐ. ܘܦܠܓܵܐ ܘܦܲܪܨܘܦܵܐ ܡܲܚܙܝܼܬܵܐ ܠܡܲܬܠܵܐ ܒܟܠ ܝܘܡܐ. ܘܒܟܠܝܵܬܵܐ ܐܲܢ̈ܫܹܐ ܢܝܫܵܐ. ܗ̄ܝ ܩܵܐ ܒܪ ܥܵܡܵܐ ܘܐܲܢܵܫܹܐ ܘܚܲܝܘܵܬܵܐ. ܦܲܪܵܐ ܒܪ ܓܲܪܒܵܐ ܘܒܲܟܹܐ. ܘܒܲܬܲܪ ܕܫܥܵܬܵܐ ܕܐܘܼܡܵܢܘܵܬܵܐ ܡܲܟܪܸܙܵܐ ܩܵܐ ܕܘܼܡܵܪܵܐ ܕܘܼܪܵܐ. ܘܒܟܠ ܐܲܢ̈ܫܹܐ ܥܵܡܠܝܼܢ ܕܘܼܡܵܪܵܐ ܗ̄ܝ ܒܚܹܠܵܐ ܘܢܲܟܠܝܢܵܐ ܡܲܢܝܵܢܵܐ ܠܲܕܥܬܵܐ. ܘܒܗܘܵܐ ܚܡܫܵܐ ܐܲܪܒܥܵܐ ܚܕܵܐ ܕܘܼܡܵܪܵܐ ܕܘܼܪܵܐ ܡܲܡܠܝܵܢܵܐ܀

ܒܲܡܦܲܢܝܵܬܵܐ ܕܦܲܢܝܵܐ ܟܠ ܐܲܢ̈ܫܹܐ ܡܲܦܩܝܼܢ ܒܲܢܘܼܗܪܵܢܵܝܘܼܬܵܐ ܘܥܵܡܠܝܼܢ ܐܲܪܥܵܐ. ܘܡܲܥܵܐ ܒܫܠܝܵܐ ܐܘܼܠܨܵܢܵܐ ܕܒܲܪܢܵܫܵܐ ܐܲܠܡܲܢܝܵܐ. ܘܒܟܠ ܚܲܕܘܼܬܵܐ ܕܝܵܘܡܵܐ. ܐܲܢ̈ܫܹܐ ܟܹܐ ܒܲܠܥܵܐ ܕܐܲܡܥܵܐ ܐܲܦܝܵܐ ܐܘܼܩܵܐ ܕܒܲܠܒܵܐ. ܘܒܚܲܕܘܼܬܵܐ ܕܐܲܡܥܵܐ ܚܕܘܼܬܵܐ ܕܫܲܒܵܐ. ܐܲܢ̈ܫܹܐ ܒܡܲܥܒܵܐ ܥܘܼܠ ܦܠܵܓܵܐ ܕܦܘܼܫܵܐ ܘܐܲܓܠܵܐ ܟܠ̈ܝܬܵܐ ܡܲܕܢܵܐ. ܡܢ ܐܲܡܠܵܐ ܕܕܝܼܢܵܐ ܘܒܲܒܝܼܬܵܐ ܗܘܵܐ. ܘܒܚܲܝܘܵܬܵܐ ܫܲܪܒܵܐ ܟܵܪܘܼܦܵܐ ܘܡܲܚܫܠܢܵܐ ܕܚܲܠܒܵܐ ܘܡܲܟܪܵܐ ܕܡܵܪܝ. ܘܒܲܒܝܬܵܐ ܥܲܕܵܒܵܐ ܠܝܠܝܐ ܟܠܗ ܒܝܘܡܐ܀ ܒܥܵܡܵܐ ܕܝܘܼܗܵܐ ܒܚܲܝܘܵܬܵܐ ܩܵܐ ܚܠܵܦܵܐ ܕܐܲܡܥܵܐ ܡܲܢܝܵܢܵܐ ܗ̄ܝ ܐܲܪܒܥ ܕܦܠܵܓܵܐ ܕܠܝܠܝܐ. ܘܒܲܒܝܬܵܐ ܕܐܲܡܗܵܐ ܠܒܝܬܵܐ ܡܲܗܘܵܐ ܐܲܡܝܵܢ ܒܲܬܲܪ ܥܠܝܡܐ. ܘܐܲܢܫ ܩܵܐ ܡܲܬܪܝܵܐ ܕܢܵܚܝܵܐ ܡܵܪܝ. ܘܩܵܐ ܐܲܪܒܥ ܟܠ ܐܲܢ̈ܫܹܐ ܗܘܝܵܐ ܒܲܬܲܪ ܘܐܲܝܟܢܵܐ. ܘܢܲܦܪܝܵܐ ܠܲܐܲܠܵܗܵܐ ܘܠܡܵܪܝ ܝܠܝܦܐ ܦܘܼܫܵܢܵܐ. ܘܒܡܲܫܠܡܵܐ ܫܢܝ ܫܢܝ: ܘܒܝܘܡܵܐ ܢܝܚܐ ܡܵܪܝ. ܥܘܼܩܵܢܵܐ ܠܥܠܡܐ܀

VOCABULARY

English	Aramaic	English	Aramaic
hoe	ܡܪܐ	the way	ܐܘܪܚܐ
curecuma, turmeric	ܟܘܪܟܡ	egg	ܒܥܬܐ
to cut the weed	ܟܫܦܠܗ	angelica	ܓܘܪܓܡܐ
mouse	ܥܩܘܒܪܐ	greens	ܓܠܬܐ
plant with prickles	ܥܩܦܠܐ	to look for	ܓܠܗ
weed		branch	ܕܘܩܫܐ
Friday	ܥܪܘܒܬܐ	weed	ܕܓܠ
good Friday	ܥܪܘܒܬܐ ܕܚܫܐ	to return	ܕܥܪܗ
banner	ܒܝܪܩܐ	Underground roots	ܙܥܚ
Passover, Pascal	ܦܨܚܐ	darnel	ܙܝܙܢܐ
lilies	ܦܩܬܐ	to give	ܝܗܒܠܗ
room	ܩܘܛܐ	mushroom	ܟܠܦܬܐ ܕܚܓܒ
to cut	ܩܛܥܠܗ	arch	ܟܦܬܐ
resurrection	ܩܝܡܬܐ	to announce	ܡܒܘܫܪܗ
glory	ܫܘܒܚܐ	to confess	ܡܘܕܝܠܗ
festival, feast	ܥܐܕܐ	blowpipe	ܡܢܦܚ
Wild roots	ܥܩܪܐ	bitter	ܡܪܝܪܐ
boiled	ܫܠܝܩܐ	to wash	ܡܚܘܠܠܗ
to brake	ܬܘܝܪܗ	for procession	ܡܘܒܠܗ
there	ܬܡܐ	to carry around	
poppy	ܚܬܐ	to transport,	ܢܘܒܠܗ
Medicanal plant	ܓܢܓܬܐ ܛܒܬܐ	to move, to deliver	
		hole, puncture	ܢܘܩܒܐ

LESSON TWELVE ܦܸܪܩܵܐ ܕܬܪܸܥܣܲܪ
PARTICLES ܐܸܣܘܵܪ̈ܐ

Particles in Modern Aramaic consist of four parts:

	Particles		Examples	
1	**Adverbs**	ܒܲܪ ܡܸܠܬܵܐ	now	ܕܵܗܵܐ
2	**Conjunctions**	ܐܸܣܘܵܪܵܐ	may be	ܒܲܠܟܝ
3	**Interjections**	ܡܸܬܟܲܪܝܘܼܬܵܐ	oh	ܐܘܿ ܐܲܢܵܐ
4	**Prepositions**	ܩܕܝܡܘܼܬ ܫܡܵܐ	with	ܐܸܡܲܕ

ADVERBS ܒܲܪ ܡܸܠܬܵܐ

Adverbs may be classified into

A - Adverbs of time ܒܲܪ ܡܸܠܬܵܐ ܕܙܲܒܢܵܐ

today	ܐܸܕܝܘܿܡ
tomorrow	ܝܼܦܕܵܐ
the day after tomorrow	ܐܘܿܡܚܪܵܐ
two days after tomorrow	ܐܘܿܚܪܵܐ
yesterday	ܬܸܡܵܠ
before yesterday	ܩܕܡ ܬܸܡܵܠ
this night	ܗܲܕܠܸܠܝܐ
this time	ܐܵܗ ܓܵܗܵܐ
first	ܩܲܕܡܵܝܬܵܐ
last	ܚܲܪܵܝܬܵܐ
before	ܩܕܡ
after	ܒܵܬܪ
now	ܕܵܗܵܐ
last year	ܫܸܬܩܵܐ
immediately	ܚܝܼܕܵܢܵܗ

same day	ܒܝܘܡܗ
once upon a time	ܚܕ ܙܒܢܐ
from now	ܡܢ ܕܗܫܐ
from now on	ܡܢ ܕܗܫܐ
	ܘܠܗܠ (ܘܠܩܕܡ)
night	ܠܠܝܐ
day and night	ܠܠܝܐ ܘܝܘܡܐ
in one hour, in time	ܒܫܥܬܐ
at that time	ܒܗܝ ܫܥܬܐ
day	ܝܘܡܐ
that time	ܒܙܒܢܐ
to hurry, to rush	ܒܥܓܠܐ
slowly	ܗܝܕܝ ܗܝܕܝ
how often	ܐܟܡܐ ܙܒ̈ܢܬܐ
until	ܗܘܠ
until when	ܗܘܠ ܐܝܡܡ
for ever	ܗܘܠ ܐܒܕ
perhaps, may be	ܒܠܟܝ
of an eye, a blink in the twinkling	ܒܪܦܦܬܐ ܕܥܝܢܐ

ܥܐܕܐ ܐܘܡܬܢܝܐ : ܪܝܫܐ ܕܫܢܬܐ ܚܕܬܐ ܕܫܘܪܝܐ ܘܚܘܕܬܐ

ܒܠܘܢ̈ܐ ܕܡܬܡܘܬܐ ܕܝܕܝܥܐ. ܐܝܟ ܕܒܡܟܠܝ ܒܫܢܐ ܕܢܫܘܝ ܠܡܘܬܘܬܢܝܬܐ. ܒܡܟܪܟ ܥܢܢܐ ܒܠܗ ܠܐܝ ܬܘܡܬܐ. ܕܫܢܝܐ ܘܡܬܡ ܕܓܠܝܘܢ ܠܥܡܡ̈ܐ. ܘܕܡܝ (ܦܪܚܝ) ܕܫܢܝܐ ܕܝܬܘܬܐ ܝܠܝܘܢ ܒܬܘܡܬܐ ܕܡܘܬܐ܀

ܒܪܫܐ ܕܫܢܬ ܕܗܘܐ ܒܐܢܫܐ. ܘܐܢܫܐ ܒܡܟܪܟ ܕܡܬܡܬܡ ܥܘܢܝܬܘܢ ܠܐܬܘܪܝܐ. ܐܢܫܐ ܘܡܠܟܐ ܒܪܬܝ ܡܢ ܐܪܥܐ ܠܐܬܪܐ ܒܐܒܒܠܐ. ܘܐܝ ܢܬܦܬܐ ܘܡܬܒܬܐ ܪܒܐ. ܒܦܬܚ ܘܒܚܒܪܝ ܗܟܪܐ ܕܒܝܬܐ. ܗܕ ܐܝܘܢ ܐܝܬ ܐܒܕܢܐ. ܘܥܡܡ ܘܡܫܚ ܡܫܝܚܢܝܬܐ ܘܫܚܬܐ ܕܡܘܬܐ. ܒܬܘܕܡܝܐ ܒܥܢܐ ܒܦܝܪ ܡܘܗܡܐ ܠܐܬܪܐ ܒܝ ܠܐܬܪܝܬܐ. ܘܐܢܫܐ ܕܒܝܬܐ ܒܫܢܝܐ ܕܦܪܡܝܪ ܕܠܐܟܐ ܒܝ ܝܘܡܝܐ. ܘܐܬܒܡ ܡܠܟܐ ܡܢ ܠܫܡܐ ܕܪܡܐ. ܒܝ ܐܓܪܬܐ ܐܝܕ ܐܘܦܡܐ ܒܝ ܐܝܟܐ ܘܐܝܬܐ. ܒܝ ܐܝܬ ܘܐܝܟܠ .ܐܝ ܟܐ ܗܘܐ ܒܘܬܟܐ ܡܘܫܝܪܐ. ܦܝܫܘܬܐ ܕܢܬܦܬܐ ܒܝܬܪܐ ܘܦܘܫܐ ܒܗܝܡܢܐ ܕܒܪܝܐ. ܘܐܚܘܬܐ ܘܡܦܪܢܝܬܐ ܕܫܚܡܐ ܪܒܐ. ܒܝ ܐܝܟܠ ܘܪܒܐ ܕܐܝ ܕܐܬܐ ܐܠܟܐ ܒܝ ܕܟܦܐ. ܘܐܚܘܬܐ ܡܦܝܪܐ ܕܫܠܝ ܕܐܝܠܗ ܒܘܐܝܟܐ ܘܐܦܪܐ. ܒܡܦܝܪܝܠܗ ܒܐܪܝ ܒܐܡܠܗ ܦܪܓܐ ܕܦܫܡܐ. ܘܒܝܪܝ ܐܠܗ ܐܘ ܘܒܡܝܠܡܝܠܗ ܒܡܝܠ. ܘܒܠܝ ܐܢܫܐ ܘܐܦܪܐ ܒܡܝܡܝ ܐܘܠܗ ܐܘܠܗ ܒܫܠܝ. ܒܠܝ ܐܝ ܡܝܕܝܬܐ. ܒܐܘܝܠܗ ܕܡܓܐ ܠܐܬܘܪܝܐ ܫܐ ܘܒܢܐ ܒܗܝܡܐ ܕܟܐ ܒܐܗܘ ܠܝܬܢܐ܀

ܒܝܬܐ ܡܢ ܪܒܐ. ܒܫܝܕܝ ܐܬܪܐ ܘܡܠܟܘܬܐ ܘܒܝܬܐ. ܘܒܠܡܝܬܝ ܐܬܘܪܝܐ. ܘܪܒܐ ܘܡܕ ܕܡܡܠܟܐ ܐܪܒܥܐ ܦܬܠܐ. ܕܗܘܘܐ ܣܡܝܠܐ ܒܥܘܡܐ ܘܥܡܠܝܬܐ ܕܦܠܚܝܬܐ ܒܫܡܠܝܬܘܢ. ܘܒܠܝ ܥܦܦܐ ܘܐܘܪܫܝܬܐ ܘܡܫܘܡܐ. ܒܡܠܟܐ ܒܐܝ ܬܘܡܬܐ ܡܢ ܐܘܟܐ ܘܐܝܬܐ ܠܥܘܠܐ. ܒܟܪܝܣܛܝܢܘܬܐ ܗܘܟܐ ܘܐܝܟ ܒܝܬܐ ܡܝܬܝܢܘܢ. ܡܠܟܐ ܥܒܕܐ ܡܚܘܬܝܐ ܡܢ ܐܬܪܐ ܒܝ ܡܠܟܘܬܐ ܕܡܬܘܠܐ ܠܚܘܕܬܐ. ܘܐܪܒܥܐ ܗܘܟܐ ܒܡܠܐ ܚܕ ܒܡܠܐ. ܗܘܐ ܟܢܢܐ ܕܫܡܐ. ܘܦܫܝܛܐ ܗܘ ܝܘܡܐ ܫܪܝܬܐ ܐܢܫܐ. ܪܒܝܒܐ ܠܐܪܥܢܐ ܒܝܬܥܢܐ ܫܡܪܐ ܒܝ ܚܘܕܬܐ ܘܐܝܬ ܒܘܡܪܐ ܒܝ ܒܝܠܦܝܬܐ. ܘܐܝܡܢܘܢ ܒܝܬܐ ܕܥܡܢܐ ܒܘܡܘܦܝܐ. ܡܚܝܕ ܝܬܝܠܐ ܕܢܦܠܝܬܐ ܡܢ ܥܒܕܐ ܘܡܢ ܒܬܦܐ. ܥܦܝܬܐ ܗܐ ܦܪܢܐ ܐܒܓܠܐ ܒܝܬܐ܀

ܥܡܐ ܕܡܪܢܐ ܐܠܗܐ. ܘܐܬܠܦܬܐ ܗܘܐ ܒܥܡܐ ܕܒܠܝ ܐܢܫܐ. ܐܝ ܫܢܝܐ ܒܡܦܘܬܝ ܕܓܠܐ. ܘܐܝ ܦܠܝܬܐ ܒܝܬܠܐ ܢܦܝܫܘܬܘܢ ܒܝܬܐ ܡܢ ܡܪܝ ܘܪܒܝܬܐ. ܘܐܝܬ ܒܝܪܫܐ ܒܝ ܒܝܦܠܢܐ ܡܢܠܦܐ ܦܪܝܢܐ. ܘܡܘܡܪܝܬܐ ܕܦܪܝܚܢܝܬܐ. ܒܟܪܝܣܛܝܢܘܬܐ ܕܦܪܝܚܘܬܐ ܕܡܪܝ ܡܪܝܡ: ܒܝܡܐ ܕܒܢܝܐ ܘܒܢܘܬܐ܀

ܒܪܡܫܐ ܕܫܡܫܡܫܐ ܒܢܚ ܢܪܫܐ ܓܠܕܝܬܐ ܒܡܟܝܕܝܒ ܒܪܕܐ ܕܡܕܘܬܝ ܡܕܝܡ ܢܛܪܬܐ
ܕܘܪܟܝܐ. ܒܪܝ ܬܘܡܬܐ ܒܛܠܒܝܢ ܡܢ ܝܡܐ ܕܐܠܗܐ. ܒܥܦܪܐ ܕܝܢܗ ܓܒܝܪ ܬܥܘܕ ܒܪܘܢܗ
ܗܕܦܝܥܒ ܠܗܒܪܐ ܘܪܟܝܐ ܘܒܗܡܢܬܐ. ܡܢ ܡܘܦܬܐ ܘܩܡܨܐ ܦܢܪܐ ܘܩܡܨܐ ܒܢܓܐ. ܘܫܗܡ
ܕܚܛܐ ܘܗܘܠܝܬܐ ܘܦܘܚܐ ܫܡܒܪܝܒ ܘܛܝܪܐ❖

❖ ❖ ❖ ❖ ❖ ❖ ❖ ❖ ❖

VOCABULARY

English	Aramaic	English	Aramaic
to uplift	ܡܘܫܡܠܝܗ	together	ܥܡܕ ܐܚܕܕܐ
to pay back	ܡܘܦܝܠܝܗ		(ܒܚܕܕܐ)
crop, plant	ܡܝܘܪܘܟܢܬܐ	to run	ܐܪܡܠܝܗ
pilled up	ܡܟܘܒܢܐ	evening	ܒܪܡܫܐ
packed		terrace	ܓܪܐ
trip	ܢܦܠܐ	lower terrace	ܓܪܝܬܐ
deliverer of	ܗܘܟܐ	to pull	ܓܪܫܠܝܗ
the harvest		Religious story	ܕܘܪܟܬܐ
small wall	ܗܬܪܐ	loan, debt	ܕܝܢܐ
between		peep chirping	ܨܘܨܝܐ
houses' roofs		weevil	ܫܗܡ ܕܚܛܐ
to cross	ܒܥܒܪܗ	wheat rust	
wagon	ܥܪܒܢܐ	drum	ܛܒܠ
supper	ܚܫܡܐ	straw plate	ܛܒܩ
hot wind	ܦܘܚܐ ܫܡܒܪܝܒ	bird	ܛܝܪܐ
to step	ܦܫܝܠܝܗ	to guide	ܛܪܝܠܝܗ
tray	ܝܡܝܢܐ	to drive	
plant louse	ܡܘܦܬܐ	daily wage	ܝܘܡܝܐ
aphid		large metal	ܠܓܢ
locust	ܩܡܨܐ	plate, salver	

VOCABULARY Cont.

English	Aramaic	English	Aramaic
worm	ܣܘܠܝܬܐ	grass hopper	ܩܡܨܐ ܚܢܓܐ
depended on	ܣܟ݂ܠܗ	crawling locust	
story, news	ܚܒ݂ܪܐ	to get drunk	ܪܘܝܠܗ
life	ܚܝܐ	large thin	ܪܩܐ
to rotate	ܚܕܪܗ	bread	
to go around		ear of wheat	ܫܒܠܬܐ
wood bearer	ܚܛܒ݂ܐ	bed	ܥܪܣܐ

LESSON THIRTEEN ܦܣܘܩܐ ܕܬܠܬܥܣܪ

CONTINUED - THE ADVERBS ܒܪ ܡܠܬܐ

B. ADVERBS OF PLACE ܒܪ ܡܠܬܐ ܕܕܘܟܬܐ

here	ܗܪܟܐ (ܡܢ ܕܗܪܟܐ) (ܡܢ ܗܪܟܐ)
here and there	ܡܢ ܗܪܟܐ ܘܬܡܢ
there	ܬܡܢ
where	ܐܝܟܐ
from where	ܡܢ ܕܐܝܟܐ
inside	ܓܘܝܐ
outside	ܒܪܝܐ (ܡܒܪܝܐ)
place	ܕܘܟܬܐ
everywhere	ܟܠ ܕܘܟܬܐ
in front, forward	ܠܩܡܐ
behind	ܠܒܬܪܐ
right ward	ܠܝܡܝܢܐ
left ward	ܠܣܡܠܐ (ܠܓܒܝܐ)
downward	ܠܬܚܬ (ܡܢ ܠܬܚܬ)
over upward	ܠܥܠ (ܡܢ ܠܥܠ)
from far	ܡܪܚܘܩܐ
by, with	ܓܒܝ
near	ܩܪܝܒܐ

C . ADVERBS OF COMPARISON ܦܠܓ ܡܠܬܐ ܕܕܘܡܝܐ

so, like this	ܗܵܕܵܟ݂
like what	ܕܐܟ݂ (ܐܝܟ ܡܘܕܐ)
likewise	ܐܝܟ

D . ADVERBS OF MANNER, AFFIRMATION ܦܠܓ ܡܠܬܐ ܕܐܘܪܚܐ ܘܫܪܝܪܘܬܐ ܐܝܟ ܕܝܢܐ

yes	ܐܝܢ (ܢܥܡ)
truly, for sure, justly	ܒܫܪܝܪܘܬܐ
Amen , let it be so	ܐܡܝܢ
enough, sufficiently	ܣܦܩܐ
no	ܠܐ
no not	ܠܐ ܠܐ

E . ADVERBS OF DOUBT ܦܠܓ ܡܠܬܐ ܕܡܫܟܚܢܘܬܐ ܐܘ ܡܫܟܚܢܐ

perhaps	ܟܒܪ
it might be	ܡܡܟܢ (ܟܒܪܐ)
what?	ܡܐ (ܡܘܢ)
why is it?	ܩܡܘ
therefore, what else	ܟܕܡ (ܠܟܕܟ)
in this case, why?	ܐܟܕܡ ܩܡܝ

❖ ❖ ❖ ❖ ❖ ❖ ❖ ❖ ❖

ܝܘܢܢܐ ܘܐܠܟܣܢܕܪܐ : ܣܘܪܝ̈ܝܐ ܒܐܬܪܐ ܕܝܘܢܝ̈ܐ

ܡܢ ܒܝܘܢܝ̈ܐ ܚܫܝܒܝ ܠܗܝ ܬܠܡܝܕܐ. ܗܘ ܠܡܛܝ ܗܕܟܘܢ ܘܫܪܒܬܐ ܘܟܬܝܒܬܐ. ܡܢܗܘܢ ܚܫܝܒܝ ܠܦܝܠܣܘܦܐ. ܘܡܢܗܘܢ ܗܘ ܕܚܘܝ ܚܟܡܬܐ ܒܗ ܗܘ ܡܝܬܘܬܐ. ܘܡܢ ܚܟܝܡܐ ܗܘ ܢܦܠܣܘܦ ܠܟܠܗ ܚܟܡܬܐ܀ ܫܢ̈ܝܐ ܚܢܢܝܐܝܬ ܒܟܬܒܐ. ܒܗ ܒܬܪܟܢܗ ܒܗ ܒܝܬܘܬܗܝܢ ܠܚܘܪܬܐ. ܘܒܡܠܦܢܘܬܐ ܒܝܘܢܝܐ ܒܬܫܡܫܬܐ ܘܚܘܒ̈ܝܐ ܒܐܬܪܬܐ ܝܘܢܝ̈ܐ ܘܐܬܪ̈ܘܬܐ ܘܫܢ̈ܝܐ. ܚܘܕ ܢܦܩ ܒܕܝܪܬܐ ܒܟܬܒܐ ܒܡܬܝܚܒ ܠܐܘܪܗܝ ܗܘ ܠܡܫܚܐ ܕܝܘܢܝܐ. ܒܬܘܕ ܡܕܡܢܐ. ܒܪܘܡܐ ܠܡܠܦ̈ܢܐ. ܘܒܪܟܒ ܐܝܟ ܡܟܬܒ ܕܡܟܘܪܟ. ܘܡܢܡܢ ܕܒܗܪܐ ܕܘܒܝ. ܒܫܘܬ ܠܝܘܢܝܐ. ܘܗܢܐ ܐܝܟ ܟܬܒܐ ܕܡܟܬܒ ܒܠܫܢܐ ܒܣܘܪܬ ܕܝܢܗܘܢ. ܘܡܢ ܕܝܪܬܐ ܐܝܟ ܟܬܒܐ ܒܗܦܟܝܢ ܦܪܝܫܐ ܫܪܒܬܐ ܘܒܦܘܫܩ ܒܝܘܢܝܐ ܘܥܒܕܐ. ܘܒܦܘܫܩܐ ܐܝܟ ܟܬܝܒܬܐ ܟܬܒܐ ܡܫܝܚܝܐ. ܘܗܕܐ ܒܡܕܡܢܐ ܘܟܬܒܐ ܠܐܪܟܐ. ܐܝܟ ܟܬܒܐ ܗܢܝ ܕܗܝܠܝܢ ܡܢ ܒܝܬܐ. ܒܡܟܬܒ ܒܠܫܢܐ ܘܡܟܬܒ ܡܢ ܡܕܝܢܐ. ܒܘܟ ܟܬܒܬܐ ܠܕܘܟܬܗ ܒܘܡܐ ܫܪܒܐ. ܒܫܘܬܐ ܟܬܒܐ ܒܠܫܢܐ ܒܗ ܒܘܪܒ ܠܚܘܕܐ. ܒܗ ܒܦܘܫܩܐ ܕܐܝܟ ܟܬܘܒܐ ܕܪܐ ܘܟܬܒܝܗܘܢ܀ ܒܠ ܡܢ ܕܐܝܬܘܗܝ ܡܕܘܒܪܐ. ܘܒܝܬܐ ܡܘܟܪܐ. ܘܡܟܬܒܐ ܒܗ ܕܡܟܬܒ ܒܝܘܢܝܐ. ܠܐ ܒܢܝܫܐ ܐܝܟ ܬܠܡܝܕܐ ܟܬܒܢܐ ܡܢܐ ܕܐܝܬܘܗܝ ܒܝܫܐ. ܡܢܠܗ ܟܬܒܐ ܒܘܕ ܒܡܫܬܡܥ ܡܢ ܒܝܘܢܝ̈ܐ. ܟܫܘܠܐ ܘܟܫܘܪ ܘܟܬܒܐ. ܘܒܦܘܫܩ ܢܘܗܪܐ ܗܘܟ ܕܒܪܢܫܐ ܝܕܥܝܢܘܗܝ. ܘܒܘܕ ܫܢܐ ܡܢܗܘܢ ܒܬܠܗ ܕܐܡܝܢ ܒܣܘܟܐ ܕܝܠܗ ܒܝܘܢܝܐ܀

ܒܐܬ ܐܬܪܐ ܝܘܢܝܐ ܟܠܕܝܐ. ܒܡܕܝܢܬܐ ܐܬܪܐ ܕܠܟܐ ܕܐܝܬܘܗܝ ܡܕܝܢܬܐ. ܘܡܕܝܢܬܐ ܕܦܝܠܣܘܦܘܬܐ ܢܦܩܐ ܕܝܘܢܝܐ ܕܪܘܡܝܐ ܕܡܘܕܥܐ ܐܝܟ ܥܠܡܝܐ ܒܝܠܝܬܐ ܒܦܪܓܡܐ܀

ܡܕܝܢܬܐ ܒܐܬ ܐܬܪܐ ܟܠܕܝܐ. ܘܐܢܫܐ ܘܟܬܒܐ ܘܐܬܘܪܝܐ ܒܝܬ ܢܗܪܝܢ. ܐܝܟ ܕܒܝܬ ܢܗܪܝܢ. ܘܐܝܟ ܕܝܘܡܢܐ ܘܐܝܟ ܕܒܫܢܝܐ. ܐܝܟ ܕܒܢܝܢܐ ܟܬܒܐ. ܘܐܫܬܝܢ ܒܢܝܢܐ ܝܘܢܝ̈ܐ. ܒܗ ܒܠܫܢܐ ܟܬܒܐ ܘܐܬܟܘܢ. ܘܒܢܝܢܐ ܡܢ ܝܘܢܝܐ ܠܟܘܠܐ ܒܗ ܠܟܬܒܐ. ܘܐܝܟ ܕܒܪܟܘܬ ܠܐܬܪܘܬܐ. ܟܘܠܐ ܐܝܬܘܗܝ ܡܕܝܢܬܐ. ܗܘ ܐܬܘܪ̈ܝܐ ܒܢܦܫܐ ܘܟܬܒܐ ܘܟܬܒܐ ܘܐܝܬܝܗ. ܘܗܘ ܐܝܬ ܕܐܝܬ ܐܬܪܐ ܒܟܘܢܐ. ܗܘ ܫܠܡܐ ܠܗ ܕܒܠܗ ܡܢܐ ܒܗܦܟܐ ܡܢ ܝܘܡܐ ܕܝܒܫܬܐ ܒܐܘܪܗܝ ܘܒܐܬܪܐ ܡܒܠ ܟܬܒܐ܀

ܐܬ ܐܬܪܐ ܕܒܘܪܟܬܐ. ܒܫܢ̈ܝܐ ܫܢܝ ܒܒܠ ܐܢܫܐ. ܘܐܝܟ ܕܗܦܟܐ ܒܠܗ ܗܘܦܐ ܘܟܬܒ. ܒܬܘܪ ܦܬܐ ܠܦܝܠܣܘܦ̈ܐ ܘܒܦܬܝܦ ܕܝܢܗܘܢ. ܘܒܡܫܡܫ ܗܘ ܗܦܝܠܣܘܦ̈ܐ ܘܟܬܒܝܗܘܢ ܡܟܘܪܐ ܕܐܬܪܘܬܐ. ܒܗ ܗܘ ܒܚܢܐ ܐܦ ܗܘ ܘܦܢܐ ܕܝܘܢܝ̈ܐ ܘܐܬܪܬܐ. ܒܗ ܗܘ ܡܦܫܩܢܐ ܠܐܬܪܘܬܐ ܕܣܘܪܝܐ܀

VOCABULARY

English	Aramaic	English	Aramaic
automobile, car	ܛܪܘܡܒܝܠ	country	ܐܬܪܐ
wallet, bag or	ܟܝܣܬܐ	sun rise	ܒܗܪܐ ܕܝܘܡ
pouch for		cantaloupe, melon	ܫܛܒܓܬܐ
to pick, to pluck	ܠܩܛܠܗ	alive	ܒܣܝܡܐ
to gather, to reap		to build	ܒܢܝܠܗ
school	ܡܕܪܫܬܐ	gravel, pebbles	ܒܩܪܐ
how much	ܟܡܐ	boy, boys	ܒܪܘܢܐ (ܒܢܘܢܐ)
as much		girl, girls	ܒܪܬܐ (ܒܢܬܐ)
to renew	ܡܚܘܕܬܠܗ	to the side	ܡܟܪܐ
age	ܥܘܡܪܐ	long large melon	ܫܥܒܠܐ
upper room	ܥܠܝܬܐ	oval shape	
thistle	ܥܟܘܒܐ	man	ܓܒܪܐ
to leave to exit	ܦܠܛܠܗ	marriage	ܓܘܪܐ
Paver, grave stones	ܦܪܫܐ	sack, burlap	ܓܘܢܝܐ
small booth	ܡܘ ܦܪܢܐ	gunny	
shack		near by	ܓܢܒܝ
sapling, vine	ܡܘܪܡܐ	flea market	ܓܒܘ
transplant, plant		farmer market	
market	ܫܘܩܐ	hay thrasher	ܓܪܓܪܐ
nap, sleep	ܫܢܬܐ	side	ܕܦܢܐ
ant	ܫܚܦܢܐ	to pound	ܕܩܠܗ
cucumber	ܚܪܡܘܙܐ-ܚܪܡܘܙܬܐ	container made	ܙܒܘܠ
large bag for	ܓܪܪܐ	of reeds	
carrying the hay		hay bed, nest	ܣܘܟܐ
		thistle bed	

LESSON FOURTEEN ܩܪܝܢܐ ܕܐܪܒܥܣܪ

CONTINUED - THE ADVERB ܒܪ ܡܠܬܐ

F. ADVERB OF DESIRE ܒܪ ܡܠܬܐ ܕܡܬܡܢܝܢܘܬܐ

when	ܐܡܬܝ
who can give me	ܡܢ ܢܬܠ ܠܝ
who can make	ܡܢ ܢܥܒܕ
then when	ܐܡܬܝ ܟܝܬ

G. ADVERBS OF INTERROGATION OR DEMAND ܒܪ ܡܠܬܐ ܕܫܘܐܠܐ

where	ܐܝܟܐ
from where	ܡܢ ܕܐܝܟܐ
how	ܐܝܟܢ
if, whether	ܐܢ
what	ܡܢܐ
why	ܠܡܢ
how many	ܐܟܡܐ
when	ܐܡܬܝ
how much then	ܟܡܐ ܟܝܬ
like what , what sort of	ܐܝܟ ܡܢܐ

H. ADVERBS OF EXPLANATION ܦܵܬܼ ܡܸܠܬܵܐ ܕܦܘܼܫܵܩܵܐ

more	ܒܝܼܫܝܲܬܝܼܪ
less	ܒܝܼܫ ܒܨܝܼܪܵܐ
plenty	ܟܲܒܝܼܪܵܐ
very much	ܒܠܝܼܫ ܟܲܒܝܼܪܵܐ
less or more	ܒܨܝܼܪܵܐ ܘܟܲܒܝܼܪܵܐ
a little	ܟܨܝܼܪܵܐ
a little less	ܟܨܝܼܪܵܐ ܒܝܼܫ ܒܨܝܼܪܵܐ
a little more	ܟܨܝܼܪܵܐ ܒܝܼܫ ܟܲܒܝܼܪܵܐ
only	ܒܲܣ
never	ܐܲܒܕܝܼ
alone	ܒܠܚܘܿܕܹܗ
soon after	ܒܵܬܲܪ ܟܨܝܼܪܵܐ
for a long time	ܡܢ ܙܲܒܢܵܐ
centuries ago, ancient time	ܒܕܵܪܹܐ ܩܲܕܡܵܝܹܐ

I. ADVERBS OF QUALITY ܦܵܬܼ ܡܸܠܬܵܐ ܕܕܝܼܠܵܝܘܼܬܼܵܐ

very well	ܪܵܒܵܐ
good	ܛܵܒܵܐ
free, in vain	ܒܲܠܫ

ܩܛܠܐ ܐܪܡܢܝܐ : ܐܪܒܥܐ ܕܐܡܣܘ ܫܢܝܬܐ

ܟܝ ܬܦܩܐ ܕܥܡܡܐ ܒܢܘܗܪܝܢ ܒܠ ܒܘܪܟܬܗܘܢ. ܘܦܪܝܩ ܦܪܝܩ ܡܘܪܟܐ ܒܡܫܟܢܐ ܕܝܘܡܐ. ܐܪܒܘܢ ܠܐ ܒܦܝܫ ܡܢܝܢܝ ܐܠܐ ܥܠܬܢܝ ܕܒܣܠܒ ܒܘܠܝܢܝ ܗܐ ܬܪܘܢܐ ܗܐ ܕܝܪܝ ܬܪܝܢܐ❖

ܐܝܟ ܫܘܒܥܐ ܡܢ ܐܢܫܐ ܒܢܘܒܢ ܘܪܘܚܘܢ. ܗܐ ܓܘܪܐ ܒܝܪܐܗܐ. ܘܕܓܠܐ ܒܡܢܛܡܝܢܗ ܒܢܘܝܢܐ. ܘܒܢܡܠܝܢܗ ܠܟܢܫܐ ܒܝ ܠܥܘܦܐ ܗܐ ܘܒܦܝܪܐ. ܘܐܝܟ ܐܫܬܐ ܒܢܘܒܝܢܗ ܘܪܘܚܘܢ ܗܐ ܓܘܪܐ ܒܡܓܠܐ ܘܒܡܢܛܡܝܢܗ ܒܡܓܘܪܐ ܘܒܢܡܠܝܢܗ ܒܥܓܪܐ ܠܒܘܝܪܐ. ܒܝܡܢܝܢܗ ܒܓܕܓܕܐ ܘܒܡܝܕܪܠܗ. ܘܗܘܝܐ ܒܢܡܠܝܢܗ ܠܟܢܫܐ ܒܓܪܕܐ. ܗܐ ܐܝܓܠܐ ܕܝܣܘܬܐ ܘܗܐ ܐܝܦܢܐ. ܒܘܕ ܟܢܫܐ ܐܝܗܘܠܗ ܒܘܝܕܐ (ܐܪܟܐ ܘܟܦܪܐ ܕܦܪܡܝܕܐ ܕܡܫܐ). ܘܠܐ ܐܢܫܐ ܐܝܗܘܝܗ ܕܢܡܠܘܟܐ ܕܓܠܗ ܠܟܢܫܐ ܐܠܐ ܟܐܪ ܡܐ ܕܡܓܝܣܘܠܗ ܡܘܠܟܝ. ܕܢܘܒܠܘܠܗ ܘܐܡܪ ܕܝܪܒܬܐ. ܕܡܘܬܐ ܟܘܡ ܠܡܪܬܐ ܕܒܘܝܕܐ ܕܝܦܝܢܘܬܐ ܦܪܐ ܗܐ ܣܒܘܪܐ ܒܡܠܘܟܐ❖

ܐܡܝܪ ܡܓܡܠܢܐ ܘܡܘܠܟܝ. ܐܢܫܐ ܐܢܫܐ ܕܡܫܒܚܬܐ ܡܢ ܡܐܐ ܘܡܢ ܟܕܝ. ܘܒܘܕ ܫܝ ܡܢܝܢܝ ܒܒܝܬܐ ܒܝܬܦܐ. ܘܒܠ ܡܕ ܒܘܝܕܐ ܢܘܒܠܦܐ. ܐܟܡܢܐ ܒܝ ܦܝܐ ܡܢ ܓܟܝܐ ܒܝ ܢܟܕܐ ܒܝ ܒܠܘܝܬܐ ܗܐ ܐܝܟ ܗܝܒܝܗ. ܟܝ ܬܦܩܐ ܐܢܫܐ ܡܐܦܐ ܡܢ ܒܘܪܐ ܦܪܐ ܡܢ ܟܬܒܐ ܒܝ ܦܐܬܐ. ܘܡܘܟܝܒܘܬܐ ܒܝܢܬܐ ܒܝ ܒܢܟܕܐ❖

ܘܟܕ ܐܪܒܥܐ ܓܒܪܐ ܒܡܥܝܒܐ ܘܦܥܝܒܐ ܒܟܬܝܐ. ܘܟܝܒܪܐ ܡܢ ܐܢܫܐ ܘܒܦܪܐ ܡܠܦܐ ܡܢܝܢܝ ܒܒܝܬܐ. ܘܡܟܝܠܝܒܘܬܐ ܒܡܦܐ ܘܡܘܟܝܒܘܬܐ ܒܟܬܒܐ❖

ܟܕ ܐܪܒܥܐ ܠܓܘܦܐ ܫܝ ܕܠܐ ܦܠܝܫܘܦܐ. ܘܠܓܘܦܐ ܫܝ ܕܠܐ ܡܫܝܠܘܦܐ. ܘܫܢܝܐ ܘܦܦܐ ܐܦܬܐ ܒܫܝܒܝܐ ܢܦܫܐ ܐܢܫܐ. ܘܡܘܕܝܢ ܘܫܘܒܚܐ ܕܐܡܣܘ❖

VOCABULARY

English	Aramaic	English	Aramaic
mini sickle	ܡܲܓ݂ܠܘܿܢܵܐ	to dry out	ܝܒܸܫܠܹܗ
to winnow	ܡܕܘܼܪܹܝܠܹܗ	to bake	ܝܦܹܝܠܹܗ
to trade, to sell	ܡܙܘܼܒܢܹܗ	hundreds	ܝܡܵܬܹ̈ܐ
to earn	ܡܫܘܼܩܠܹܗ	grapes	ܥܸܢܒܹ̈ܐ
poor person	ܡܣܟܹܢܵܐ	dry carobs	ܚܲܪܘܼܒܹ̈ܐ
to figure	ܡܫܘܼܡܹܝܗ	blessing	ܒܘܼܪܟ݂ܬܵܐ
to appraise		outdoor	ܒܪܵܝܵܐ
to gather	ܡܓܘܼܡܠܹܠܹܗ	out of town	
to carry, to transfer	ܢܩܸܠܹܗ	handful, fistful	ܟܡܫܵܐ
to forget	ܢܫܸܐܠܹܗ	next year	ܕܝܼܬܹܐ ܫܲܢ݇ܬܵܐ
needy	ܣܢܝܼܩܵܐ	winnower, tractor	ܕܪܵܫܵܐ
fruit	ܦܹܐܪܵܐ	to push, to pay	ܕܦܸܠܠܹܗ
tax appraisal	ܡܘܼܠܟ̰ܸܒ	go slowly	ܗܝܼܕܝܼ ܗܝܼܕܝܼ
overripe cucumber	ܥܲܠܝܼܩܵܐ	paper	ܦܪܵܣܵܐ
figs	ܬܹܐܢܹ̈ܐ	very hot wind	ܙܲܡܗܲܪܝܼܪ
two (feminine)	ܬܸܬܹܐ	government	ܚܸܟܘܼܡܵܐ
hot	ܫܲܚܝܼܢܵܐ (ܚܲܫܝܼܢܵܐ)	to carry	ܛܥܝܼܢܹܗ
large hay bag	ܓܪܵܪܵܐ	drinking vessel	ܛܲܣܬܵܐ
carobs	ܓܹܪܘܵܐ	must, necessary	ܠܵܙܸܡ
hot weather	ܫܘܿܡܵܐ	needed	
taxes	ܟܪ̈ܵܓܹܐ	there wasn't	ܠܲܝܘܵܐ
		sickle	ܡܲܓܠܵܐ

❖ ❖ ❖ ❖ ❖ ❖ ❖ ❖ ❖

LESSON FIFTEEN ܩܪܝܢܐ ܕܚܡܫܬܥܣܪܐ

CONJUNCTIONS ܐܣܪ̈ܐ ܡܣܝܒܪ̈ܢܐ – ܡܘܩܦ̈ܢܐ

Conjunctions are words which link words or sentences together. In scholastic Aramaic there are two divisions: ornamental and necessary

A - ORNAMENTAL ܨܒܬܢܝ̈ܐ

There are seven ornamental words in scholastic Aramaic they have no meaning ܦܝܢ ܕܝܢ ܓܝܪ ܟܝܬ ܬܘܒ ܟܝ ܠܡ These words are not used in Modern Aramaic: Example: when: ܟܕ ܓܝܪ

B - NECESSARY ܐܠܨܝ̈ܐ

These words are used in Modern Aramaic:

			Example
a	CAUSE	because	ܐܠܐ.ܡܛܠ ܐܝܟ ܡܕܡ
b	CONCESSION	I say	ܒܐܡܪܝ
		although	ܥܘܕ ܗܡ
		and also	ܘܗܡ
		maybe	ܒܠܟܝ
c	CO-ORDINATION	also	ܒܕܡ
		nor	ܘܠܐ
		but	ܐܠܐ or ܐܘ ܒܪ
d	CORRELATION	like	ܡܟܘܝܕ
		either or	ܐܝ ܐܘ
		neither nor	ܠܐ ܐܝܟ ܘܠܐ ܐܝܟ
e	EXPLANATION	I mean	ܝܥܢܝ
f	ADVERSITY	never mind	ܠܒܘܝܫܐ
g	CONCLUSION	because of	ܒܝܕ ܐܝܟ ܗܕܒܪ
		finally	ܒܗܪ ܟܠ

INTERJECTIONS ܡܸܠܘܵܬܹ̈ܐ ܗܲܢܝܵܢܹ̈ܐ

Interjections are words which expresses emotion.
Some of these words are:

			Examples		
			MS	FS	MP & FP
a	CALLING WORDS	you	ܐܲܢ݇ܬ	ܐܲܢ݇ܬܝ	ܐܲܚܬܘܿܢ
		you there	ܐܲܢ݇ܬ ܗܵܡܵܐ	ܐܲܢ݇ܬܝ ܗܵܡܵܐ	ܐܲܟ݂ܬܘܿܢ ܗܵܡܵܐ

b	SURPRISE	what is this?	ܡܘܼܕܝܼܠܹܗ ܗܵܕܹܐ
		what a?	ܗܘܿ
c	GRIEF	woe is me	ܘܵܝ ܐܸܠܝܼ ܡܵܐ ܒܕܝܼܠܹܗ ܒܓܵܘܝܼ
		alas	(ܚܸܣ ܐܸܠܝ ܐܸܠܘܼܟ݂)
			ܘܵܝ ܚܸܣ (ܘܵܝ ܘܵܝ)
d	DEPRECATION	let it not be	ܕܫܘܵܐ ܡܝܼܢ
		God forbid	ܚܵܫܠܹܗ
e	OF PRAISE	well done	ܒܦܲܢܵܐ ܒܦܲܩܕܵܐ
f	TO CALL ATTENTION	hey	ܗܵܝ
g	OF WONDER	what?	ܡܵܗܵܐ
		is that right	ܡܢܡܵܐ؟
h	OF JOY	yes	ܐܝܼܢ : ܒܲܠܝ
i	OF ENTREATY	I beg you	ܒܡܕܵܟ݂ܝ ܡܝܼܬܝ ܒܡܝܼܬܘܿܢ ܡܝܼܬܝ

❖ ❖ ❖ ❖ ❖ ❖ ❖ ❖ ❖

ܝܲܪ̈ܚܹܐ ܫܲܡܫܵܢܵܝܹ̈ܐ : ܝܲܪܚܵܐ ܕܐܵܒ݂ (ܐܵܒ݂) ܒܝܼܪܵܐ ܕܝܠܠܢܐ

ܝܲܪܚܵܐ ܕܐܵܒ݂ ܐܲܕܫܵܐ. ܚܘܼܟ݂ܠ ܒܝܼܪܵܐ ܕܝܠܠܢܐ ܕܡܕܝ ܠܬܘܕܐ ܕܐܬܚܘܕ ܗܵܐ ܡܘܥܕܐ ܘܐܠܢܐ. ܘܒܐܘܗ ܐܢܫܐ ܒܐܡܕܝ: ܡܝܟܐ ܘܝܠܗ ܓܠܝ ܘܬܘܡܟܐ ܦܬܘܚܐ ܘܝܠܗ ܐܬܐ. ܘܡܥܒܕܢܘܬܐ ܒܐܕܫܐ. ܚܘܼܟ݂ܠ ܒܝܼܪܵܐ ܕܥܘܢܐ ܕܡܕܢܚܐ ܡܕܝܢ ܒܓܢܢܐ ܘܦܓܪܐ ܠܥܡܢܐ. ܘܡܕܚܡܐ ܡܢ ܡܘܫܝܚܐ ܝܫܘܥܐ ܗܥܕܐ ܬܘܡܟܐ ܡܢܡ ܒܝܼܪܵܐ. ܘܟܐ ܐܓܠܝܐ ܦܝܪܐ ܘܡܚܕܘܬܐ(ܘܐܡܐ). ܐܟܐ ܕܐܘܐ ܒܠܝܢܐ ܝܩܕܐ ܕܝܠܗ ܚܕܝܘܬܐ ܡܢ ܚܘܠܐ ܝܠܕܐ ܕܡܫܝܚܐ ܘܒܥܠܡܝܐ ܝܠܕܐ ܘܐܘܡܬܐ. ܒܓܕܕܐ ܐܡܝܪ ܗܡܘܬܐ ܘܗܘܝܐ ܒܪ ܥܢܕܐ✧

ܐܢܫܐ ܡܫܢܕܝܐ ܗܐ ܒܢܢܐ. ܡܡܫܒܚܢܐ ܦܠܚܝܐ ܠܦܠܚܐ ܒܡܫܒܚܢܐ ܕܒܪܩܐ ܒܪ ܕܓܒܝܪܐ. ܡܢ ܡܫܒܚܢܐ ܕܒܪܩܐ ܡܚܟܝܐ ܡܕܝܢܬܐ ܒܡܕܝܢܬܐ. ܘܕܐܘܐ ܗܟܝܢܐ ܕܫܕܝܕ ܒܥܡܝܕܬܐ ܫܢܕܐ ܒܦܠܟܐ ܕܡܕܝܢ ܘܗܘܕܝܘܬܗ. ܟܠܢ ܒܘܕ ܒܝܢܐ ܡܕܝܢ ܡܫܘܟܗ ܒܗܘܦ. ܢܡܒܝܐ ܒܦܠܟܐ ܒܘܡܟܐ ܒܡܘܡܐ. ܘܡܟܘܟܠܗ ܒܟܕܘܕ. ܘܟܕܥܝܘܬܗ ܦܡܝܟܐ ܡܢ ܣܠܝܟܐ ܠܟܕܝܐ ܘܡܠܗܘܟܗ. ܘܚܘܦ ܡܦܠܥܘܟܠ ܠܡܕܝܢܬܐ. ܘܡܥܕܘܐ ܡܫܒܚܢܐ ܒܡܫܟܐ ܒܪܩܐ ܠܦܕܓܢܬܐ ܘܚܘܕܐ. ܘܡܓܘܐ ܫܡܕܐ ܡܕܘܥܘܢܐ ܘܕܘܐ ܠܫܝܗ ܡܫܝܚܟܐ ܕܡܫܚܐ. ܘܝܫܝܒܐ ܠܡܕܐ ܕܡܫܝܚܟܐ ܒܪܩܐ ܗܒܝܕܐ. ܘܢܡܠܝܘܟܠ ܠܡܓܐ ܗܐ ܒܢܢܐ. ܘܡܢ ܡܫܒܚܢܐ ܕܓܒܝܪܐ ܗܘܕܝܐ ܦܕܝܓܐ ܠܡܚܟܝܐ ܘܚܘܕܐ. ܘܢܚܠܝܘܟܠ ܠܐܘܢܐ ܕܡܟܘܟܠ✧

ܐܒܘܐ ܐܢܫܐ ܡܘܒܕܐ ܥܘܟܠܝܘܒ ܗܘܐ ܒܢܢܐ ܕܐܘܢܐ. ܫܘܕܝܐ ܒܐܕܟܐ ܟܘܡܐ ܕܘܝܫܐ. ܘܒܢܘܐ ܡܘܟܐ ܒܐܕܟܐ ܒܟܘܕ ܠܘܬܐ ܘܡܚܕܝܘܟܗ ܐܘܢܐ ܡܢ ܠܟܠ. ܘܡܦܡܝܐ ܒܘܡܟܐ ܗܕ ܦܠܚܝܐ ܡܝܫܘܒ ܗܢܝܐ. ܝܫܝܘܐ ܦܕܓܢܬܐ ܘܚܘܕܐ ܕܓܒܝܪܐ ܕܗܘܡܕܕ ܘܠܡܕܐ ܕܡܘܟܐ ܕܐܘܢܐ. ܘܡܠܗܘܟܗ ܠܐܘܢܐ ܘܡܥܕܘܐ ܒܗܓܡܐ. ܗܠܡܝܐ ܗܘܢܐ ܕܫܟܝܐ. ܡܘܕܐ ܕܗܠܟܐ ܬܘܡܟܐ ܘܗܠܟܐ ܠܬܠܘܓܐ ܕܟܐ ܒܗܟܐ. ܗܘܠ ܕܡܠܝܘܐ ܒܠܗ ܓܒܝܪܐ. ܗܕܝܘܐ ܗܕܐ ܬܘܡܟܐ ܡܡܐ ܕܡܫܕܘܐ ܘܦܓܘܐ ܐܘܢܐ. ܟܗܕ ܕܝܢ ܢܡܠܝܘܟܠ ܦܕܓܢܬܐ ܕܓܒܝܪܐ ܝܠܢܐ ܠܡܓܐ. ܕܐܘܟܠ ܠܡܓܢܕ. ܘܟܘܕܢܐ ܓܢܕܘܐ ܘܐܘܗ ܒܟܕܥܐ ܡܓܢܕܝܘܬܐ ܕܝܠܗ ܟܕܠܘܕܘܬܐ ܕܒܪܩܐ ܡܘܢܐ ܕܡܡܕܝܣ. ܟܗܕ ܗܕ ܕܗܫܡܘܐ ܓܒܝܪܐ ܢܡܠܝܘܟܠܗ ܠܫܢܐ ܚܕܐ. ܘܡܕܝܢܘܟܠܗ ܘܡܦܠܚܝܐ ܚܦܗ ܕܓܒܝܪܐ ܗܐ ܒܢܢܐ. ܕܐܘܟܠܗ ܒܘܒܝܕܐ ܐܠܝܕ ܘܒܘܠ ܠܫܡܕܐ ܘܢܡܠܝܘܟܠܗ ܠܟܒܐ✧

ܐܢܫܐ ܕܟܒܐ ܕܡܫܡܝܐ ܠܒܢܢܐ ܡܓܘܐ ܒܢܢܐ ܘܐܡܝܗ ܡܕܘܟܢܐ ܕܡܫܟܠܘܟܠܗ ܒܪܩܐ. ܘܐܡܝܗ ܗܡ ܟܘܟܐ ܕܓܒܝܪܐ. ܘܚܘܡܝܐ ܐܢܫܐ ܕܟܒܐ ܥܘܩܐ ܘܡܚܕܐ ܠܐܒܓܟܐ ܕܗܘܕܝܐ ܘܡܟܠܚܝܐ ܡܝܫܘܒ ܕܝܫܝܘܟܠ ܒܟܠܥ. ܒܟܕܝܥܘܓܐ ܢܘܦܠܐ ܕܓܒܝܪܐ. ܐܢܫܐ ܕܡܓܘܓܐ

ܒܢܝܐ ܒܒܢܝܐ ܩܘܕܡܝܐ ܐܝܬ ܒܗ ܐܘܕܐ. ܘܦܫܝܛܐ ܝܬܝܪ̈ܐ ܘܡܝܢ̈ܐ. ܘܡܢ ܓܘ ܐܝܟ ܒܢܝܐ ܡܕܝܢܬܐ ܘܚܙܝܬܐ ܒܘܒܐ ܚܕ ܕܐܪܐ. ܘܦܫܛܐ ܕܡܕܝܢܬܐ ܥܡܝܩܐ ܒܒܬܐ ܗ̇ܝ ܣܘܕ̈ܐ. ܘܐܢ ܕܒܝܬܝܗ ܩܪܝܐ ܕܪܬܐ ܠܐܘܕܐ ܒܝܘܡܐ ܩܕܡܐ ܗ̇ܝ ܕܒܝܬܐ. ܘܫܘܒܚܐ ܠܒܝܬܐ ܗ̇ܘܝܠܗ ܡܘܟܝܐ ܗ̇ܝ ܐܪ̈ܙܐ ܘܕܓܠܐ. ܘܡܘܟܝܐ ܗ̇ܝ ܣܘܕ̈ܐ. ܠܟܡ ܐܪ̈ܙܐ ܡܝܬܝ̈ܐ. ܗ̇ܘܘܠܗ ܚܕ ܡܕܝܢܬܐ ܘܚܠܐ ܐܪ̈ܙܐ ܕܒܝܬܐ ܕܡܣܝܒܐ ܠܒܠܐ. ܘܡܢ ܒܝܬܘܬܐ ܕܐܦܕܝܬܐ ܐܪ̈ܙܐ. ܐܦܕܝܬܐ ܗ̇ܘ ܣܘܕ̈ܐ ܕܐܣܝܒܐ ܒܒܬܐ ܕܐܝܬܝܗ ܠܐܦܕܐ ܕܢܚܫܐ. ܘܒܝܬ ܬܪܥܐ ܕܡܕܝܢܬܐ ܘܚܠܐ ܚܕ ܬܪܥܐ ܕܬܪܝܢ. ܐܝܬܘܗ ܕܪܬܐ ܘܟܠܗ̇ ܡܘܕܐ ܗ̇ܝ ܐܝܬܢܐ. ܘܟܢܐ ܗ̇ܝ ܡܒܥܘܠܐ܀

❖ ❖ ❖ ❖ ❖ ❖ ❖ ❖ ❖

VOCABULARY

English	Aramaic	English	Aramaic
to mix	ܠܚܘܠܗ	room	ܐܘܕܐ :
			ܡܘܬܐ
spirit	ܠܚܢܢܐ	manger	ܐܘܪܝܐ
stucco, plaster	ܠܓܝܣܐ	Lounge, guest	ܐܝܘܢ
Transfiguration	ܠܠܚܢܢܐ	room meeting room	
wheel	ܠܓܠܓܠܘܬܐ	furnace	ܐܬܘܢܐ
living room hall	ܕܝܘܢ	for free	ܡܓܢܐ
courtyard, yard	ܕܪܬܐ	to quit, to stop	ܡܫܠܗ
barley soup with meat	ܗܪܝܣܐ	basement,	ܡܒܪ̈ܝܐ
basket, scuttle	ܙܒܝܠܐ	stable	
big basket made of reeds	ܙܒܘܠ	stairways	ܡܣܩܢܝܬܐ
to crush	ܠܚܘܓܠܗ	main entry	ܬܪܥܐ
blast, cannon	ܠܦܦܐ	gate	
dust	ܠܦܫܐ	mason, builder	ܒܢܝܐ
iron	ܦܪܙܠܐ	gunpowder	ܒܪܘܕ
door	ܬܪܥܐ	inside	ܓܘܐ
flint	ܟܐܦܐ	seeds	ܠܘܒܝܐ
	ܕܡܩܕܚܢܐ		

VOCABULARY **Cont.**

English	Aramaic	English	Aramaic
to fall	ܢܦܠܗ	rock	ܟܐܦܐ
to pierce, to punch	ܢܩܒܠܗ	closet behind the	ܟܘܟܝܐ
summahk	ܣܡܩܐ	master room	
to crush	ܣܚܩܠܗ	dried mud brick	ܠܒܢܐ
wedge, cotter	ܣܦܢܐ	on top of, over it	ܠܥܠܗ
to coarse sifting,	ܣܪܕܠܗ	professional, skillful	ܡܗܝܪܐ
to garble		period	ܡܘܕܐ
		time	ܙܒܢܐ
loft	ܣܪܕܦ	to deliver to	ܡܫܘܠܠܗ
to invite	ܥܙܡܠܗ	organize transfer	
deep	ܥܡܘܩܐ	to carry and pass	ܡܫܘܘܠܗ
to disobey, to rebel	ܥܨܠܗ	small pallet, portage	ܡܣܡܟܐ
to be stuck		mattock	ܡܪܘܠ
rich	ܥܬܝܪܐ	to dismantle	ܡܦܘܠܥܠܗ
breezy, cool	ܦܘܟܐ	to demolish	
to cool down	ܦܟܠܗ	quarry	ܡܩܠܥ
corridor	ܨܘܦܐ	stones cutter	ܡܩܠܥܢܐ
middle of room	ܨܕܪܐ	rocks handler	ܡܪܦܟܢܐ
chest		pickax	ܡܪܟܐ
to arrange, to align	ܨܦܠܗ	to hit, to shoot	ܡܚܐܠܗ
garbanzo and melon	ܨܒܪܐ (ܨܦܪܐ)	rock breaker	ܡܓܠܬܐ
crushed seeds		round wheel	
large rock	ܩܕܝܐ	from rock	ܡܓܢܕܪܘܢܐ

VOCABULARY Cont.

English	Aramaic	English	Aramaic
to throw	ܬܠܩܠܗ	wood	ܩܝܣܐ
smoke	ܬܢܢܐ	to fry	ܩܠܝܠܗ
mud oven	ܬܢܘܪܐ	window opening	ܟܘܐ
nine	ܬܫܥܐ	animal	ܚܝܘܢܐ
to fuel the oven	ܬܓܗܠܗ	top of head	ܩܪܪܐ
under	ܬܚܬ	inner room	ܩܘܪܐ
dairy product	ܚܠܘܪܬܐ	wide	ܪܘܝܚܐ
to finish, to end	ܓܡܝܪܠܗ	window	ܫܒܟ
donkey	ܚܡܪܐ	to leave behind	ܫܒܩܠܗ
to dig	ܚܦܪܠܗ	Assumption	ܫܘܢܝܐ
back	ܚܨܐ	sugar	ܫܟܪ
rock	ܦܪܕܐ	rivulet, riled,	ܫܩܝܬܐ
marble rock	ܦܪܫܐ	brooklet	
primer, wick	ܦܬܝܠܐ	mulberry	ܬܘܬܐ

A lady's hair dress and jewelery

found at the Royal Tombs of Ur of Chaldeans on a reconstructed model. C. 3000. B.C.

LESSON SIXTEEN ܦܣܘܩܐ ܕܫܬܬܥܣܪ

PREPOSITION ܦܪܝܫܘܬܐ ܫܡܢܝܐ

A preposition is a letter placed before a noun or pronoun. Prepositions are:

(A) INSEPARABLE PREPOSITIONS:

Consisting of one letter always attached to the following word. There are seven:

	Prepositions		Examples	
1	at	ܒ	we have at home	ܐܝܬ ܒܒܝܬܐ
2	of	ܕ	my mother's book	ܟܬܒܐ ܕܝܡܝ
3	and	ܘ	Joseph and Mary	ܝܘܣܦ ܘܡܪܝܡ
4	to	ܠ	he went to church	ܙܠܗ ܠܥܕܬܐ
5	from	ܡܢ	from north and south	ܡܓܪܒܝܐ ܘܡܬܝܡܢܐ
6	like	ܟ	no one in the world is like you	ܟܘܬܟ ܠܝܬ ܒܥܠܡܐ
7	off	ܠ	up and down	ܠܥܠ ܘܠܬܚܬ

(B) SEPARATE PREPOSITIONS: standing alone. There 22 of them

according, like	ܐܝܟ
between	ܒܝܢܝ
after	ܒܬܪ
near, by	ܠܓܒ
with	ܥܡ
against	ܠܘܩܒܠ (ܠܩܘܒܠ)
from	ܡܢ
within, through	ܒܓܘ

without	ܕܠܐ
instead of	ܡܚܠܦ
upon	ܥܠ
inside, from within	ܓܘܐ
from outside	ܡܒܪܐ
before, from the front	ܡܩܡܐ (ܡܩܡ)
behind	ܒܬܪܐ
from behind	ܡܒܬܪܐ
for	ܩܐ
toward	ܨܘܒ
until	ܗܘܠ (ܗܘܠ)
of	ܕܝ
enough	ܒܣ
from	ܡܢ ܓܢܒ

❖ ❖ ❖ ❖ ❖ ❖ ❖ ❖ ❖

ܥܐܕܐ ܫܘܒܚܬܐ : ܢܘܗܪܐ ܕܝܠܕܐ

ܒܥܕܢܬܐ ܕܢܘܗܪܐ ܕܐܝܠܘܠ (ܐܝܠܘܢ) ܕܝܢ ܒܟܢܘܢ. ܘܐܢܫܐ ܒܢܛܪܝܢܐ ܡܫܬܘܚܕܐ ܡܢ ܘܕܘܟܐ ܕܘܟܐ ܕܡܬܚܙܐ. ܘܐܢܟܐ ܘܒܦܘܪܐ ܡܫܬܕܪܝܢܐ ܝܕܥܐ ܘܡܫܚܐ ܘܡܘܗܒܬܐ (ܡܢ ܡܩܡ ܘܒܦܘܪܐ ܕܝܠܕܐ). ܘܡܫܚܐ ܩܐ ܐܝܬܘܪܐ ܒܢܘܗܪܐ ܕܥܕܢܬܐ ܕܥܐܕܐ ܕܝܠܕܐ. ܒܘܕܝܘܡ ܡܬܝܠܝܕܐ ܒܡܫܠܡܬܐ ܒܝܬܐ. ܒܘܕ ܓܒ ܡܢ ܓܘܢܝܐ ܫܦܝܪܐ ܫܡܫܐ ܕܗܒܐ. ܘܡܬܝܠܕܐ ܥܠܝܗ ܦܬܝܓܐ ܐܘܪܚܐ ܘܕܘܟܐ ܚܕ ܡܢܐ ܝܕܥܐ. ܐܢ ܟܘ. ܘܡܬܚܙܝܢܐ ܒܠܒ ܒܢܝܢܐ ܕܡܫܝܚܐ. ܘܡܠܘܐ ܦܬܝܓܐ ܕܒܝܬܐ. ܘܡܝܬܝܐ ܓܘܢܝܐ ܘܠܕܝܬܗ ܫܡܫܐ ܘܡܘܕܐ ܠܟܠ ܡܢܗ ܘܐܢܫܐ ܒܡܕܘܟܐ. ܘܡܫܬܕܪܝܢܐ ܒܐܠܗܐ ܗܘܠ ܕܕܝܓܝܐ ܒܘܕܐ ܒܫܡܫܐ ܕܢܚܬܐ. ܘܠܐ ܡܫܬܚܪܐ ܡܢ ܓܒܐ ܟܘܐ ܥܠܐ ܡܬܢܘܐ ܥܡܕ ܒܢܝܢܐ ܐܢܫܝܢ ܕܥܡܘܠ ܒܝܬܐ. ܘܒܘܕ ܡܕܘܟܐ ܓܒܐ ܕܝܠܕܐ. ܟܕܘܓܐ ܕܡܫܚܐ ܡܦܠܘܐ ܒܘܕܐ ܕܡܘܗܒܬܐ. ܕܘܐ ܡܩܝܕܐ ܡܢ ܫܒܬܐ ܗܡܘܬܐ ܡܢ ܫܡܫܐ. ܘܡܠܝܐ ܒܘܕܐ ܐܢ ܡܢܗ ܒܠܘܢܐ❖

ܚܠܝ ܓܠܕܪ̈ܐ ܚܡܒܪܝ. ܚܒܝܪܐ ܕܝܠܒܝܐ ܪ̈ܕܚܫܐ ܚܝܠܘܠ. ܗܘܐ ܕܒܟܘܗ
ܡܕܝܚܢܬܐ ܗܠܝܢ. ܝܗܐ ܕܡܘܗܒܝܗܒܝܘܗ ܡܠܟܐ. ܚܢܝܬܐ ܕܗܠܟܬܐ ܪܩܐ ܘܫܢܝܐ ܘܟܗܘܒ
ܠܦܬܐ . ܗܘܝܠܐ ܦܪܐ ܗܐ ܦܠܝ̈ܢܐ . ܓܦܒܪܝ ܕܦܪܡܕܪܐ ܕܝܚܘܪܐ ܕܟܠܒܦܠܬܐ ܒܦܪܝܥܠܡ.
ܡܓܘܝܠܝ ܝܠܒܝܐ ܫܢܐ ܕܝܐܠܝܗ ܦܝܥܠܝܗ ܝܠܒܝܐ ܡܪܝ . ܘܡܢ ܦܝܫܘܦܐ ܕܡܥܝܫܢ̈ܬܐ.
ܡܘܠܗܝܠܝ ܒܗܘ ܘܚܢܐ ܢܘܪܐ. ܘܦܪܗܠܝܗ ܓܒܪ̈ܐ ܡܦܝܫܢܐ ܒܢܓܘܦܐ ܕܡܕܝܢܬܐ. ܘܪܓܥܠܝܗ
ܢܐ ܢܓܦܐ ܒܢܓܘܦܐ ܕܚܪܝܣܛܝܢ̈ܐ ܗܘܠ ܢܪܝܘ ܗܘܐ.

❖ ❖ ❖ ❖ ❖ ❖ ❖ ❖ ❖

VOCABULARY

English	Aramaic	English	Aramaic
small brazier	ܡܘܓܚܢܬܐ	sheep droppings	ܟܘܪܐ
	ܡܢ ܡܢܦܠ	gas	ܓܙ
	ܕܝܠܒܝܐ	to find, to discover	ܓܘܝܠܝܗ
	ܘܠܦܪܐ	to be extinguished	ܕܥܟܠܝܗ
district	ܡܚܠܐ	to turn off, to die	
neighborhood quarter		fear, panic	ܘܪܦܐ
to clap, to applaud	ܡܚܘܦܩܠܝܗ	a down pour	ܘܓܐ
to glow, to brighten	ܡܘܠܗܠܝܗ	heavy rain	
torch, hot surface	ܠܒܝܒܐ	alive	ܚܝ̈ܐ
little, small, few	ܒܝܪܐ		(ܚܝܫܝܐ)
to get near, to get closer	ܡܩܘܒܠܝܗ	mud	ܚܒܝܐ
candle	ܫܡܥܐ	Christian	ܚܪܝܣܛܝܢܐ

❖ ❖ ❖ ❖ ❖ ❖ ❖ ❖ ❖

LESSON SEVENTEEN ܦܘܫܩܐ ܕܫܒܥܣܪܐ

RELATIVE ADJECTIVES ܫܡܗ̈ܐ ܕܝܚܣܘܬܐ

The relative adjective is formed by adding certain suffixes to either a noun or a particle. These suffixes are added to proper names, names of an occupation, names of tribes, lands, cities, places, sects, or time and the like. In the tables below are the feminine and masculine forms of a word with the original word appearing in Aramaic in the far left hand column.

1. Suffixes indicating the nature of a noun:

For masculine: ܵܝܵܐ

For feminine: ܝܼܬܵܐ or ܵܝܬܵܐ or ܝܼܬܵܐ

Noun	Feminine	Masculine	
Christ	ܡܫܝܚܝܬܐ	ܡܫܝܚܝܐ	ܡܫܝܚܐ
Angel	ܡܠܐܟܝܬܐ	ܡܠܐܟܝܐ	ܡܠܐܟܐ
Chaldean	ܟܠܕܝܬܐ	ܟܠܕܝܐ	ܟܠܕܘ
Nineveh	ܢܝܢܘܝܬܐ	ܢܝܢܘܝܐ	ܢܝܢܘܐ
Aramaic	ܐܪܡܝܬܐ	ܐܪܡܝܐ	ܐܪܡ
Mosul	ܡܘܨܠܝܬܐ	(ܡܨܠܝܐ) ܡܘܨܠܝܐ	ܡܘܨܠ
Karamlaish	ܟܪܡܠܫܝܬܐ	ܟܪܡܠܫܝܐ	ܟܪܡܠܫ
Basra	ܒܨܪܝܬܐ	ܒܨܪܝܐ	ܒܨܪܐ
Babylon	ܒܒܠܝܬܐ	ܒܒܠܝܐ	ܒܒܠ
human	ܐܢܫܝܬܐ	ܐܢܫܝܐ	ܐܢܫܐ
country	ܐܬܪܝܬܐ	ܐܬܪܝܐ	ܐܬܪܐ
American	ܐܡܪܝܟܝܬܐ	ܐܡܪܝܟܝܐ	ܐܡܪܝܟܐ

2. Suffixes added to nouns and adjectives:

For masculine: ܢܐ

For feminine: ܢܝܬܐ

Noun	Feminine	Masculine	
smart	ܗܘܢܢܝܬܐ	ܗܘܢܢܐ	ܗܘܢܐ
heaven, sky	ܫܡܝܢܝܬܐ	ܫܡܝܢܐ	ܫܡܝܐ
Earth	ܐܪܥܢܝܬܐ	ܐܪܥܢܐ	ܐܪܥܐ
Light	ܢܘܗܪܢܝܬܐ	ܢܘܗܪܢܐ	ܢܘܗܪܐ
Fire	ܢܘܪܢܝܬܐ	ܢܘܪܢܐ	ܢܘܪܐ

3. Suffixes added to all nouns except proper nouns and nouns of place:

For masculine: ܢܝܐ

For feminine: ܝܬܐ

Noun	Feminine	Masculine	The Word
dust	ܥܘܦܪܝܬܐ	ܥܘܦܪܢܝܐ	ܥܘܦܪܐ
body	ܦܓܪܝܬܐ	ܦܓܪܢܝܐ	ܦܓܪܐ
Tilkepe	ܬܠܟܐܦܝܬܐ	ܬܠܟܐܦܢܝܐ	ܬܠܟܐܦܐ
Alkosh	ܐܠܩܘܫܝܬܐ	ܐܠܩܘܫܢܝܐ	ܐܠܩܘܫ
Telleskof	ܬܠܣܩܘܦܝܬܐ	ܬܠܣܩܘܦܢܝܐ	ܬܠܣܩܘܦ
Bikopa	ܒܝܩܘܦܝܬܐ	ܒܝܩܘܦܢܝܐ	ܒܝܩܘܦܐ
Butnaye	ܒܝܬܒܘܛܢܝܬܐ	ܒܝܬܒܘܛܢܢܝܐ	ܒܘܛܢܝܐ
Spirit	ܪܘܚܝܬܐ	ܪܘܚܢܝܐ	ܪܘܚܐ

4. **The word ܒܝ or ܡܢ ܒܝ is put before proper nouns to represent family names.**

Names	Proper Nouns
the Yausip family	ܒܝ ܝܘܣܦ (ܡܢ ܒܝ ܝܘܣܦ)
the Kasha family	ܒܝ ܩܫܐ
the Shamasha family	ܒܝ ܫܡܫܐ
the Malakha family	ܒܝ ܡܠܐܟܐ
the Andraus family	ܒܝ ܐܢܕܪܐܘܣ

❖ ❖ ❖ ❖ ❖ ❖ ❖ ❖ ❖

ܩܪܝܢܐ ܫܒܥܣܪܝܢܐ : ܐܬܘܪ (ܐܬܘܪ) ܐܬܪܐ ܕܐܒܗܬܐ

ܐܬܪܐ ܕܐܬܘܪ. ܟܠܕܝܐ ܕܐܝܬܘܗ̇ ܒܡܕܢܚܐ ܡܨܥܝܐ ܕܥܠܡܐ. ܘܗܘܐ ܐܝܬ ܗܘܐ ܠܗ̇ ܢܗܪܘܬܐ ܕܘܪܬܐ. ܐܝܟ ܐܢܝ ܕܒܘܪܟܐ ܡܢܗܪܢܐ. ܡܢ ܢܗܪܐ ܗܘܠ ܐܬܘܪ. ܐܢܫܝܐ ܒܘܪܟܐ ܒܘܢ ܒܢܝܐ ܡܕܝܢܬܐ ܡܝܬܢܐ ܒܟܪܟܐ. ܘܐܢܫܝܐ ܒܘܪܟܐ ܦܪܝܐ ܡܢ ܒܝ ܢܗܪܐ ܗܘܠ ܐܪܥܐ ܕܐܬܘܪ ❖ ܐܢܝ ܢܗܪܐ ܐܢܫܐ ܒܘܪܟܐ ܚܝܐ ܘܚܕܐ. ܟܠܗ ܡܠܟܘܬܐ ܘܫܘܠܛܢܐ ܒܘܪܟܬܐ ܒܙܒܢܐ ܕܩܕܡܐ. ܘܒܬܫܡܫܬܐ ܐܪܥܐ ܕܐܬܘܪ. ܘܡܠܟܘܬܐ ܘܡܕܝܢܘܬܐ ܪܒܬܐ. ܐܢܫܐ ܪܒܬܐ ܘܦܪܝܫܐ ܗܕܐ ܗܘܘ ܡܢ ܢܗܪܐ. ܐܢܝ ܚܕܬܐ ܘܐܢܫܝܐ ܒܟܪܟܐ (ܕܕܝܢܐ). ܝܠܗ̇ ܒܟܠܝܬܐ ܒܐܪܥܐ ܡܝܬܢܐ ܒܘܪܟܘܬ ܫܡܫܐ. ܘܝܠܗ̇ ܒܪܢܫܐ ܗ̇ܝ ܒܘܪܟܬ ܚܕܬܐ. ܒܝܬ ܐܢܫܝܐ ܗ̇ܝ ܗܘܝܐ (ܦܣܩܐ). ܘܝܠܗ̇ ܐܠܗܝܐ ܘܒܝܬܐ ܗ̇ܝ ܠܚܡܐ ܘܕܝܢܐ ❖

ܟܠܕܝܐ ܕܐܝܬܘܗ̇ ܐܝܬ ܡܘܬܒܐ ܒܟܪܟܐ ܕܒܘܪܟܘܬ. ܒܫܢܬ ܐܢܫܐ ܕܒܝܬܐ ܝܠܗ̇ ܘܡܢܬܢܬܐ. ܘܒܥܠܡܝܬܐ ܒܕܝܢܐ ܘܡܫܬܥܝܬܐ ܠܟܠܗ. ܗܕܐ ܕܝܢ ܒܫܠܡܝܬܐ ܕܕܡܝܬܐ ܒܪܝܬܐ. ܘܒܘܪ ܒܟܠܝܗ ܕܢܫܘܗ ܒܢܫܠܝܬܐ ܠܒܝܬܐ. ܘܒܪܕܘܬܐ ܒܟܪܘܟܐ ܒܢ ܒܡܕܝܢܐ. ܘܒܢܟܠܝܬܐ ܘܡܫܦܠܛܝܢ ܡܢܗܘܢ ܐ— ܟܪܘܟ ܕܫܢܐ ܒ— ܦܠܓܢܐ ܓ— ܡܢܕ ܘܡܠܟ (ܚܠܘܠܐ) ❖ ܘܐܢܝ ܕܒܡܨܥܝܬ ܗܘܝܐ (ܦܣܩܐ). ܒܫܢܬ ܐܢܫܐ ܕܒܝܬܐ ܝܠܗ̇. ܘܡܢܬܢܬܐ ܡܢ ܒܝܬܐ. ܘܒܢܟܠܝܬܐ ܠܕܝܢܐ. ܘܡܫܦܠܛܝܢ ܡܢܗܘܢ ܦܪܘܣܐ. ܘܡܕܝܢܬܐ ܒܟܘܪܝܬܐ ܠܒܝܬܐ. ܘܡܫܦܠܛܝܢ ܡܢܗܘܢ ܒܡܠܟܘܬܐ ܐ : ܦܣܩܐ ܒ :

ܡܬܬܓܪ ܓ : ܒܪܓܠ ܠܗܘܢ ܡܫܩܦܬܐ(ܪ̈ܚܝܐ ܕܐܝܕܘܬܐ) ܐܘ ܛܚܢܬܐ. ܒܪ ܬܘܩܦܬܐ ܚܠܒ ܐܢܫ̈ܐ ܕܒܝܬܐ ܒܩܠܝܒ. ܝܬܝܪ ܡܢܫܦܝ ܘܫܠܩܝ. ܘܡܒܫܠܝ ܬܢܝܐ ܘܐܢܝܢ ܘܚܘܕܪܐ. ܘܒܪܒܪܐ ܒܝܫܠܐ ܒܚܘܒܝܢܬܐ ܠܒܝܬܐ. ܘܡܒܫܠܝ ܒܗܕܝܐ ܘܒܢܓܠܝ. ܘܐܝܢܐ ܬܢܘܐ ܒܦܪܫܬܐ. ܡܢ ܗܒܢܐ ܐܘ ܕܝܢܐ ܕܕܝܕܐ ܐܘ ܥܢܡܐ ܚܠܒܗ܀ ܐܡܝܕ ܡܣܢܘܩܝ̈ܐ ܕܕܝܕܐ. ܐܢܫ̈ܐ ܗܘܡ ܒܘܦܝܒܬܐ ܐܘ ܥܢܡܐ ܚܠܒܗ. ܡܠܫܐ ܘܚܫܕܐ. ܘܒܝܬܐ ܘܐܢ̈ܝܐ ܘܫܒܠܐ ܡܢ ܡܬܪܒܐ. ܘܕܦܫܟ ܡܢ ܒܝܬܪܐ. ܚܒܝܕܐ ܡܢ ܚܠܕܝ̈ܐ ܕܝܒܝܫܐ. ܟܐ ܒܣ ܡܣܢܕܝܒܬܐ ܐܘ ܓܢܒܝܗܘܢ ܕܝܕܐ. ܐܟܐ ܗܘܡ ܐܘ ܒܬܘܡܒܗܘܢ ܒܡܦܪܓ ܘܒܓܕܕ ܘܡܘܦܬܐ ܐܢ̈ܫܐ ܕܣܘܪܝܐ. ܘܒܝܬܝ ܕܕܘܒܠܐ ܐܢܫܝ̈ܐ ܡܢ ܕܝܪܐ ܕܝܗܘܕܝ. ܐܢܫ̈ܐ ܡܘܬܒܝܒܬܐ ܕܝܕܐ ܐܘ ܡܠܟܬܐ. ܕܢܚܠܒܘܠܗ ܠܚܠܒ ܡܘܦܬܐ ܕܒܝܬ ܢܘܕܒܝ. ܘܡܝܬܗ ܠܕܘܠܒܐ ܡܕܒܪܐ. ܒܩܕܝܡܘܬܐ ܡܬܢܐ ܡܢ ܕܡܥܘܕܠܝ ܕܢܫܐ ܕܕܝܪܐ ܒܚܘܕܪܐ܀

ܒܝܠܘܟ ܡܕܪܫܬܐ ܒܡܥܪܒ. ܘܐܢܫܐ ܘܚܘܕܪܐ ܒܦܠܚܘܬܐ ܡܒܝܬܐ ܕܕܪܐ ܕܝܗܘܕܝ. ܠܦܥܝܒܐ ܓܘܠܐ ܥܘܩܬܢܝܬܐ ܘܒܠܘܫܐ. ܚܒܝܕܐ ܒܚܒܝܬܐ ܡܢ ܓܘܪܐ ܕܡܦܠܫܒܘܠܗ ܐܢܫ̈ܐ ܕܒܝܬܐ. ܟܠܡ ܚܘܕ ܕܝܢ ܓܘܟܐ ܦܪ ܘܦܒܘܠܝ ܡܢ ܥܘܡܐ. ܘܒܓܠܝ ܐܝܬܝܪ ܡܢ ܐܘܟܐ ܒܕܘܟ ܓܕܕܐ ܕܥܡܪܐ. ܘܡܢ ܠܢܦܐ ܒܕܘܟܠܐ ܡܢ ܓܕܕܐ ܕܣܠܒܝܐ. ܘܡܢ ܝܕܥܘ ܐܘ ܡܣܢܘܩܝ̈ܐ ܕܒܚܕܬܐ ܐܘ ܘܡܕܐ. ܘܒܪܒܪܐ ܡܘܒܝܒܠܝ ܒܝܫ ܕܡܥܡܘܦܝ ܕܓܕܕܐ ܒܕܪܬܐ. ܘܡܘܒܝܫܠܝ ܐܡܠܘܬܗܝ ܘܐܒܕܘܬܗܝ ܘܐܢܫܘܬܗܝ. ܡܢ ܓܡܓܡܢܬܐ ܕܕܦܐ ܘܐܚܘܬܐ ܘܡܕܐ ܒܟܘܕ ܓܘܪܐ ܀

❖ ❖ ❖ ❖ ❖ ❖ ❖ ❖ ❖

VOCABULARY

English	Aramaic	English	Aramaic
enough, only	ܒܣ	shuttle	ܐܒܘܬܐ
thread,string, yarn	ܓܕܕܐ	wool	ܥܡܪܐ
loom	ܓܘܪܐ	spinning of wool	ܐܘܠܝܗ
cream of wheat	ܒܪܓܠ	Baghdad city	ܒܓܕܕ
to crush	ܒܪܓܫܠܗ	by himself	ܒܝܢܗ
quern, hand mill	ܒܪܓܫܬܐ	spices	ܒܗܪܬ
spindle	ܕܘܟ	thread spool	ܒܚܕܐ
rotating wheel	ܕܘܟܠܐ	sweater	ܒܠܘܫ
country	ܕܘܠܬܐ	about,subject	ܒܝܫ

VOCABULARY Cont.

English	Aramaic	English	Aramaic
soil moistened	ܦܕܢܐ	crushing, ounding,	ܕܢܩܐ
middle, second grade	ܦܠܓܢܐ	ringing	
cream of wheat		mud barrel	ܟܘܪܐ
third grade of	ܡܢܬ ܘܬܠܬ	type of wheat	ܟܪܦܝܢܐ
cream of wheat		type of wheat	ܟܚܠܐ
near, neighbor,	ܩܪܝܒܐ	to twist, to spin	ܠܦܠܗ
close by		to water, to prepare	ܡܘܫܩܝܠܗ
provisions	ܙܘܕܐ	threads for weaving	
first grade of cream	ܪܝܫܢܐ	salt	ܡܠܚܐ
of wheat, burgle		machine	ܡܟܝܢܐ
country region	ܕܒܪܐ	to pick, to select	ܡܢܘܩܝܠܗ
millstone	ܪܚܝܐ	sifter	ܡܢܚܠܬܐ
shallow open pot	ܕܣܬܐ	to sift, to bolt	ܢܚܠܗ
quern, hand mill,	ܕܦܐ	to rest	ܢܝܚܠܗ
panel		barley	ܣܥܪܐ (ܦܩܦܬܐ)
step on to	ܕܥܣܠܗ	second grade	ܡܟܪܒܠ
to weave	ܘܙܩܪܗ	of barley	
to plant	ܘܙܪܥܠܗ	to return,	ܡܘܕܥܪܗ
cotton	ܣܠܒܓܐ	to put back	
meat stuffed wheat	ܟܘܒܝܬܐ	food supplies	ܡܘܢܐ
shirt	ܫܦܩܬܐ	to dry up,	ܡܘܝܒܫܠܗ
to boil	ܫܠܩܠܗ	to hydrate	
trader merchant,	ܬܓܪܐ	to hire	ܡܘܦܠܚܢܠܗ
type of wheat	ܚܡܪܝ	wheel weaving	ܢܪܟܣ
noise	ܚܡܚܡܬܐ	bran,shell of wheat	ܦܪܩܬܐ

LESSON EIGHTEEN ܦܣܘܩܐ ܕܬܡܢܬܥܣܪ

DIMINUTIVE ܡܙܥܪܢܘܬܐ (ܙܥܘܪܐ)

The diminutive is derived from nouns to express the smallness of things. Diminutives are formed by adding a suffix.

The nouns set out below are grouped together according to which suffix is used.The original noun is on the right and its diminutive form is on the left:

1- ܝܬܐ or ܬܐ or ܬܐ

ܡܕܝܢܬܬܐ	ܡܕܝܢܬ
ܡܓܠܬܐ	ܡܓܠܐ
ܓܘܪܝܬܐ	ܓܘܪܝܐ
ܓܒܣܬܐ	ܓܒܣ
ܒܪܝܬܐ	ܒܪܐ (ܠܒܘܪܐ)
ܟܬܒܝܬܐ	ܟܬܒܐ
ܡܕܘܟܝܬܐ	ܡܕܘܟܐ

2- ܘܢܐ or ܝܢܐ or ܘܢܐ ܢܐ or ܢܐ

ܥܕܘܢܐ	ܥܕܐ
ܡܐܝܢܐ	ܡܐܐ
ܓܠܒܘܢܐ	ܓܠܒ
ܓܕܘܢܐ	ܓܕܝܐ
ܠܚܡܢܘܢܐ	ܠܚܡ
ܒܝܬܘܢܐ	ܒܝܬ
ܢܗܪܘܢܐ	ܢܗܪ
ܢܗܪܝܢܐ	ܢܒܝܐ
ܓܒܘܢܐ	ܓܒܐ
ܟܠܒܘܢܐ	ܟܠܒ

ܡܝܬܐ	ܡܝܬܗ			3- ܝܬܗ
ܚܕܝܬܐ	ܚܕܝܬܗ			
ܡܕܝܢܬܐ	ܡܝܢܐ	ܡܝܢܝ	ܡܝܢܐ ܕܡܝܢܐ	4- ܝܢܝ or ܢܐ
ܟܬܒܐ	ܟܬܒܢܐ			
ܣܝܦܐ	ܣܝܦܝ			
ܠܘܚܐ	ܠܘܚܢܐ			
ܡܝܐ	ܡܝܢܐ			
ܚܟܡ			ܚܟܡܘܝ	5- ܘܝ
ܡܕܝܢܬܐ	(ܡܕܝܢܬܐ)		ܡܕܝܢܬܘܝ	
ܓܠܝܠܐ	(ܓܠܝܠ)		ܓܠܝܠܘܝ	
ܦܪܢܣܐ	(ܦܪܢܣ)		ܦܪܢܣܘܝ	
ܡܘܕܢܚܐ	(ܡܘܕܢܚ) ܡܘܕܢܚܘܬܐ			6- ܘܬܐ
ܦܪܢܣܐ (ܦܪܢܣ)	ܦܪܢܣܘܬܐ			
ܡܕܢܚܐ	ܡܕܢܚܘܬܐ			
ܟܬܒܐ (ܟܬܒ̈ܐ)	ܟܬܒܘܢܐ			7- ܘܢܐ
ܝܠܕܐ	ܝܠܕܘܢܐ			
ܚܡܪܐ	ܚܡܪܘܢܐ			
ܫܡܫܐ	ܫܡܫܘܢܐ			
ܥܨܦܘܪܐ	ܥܨܦܘܪܘܢܐ			

❖ ❖ ❖ ❖ ❖ ❖ ❖ ❖ ❖

ܡܪ̈ܢܝܐ ܫܡܝܫܝܬܐ
ܐܪ̈ܫܐ ܕܒܝܬ ܢܗܪ̈ܝܢ (ܦܪܩܐ ܐ)

ܟܕ ܬܘܡܡܐ ܕܥܡܐ ܚܡܫܘܡܐ ܕܝܠܗܘܢ. ܚܡܠܟܐ ܡܢ ܫܕܘܐ ܫܕܘܐ ܕܐܬܘܪ̈ܝܐ. ܡܦܩܝܬܐ ܘܡܕܘܒܪܐ ܘܝܬܘܒܬܐ. ܘܟܝܢܘܬܐ ܘܬܘܫܒܚܬܐ ܕܐܠܗܘܬܐ. ܘܢܬܐ ܘܡܦܩܬܐ ܕܟܬܒ̈ܐ ܘܫܡܫܬܐ (ܟܝܡܘܓܡܝܢ). ܐܝܟܢܐ ܕܟܠܗܘܢ ܟܫܦܬܐ ܐܝܟ ܐܢܐ ܘܐܢܬ. ܒܡܦܠܛܝܢ ܡܢ ܚܘܒܛܐ ܦܓܪܐ ܕܢܦܫܝ. ܘܦܢܝܬܐ ܚܡܝܫܬܐ ܗܘ ܕܟܠ ܚܢܦܝܢ ܚܠܡܝܬܐ. ܘܚܘܦܝܢ ܡܚܕܟܠܗܘܢ ܐܚܪ̈ܢܐ ܫܢܬܐ. ܚܠ ܐܝܟܢܐ ܚܫܝܢ ܚܦܓܬܗ ܓܒܐ ܟܓܒܐ. ܚܕܪܝܬܐ ܕܦܪܫܢܘܬܐ ܕܫܘܥܝܬܐ ܕܡܕܒܪܢܘܬܐ. ܚܡܣܝܢܐ ܡܠܦܘܬܐ ܡܢ ܡܣܩܐ ܡܘܢܐ. ܘܡܚܡܬܐ ܗܝ ܕܢܦܫ ܕܪܕܟܐ. ܘܠܬܕܝܪܐ ܕܢܝܫܐ ܡܢ ܟܦܢ. ܘܚܡܕܝܢ ܫܒܝܠܐ ܫܢܬܐ. ܘܚܢܝܡܬܐ ܘܚܡܟܢܬܐ ܠܕܪܝܐ ܚܢܫܝܐ ܕܗܘܘ ܫܢܬܐ ܗܝ ܦܓܪܐ. ܐܝܟܢܐ ܕܡܫܘܡܬܐ ܕܝܠܗܘܢ ܚܫܝܚ ܡܢ ܡܕܡܐ ܡܡܠܐ ܕܕܝܥܘܬܐ ܦܪܫܐ. ܚܘܕ ܚܡܫܟܐ ܠܐܪܥܐ ܘܟܝܢܐ ܐܝܬܗ ܚܫܦܪ ܕܘܟܬܐ ܗܝ ܦܢܝܐ. ܚܫܡܝܫܬܗ ܘܠܐ ܚܥܕܡ ܕܡܚܝܢܗ ܐܠܐ ܫܒܝܒܬܐ. ܘܚܡܟܠܠܗ ܟܠܗܘܢ ܕܦܪܫܢܘܬܐ ܕܫܒܝܒܬܐ. ܘܚܕܪܗ ܗܠܟܐ ܬܘܟܠܢܐ. ܫܪܐ ܡܕܦܢܐ ܕܢܡܝܢܐ ܘܐܣܪܢܐ ܡܟܫܪܐ ܘܐܣܪܢܐ ܠܡܪܐ ܕܦܢܐ. ܚܫܦܪ ܐܝܟܢܐ ܠܚܘܕܐ ܕܕܘܟܝ. ܚܘܕ ܚܡܥܕܝ ܟܦܪܐ ܕܐܬܘܪ̈ܝܐ ܚܣܕܘܟܝܐ. ܚܡܢܝܠܗ ܕܟܠܟܝ ܢܫܒ ܠܐܪܥܐ ܕܒܝܬܐ ܦܢܝܬܗ. ܘܟܗܢ̈ܐ ܐܘܗܘ ܚܡܝܡܠܟܐ ܡܢ ܕܘܟܝܢ ܡܕܝܢܐ ܕܐܗܝ ܠܦܢܝܬܗ. ܐܝܬܘܗܝ ܐܝܟܢܐ ܐܪܘܐ ܚܫܝܪ ܢܘܡܐ. ܟܝܢ ܟܗܢܐ ܠܫܡܥܝ ܢܬܐ ܒܢ ܢܦܩܐ ܕܟܬܒ̈ܐ ܘܫܡܫܬܐ. ܘܐܝܬ ܕܐܪܘܐ ܟܝܢ ܐܘܡܐ ܠܚܕܐ ܐܝܟܐ ܡܦܩܝܬܐ ܒܢ ܡܕܘܒܪܐ ܒܢ ܘܝܬܘܒܬܐ. ܘܫܪܚܡܐ ܐܝܟܢܐ ܢܚܠܝܬܐ ܟܦܪ̈ܐ ܘܡܫܘܬܐ ܚܕܥܡܐ ❖

ܚܠܝܕܘܬܐ ܚܘܕ ܕܐܪܝܬܐ ܐܝܟܢܐ. ܦܠܚܝܬܐ ܢܡܝܢܗ ܐܢܠܢܘܢ ܘܟܦܪ̈ܐ. ܕܥܡܠܝܬܐ ܘܝܬܘܒܬܐ ܡܢܝܗܘܢ. ܐܪܥܬܐ ܚܓܘܠܦܢܝܗܘܢ ܘܡܦܘܢܝܬܐ ܕܡܘܬܒܘܬܐ. ܘܚܘܕ ܐܘܪܚܐ ܐܝܟܢܐ ܠܟܢܫܐ ܟܡܝܬܐ ܐܢܫ̈ܐ ܕܟܢܫܐ. ܗܝ ܢܦܩܐ ܘܡܠܟܐ ܘܡܫܒܚܢܐ. ܚܕܪܐ ܕܕܥܘܬܐ ܠܦܫܛ ܚܡܝܡܠܟ. ܒܢ ܚܘܥܕܢܐ ܐܝܟܝ ܟܘܕܟܘܕ ܒܢ ܦܝܫܐ. ܦܪ̈ܕܐ ܡܘܟܝܢܘܬܐ ܗܝ ܐܢܫ̈ܐ ܘܕܪܘܬܐ ܚܡܬܢܝܬܐ. ܘܡܦܩܝܬܐ ܒܢ ܗܡܡܐ ܕܐܬܘܪ̈ܝܐ ܡܢܝܦܝܘܬܐ. ܘܡܘܟܝܢܘܬܐ ܡܟܘܥܕܐ ܚܥܘܡܐ ܠܐ ܟܗ ܐܝܟܢܐ ܕܦܢܝܬܐ ܐܝܕܝܬܐ ܟܝܢܐ. ܐܠܐ ܗܘܡ ܫܪܚܡܐ ܕܐܝܬܘܬܐ ܟܠܬܐ ܕܢܝܪܐ ܘܦܠܛ ܠܕܥܡܐ ܟܝܢܠܐ ܠܟܪܝܘܬܐ ܘܚܦܢܐ ܗܝ ܦܝܪ̈ܝܗܘܢ. ܘܠܐܝܟܠ ܗܝ ܟܠܟܝܗܘܢ. ܘܚܢܘܡܐ ܕܢܫܘܡܬܐ. ܟܝܠܝܬܐ ܫܪܚܡܐ ܐܢܫ̈ܐ ܐܚܪ̈ܢܐ ܕܦܪܫܢܘܬܐ ܕܗܠܦܘܬܐ ܕܡܢܐ. ܘܐܪܘܐ ܟܝܢܐ ܕܦܐ ܗܘܝܐ ܟܘܠܦܢܝܗܘܢ. ܘܐܝܬܘܗܝ ܐܚܪ̈ܢܐ ܦܠܛ ܠܢܝܪܐ ܕܢܘܢܝܬܐ ܚܘܟܡܬܐ ܕܐܝܬ

ܫܠܸܡ ܗܵܢܵܐ ܟܬܵܒܵܐ. ܒܝܲܪܚܵܐ ܕܫܒܵܛ ([illegible]). ܒܗ ܒܒܝܬܘܢܐ. ܒܗ ܒܝܘܡܐ ܕܡܫܝܚܝܘܬܐ.
ܒܗ ܒܝܘܡܐ ܐܪܒܥܐ ܕܥܐܕܐ ܕܫܒܘܥܐ ܕܒܥܘܬܐ ܕܢܝܢܘܝܐ ❖

❖ ❖ ❖ ❖ ❖ ❖ ❖ ❖ ❖

VOCABULARY

English	Aramaic	English	Aramaic
to insert	ܡܥܒܪܬܗ	to hold, to catch	ܐܕܝܠܗ
to clean	ܡܢܕܦܠܗ	old	ܥܬܝܩܐ
to make rise	ܡܩܝܡܠܗ	he is	ܐܘܗܘ
to soak, to soften	ܡܪܛܒܠܗ	between	ܒܝܢ (ܒܝܢܬ)
to straighten, to smoothen	ܡܫܘܝܠܗ	maybe	ܐܠܚܒ
		wing	ܓܘܠܦܐ
to move	ܡܚܪܟܠܗ	leather, skin	ܓܠܕܐ
to barbecue , to roast	ܡܫܘܘܠܗ	band, group	ܓܦܐ
to pluck feather's bird	ܡܢܬܪܗ	cotton thread	ܓܕܕܐ ܕܩܛܢܐ
to tweet, to chirp	ܡܨܘܨܠܗ	starling	ܙܒܘܒܕܐ
finch	ܡܪܘܒܚܐ	stock dove	ܫܦܢܐ
to try	ܡܓܪܒܠܗ		ܚܒܘܓܒ
fish	ܢܘܢܐ	to attend, to present, to report	ܚܙܪܗ
to be useful, helpful	ܢܦܥܠܗ		
Peg or stake	ܣܟܬܐ	deer, gazelle	ܛܦܢܐ
	ܣܢܕܬܐ	to bury, to hide	ܛܡܪܗ
pillow	(ܣܦܕܬܐ)	pigeon	ܝܘܢܐ
	ܒܣܕܐ (ܟܘܪܐ)	wild pigeon	ܝܘܢܐ ܕܓܫܒܐ
left	ܟܕܘܟܐ	right side	ܝܡܝܢܐ
rabbit	ܦܪܐ (ܦܪܪܐ)	partridge	ܢܥܐ
feather	ܝܪܠܗ	dog	ܟܠܒܐ
to hunt, to shoot	ܢܟܢܐ	hunting dog	ܟܠܒܐ ܕܨܝܕܐ
fowler, shooter	ܨܝܕܠܗ	cotton	ܩܛܢ
lay snare	ܦܘܢܐ	to show ,to display	ܡܚܘܝܠܗ
strong, hard			

VOCABULARY Cont.

English	Aramaic	English	Aramaic
to drop, to throw away	ܬܠܡܠܗ	bow	ܩܘܫܬܐ
the rest	ܬܦܣܝܬܐ	quail, skylark	ܩܦܫܝܢܐ
fog, mist	ܫܡܦܘܟܐ	wooden breach	ܩܠܦܘܪܐ
hidden ditch in ground	ܓܗܦܐ	hard piece of earth	ܩܘܠܢܐ
ax, hatchet	ܓܝܒܢܐ	to wake up	ܪܝܫܠܗ
trap, snare	ܦܢܐ	skewer, spit	ܫܦܘܕܐ
hedge sparrow	ܓܝܓܘܕ	fox	ܬܥܠܐ
		telephone	ܬܝܠܦܘܢ

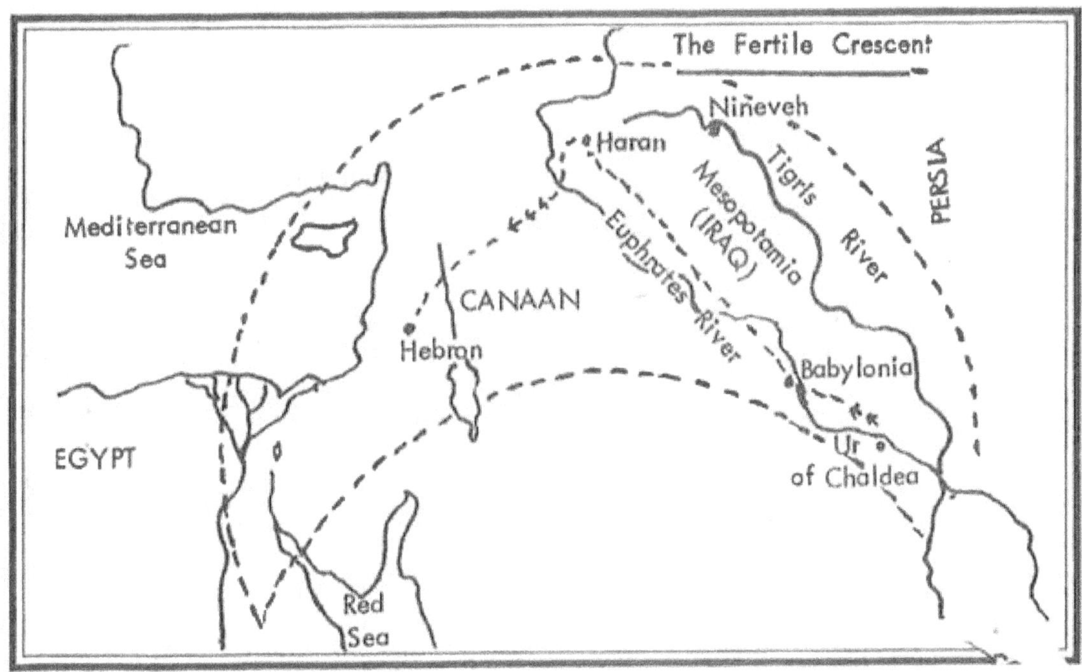

Journey of Abraham 19th Century B.C. from his home town Ur of Chaldea in Mesopotamia to Palestine (Canaan) – See Gen. 11:31-14:16.

LESSON NINETEEN ܩܪܝܢܐ ܕܬܫܥܣܪ

FOREIGN WORDS IN MODERN ARAMAIC

ܡܠܐ ܢܘܟܪܝܐ ܕܥܒܝܕܐ ܐܝܟ ܠܘܩܒܠ ܐܪܡܝܐ ܚܕܬܐ-ܟܠܕܝܐ

Modern Aramaic-Chldean, in general, and the Nineveh dialect especially, are influenced by the neighboring languages of Kurdish, Arabic, Persian and Turkish. Some of the words which are adopted from these languages by Modern Aramaic-Chaldean and the dialect of Nineveh are formed either by adding a prefix or suffix to the words.

I- Nouns formed by the addition of a particular prefix:

1- ܢ	patron, mediator	ܢܩܝܒ
	ignorance	ܢܘܢܘܚܐ
2- ܒ	out law	ܒܢܡܘܣ
	shameless	ܒܣܢܐ
	without honor	ܒܓܒܕܐ
	foolish	ܒܥܩܠ
3- ܒܝܡ	without brain	ܒܝܡ ܡܘܚܐ
	without food	ܒܝܡ ܕܐܟܠܐ
	without money	ܒܝܡ ܙܘܙܐ
4- ܣܪ	captain	ܣܪܟܗܒܐ
	extra	ܣܪܒܪ

II- Nouns formed by the addition of a particular suffix:

1-	ܓ̰ܝ	the best	ܒܝܪܝܢܓ̰ܝ
		tax collector	ܡܘܠܓ̰ܝ
2-	ܓ̰ܝ	tahini maker	ܛܚܝܢܓ̰ܝ
		Gunsmith, weapon seller	ܓ̰ܒܗܟܓ̰ܝ
		carriage driver	ܥܪܒܓ̰ܝ
		guard	ܩܪܘܠܓ̰ܝ
3-	ܠܝ	Ottoman	ܥܘܣܡܢܠܝ
4-	ܠܝܟ	noise	ܩܠܒܠܝܟ
5-	ܒܢܕ	horse shoe worker	ܢܥܠܒܢܕ
6-	ܕܐܢ	candlestick	ܫܡܥܕܐܢ
7-	ܕܐܪ	lawyer	ܥܕܠܕܐܪ
		wise man	ܚܟܡܬܕܐܪ
		helper	ܗܕܠܕܐܪ
8-	ܒܐܙ	Juggler	ܚܘܩܒܐܙ
		porter	ܕܪܘܒܐܙ
9-	ܚܐܢܐ	hospital	ܚܣܬܚܐܢܐ
		sitting room	ܕܝܘܐܢܚܐܢܐ
		bathroom	ܐܕܒܚܐܢܐ

10-	ܟ݂ܳܪ	artisan	ܨܰܢܥܰܬܟ݂ܳܪ
		guilty	ܓܘܢܰܗܟ݂ܳܪ
		greedy	ܛܰܡܰܥܟ݂ܳܪ
		trickster	ܚܺܝܠܶܟ݂ܳܪ
11-	ܡܳܢܺܝ	Turkish	ܬܘܪܟܡܳܢܺܝ
		Indian	ܗܶܢܕܡܳܢܺܝ
12-	ܒܳܙ	fraud	ܚܺܝܠܰܒܳܙ
		cheater	ܩܘܡܰܪܒܳܙ
13-	ܣܶܙ	uncaring	ܕܶܪܬܣܶܙ
		unbalanced	ܗܰܕܣܶܙ
14-	ܡܰܐ	button	ܕܘܓܡܰܐ
		grape leaves stuffed with meat and vegetables	ܕܘܠܡܰܐ
		dried salami	ܦܶܣܛܘܪܡܰܐ
		ice cream	ܕܘܢܕܘܪܡܰܐ

ܝܘܡܢܐ ܡܫܝܚܝܬܐ

ܒܘܪܟܬܐ ܒܒܢܬܐ

ܠܓܘܦܐ ܒܫܢܬܐ ܕܡܫܝܚܝܘܬܐ ܕܒܝܬܘܢܐ. ܕܠܓܘܦܝܗ ܓܒܪܐ ܡܘܕܥܐ ܚܕ ܕܟܢܫܘܬܐ. ܘܡܢ ܡܓܘܫܡܐ ܡܫܝܕܝܢܘܬܗ ܡܘܕܥܐ ܠܟܘܡܪܐ. ܘܡܫܝܕܥܐ ܕܪܘܫܐ ܘܐܝܬܘܗܝ ܡܣܘܡܟܬܐ ܒܝܠܢܐ. ܫܠܡܘܬܗ ܘܡܫܝܢܝܘܬܐ ܒܝܠܢܗ. ܘܟܕ ܡܠܟܘܬܗ ܕܫܡܝܐ. ܐܢܟܐ ܘܠܦܘܬ ܐܦܝܢܐ ܥܕܬܐ ܠܒܫܡܐ ܕܝܠܢܐ. ܡܪܕܘܬܗ ܒܝܠܢܐ. ܘܕܝܢ ܢܦܫܐ ܦܝܫܐ ܫܠܛܐ. ܐܢ ܐܦܝܢܐ ܡܢ ܝܠܕܐ ܟܘܟܒܐ. ܘܡܘܠܕܬܐ ܕܫܠܛܐ ܗܘܐ ܗܘ ܦܠܚܝܐ ܩܕܝ ܟܘܡܪܐ ܡܢ ܐܢܫܐ ܕܒܫܝܐ.

ܘܡܦܠܚܝܢܐ ܡܢ ܫܠܛܐ ܟܕ ܡܢܝܗ ܚܕܪܐ. ܗܐ ܟܦܠܚ ܘܕܦܪܐ ܡܢܝܢܐ ܐܢ ܟܦܝܢܐ ܐܘ ܫܡܘܝܐ. ܫܠܛܐ ܕܟܝܢܘܬܐ ܒܝܬ ܟܗܢܐ ܗܘܐ ܡܢ ܟܠܗ ܥܡܡܐ. ܡܟܝܢ ܫܠܛܐ ܕܡܫܪܕܠܗ ܒܢܦܫܐ ܦܠܚܢܐ ܟܘܠܗ ܫܡܘܝܐ. ܘܟܗܢܐ ܦܝܫܐ ܡܢܢܐ. ܟܠܝܢ ܟܝܢܘܬܐ ܕܘܒܝ ܗܘܢܐ ܟܐ ܥܠܡܐ ܘܟܠ ܡܕܝܢܬܐ. ܫܠܛܐ ܒܪܝܢܐ ܕܝܢܐ. ܗܘܠ ܕܐܡܪܝܢܐ ܡܢ ܫܠܛܐ ܕܟܝܢܘܬܐ. ܫܡܐ ܟܐ ܒܡܟܠܐ ܫܡܗ. ܘܫܘܚܠܦܐ ܒܡܫܝܚܝܘܬܐ ܕܒܝܬܐ ܒܗܘܐ ܐܦܝܐ. ܘܡܢ ܝܠܢܐ ܕܐܦܝܐ ܗܡ ܒܐܦܝܢܐ ܫܠܛܐ ܘܟܘܟܒܐ. ܘܡܫܝܕܐ ܒܝ ܢܦܫܐ ܕܟܠܝܢܐ ܦܪܐ ܐܢ ܥܪܒܐ. ܘܢܓܕܝܢܘܬܐ ܒܫܡܐ ܕܡܪܝܐ ܕܟܝ ܢܠܕܐ ܐܢ ܕܡܪܝܐ ܪܒܐ❖

ܡܫܡܫ ܕܐܘܪܚܐ ܒܗܕܐ ܠܡܫܝܚܐ. ܐܝܓܘܦܐ ܫܘܚܠܦܐ ܢܣܒܝܢܐ ܪܒܝܬܐ ܥܪܒܐ ܐܢ ܗܘܪܐ ܐܢ ܦܪܐ. ܡܓܘܐ ܡܢܐ ܘܡܠܟܝܢܐ ܒܟܘܬܒܐ ܡܠܟܐ. ܘܗܕ ܢܝܫܝܢܐ ܕܡܠܟܐ ܒܡܠܟܐ. ܡܫܝܚܝܢܐ ܒܝܗܐ ܒܡܢܐ ܡܠܘܫܐ. ܝܝ ܡܫܘܦܐ. ܡܠܟܘܬܐ ܡܢܐ ܡܠܘܫܐ ܒܟܘܪܡܐ. ܘܪܘܚܐ ܒܟܘܬܗ ܦܪܨܘ ܕܦܝܪܐ. ܘܗܝܝܢܐ ܒܡܐ ܕܡܦܓܐ ܐܢ ܕܟܘܪܡܐ. ܘܡܫܪܝܢܘܬܗ ܒܕܘܟܬܐ ܡܪܝܢܬܐ ܒܒܒܕܐ (ܒܫܡܐ ܕܐܒܪܐ). ܘܗܘܝ ܗܡ ܐܦܝܢܐ. ܟܘܪ ܒܒܟܘܐ ܕܡܫܪܝܢܐ ܠܘܦܐ ܘܐܢܫܐ ܕܐܠܗܝܢܐ ܡܢܚܡ ܗܘܐ ܟܠܗ❖

❖ ❖ ❖ ❖ ❖ ❖ ❖ ❖ ❖

VOCABULARY

English	Aramaic	English	Aramaic
to slaughter	ܢܚܪܗ	sheep	ܥܪܒܐ
action, behavior	ܥܒܕܐ	cattle area,	ܒܘܩܪܐ
lamb, money	ܦܪܐ	cow herd	
fruit	ܦܐܪܐ	large ceramic jar	ܒܘܪܩܐ
to become, to stay	ܦܝܫܠܗ	light butter milk	ܕܘܓܐ
thick rich cream	ܩܘܠܡܥܡܬܐ	thick butter milk	ܕܘܓܐ ܚܡܝܪܐ
small jar, crock	ܩܘܓܬܐ(ܩܘܦܐ)	cooking pot	ܕܣܬܐ
to pour forth,	ܩܠܒܠܗ	to shelter,	ܣܘܚܠܗ
to flip to turn over		to raise cattle	
to raise cattle for	ܕܒܗܠܗ	crispy bottom of	ܚܟܟܐ
slaughter,		certain food	
to tie the cattle		enough	ܒܣܝܐ
well fed cattle	ܕܒܗܠܐ	butter	ܟܪܐܐ
fine, good	ܕܥܝܐ	thick	ܓܥܝܐ
calf	ܥܪܓܐ	enzyme, yeast	ܡܐܪܕܬܐ
fight, war, dispute	ܥܪܝܐ	to cook	ܡܒܘܫܠܐ
bull	ܬܘܪܐ	to make yogurt	ܡܘܐܕܪܠܗ
milk	ܚܠܒܐ	to float	ܡܘܛܦܠܐ
yogurt	ܚܠܝܒܐ	to warm, to heat	ܡܘܫܚܢܗ
to milk	ܚܠܘܒܠܗ	to load	ܡܣܘܩܠܐ
sour	ܚܡܘܨܐ	churning, shaking	ܡܒܐܐ

LESSON TWENTY ܦܘܫܩܐ ܕܥܣܪܝܢ

THE NAMES OF THE PARTS OF THE HUMAN BODY IN MODERN ARAMAIC

ܫܡ̈ܐ ܘܗܕ̈ܡܐ ܘܓܒ̈ܐ ܘܐܢ̈ܫܝܐ ܠܓܘܫܡܐ (ܦܓܪܐ) ܕܒܪ̈ܢܫܐ

SECTION ONE

THE HEAD ܪܝܫܐ

nostrils	ܢܚܝܪ̈ܐ ܕܦܘܢܐ	skull	ܩܪܩܦܬܐ
mouth	ܦܘܡܐ	the skin of the head	ܓܠܕܐ ܕܪܝܫܐ
tongue	ܠܫܢܐ	hair of the head	ܒܦܫܐ
epiglottis	ܠܫܢܐ ܙܥܘܪܐ	hair	ܡܘܙܐ
saliva	ܪܘܩܐ (ܬܘܦܐ)	hair plural	ܡܙ̈ܐ
lower jaw	ܦܟܐ ܬܚܬܝܐ	hair in general	ܣܥܪܐ
upper jaw	ܦܟܐ ܥܠܝܐ	brain	ܡܘܚܐ
mouth, gums	ܒܣܪܐ ܕܦܘܡܐ	forehead	ܒܘܠܘܒܢܐ
palate	ܣܩܦ ܕܦܘܡܐ	face, cheek	ܦܬܐ
tooth	ܟܟܐ	ear	ܢܬܐ
canine tooth	ܢܝܒܐ	ear drum	ܛܒܠܐ ܕܢܬܐ
molar	ܓܪܣܬܐ	eye	ܥܝܢܐ
baby milk tooth	ܟܟܐ ܕܚܠܒܐ	eye - lashes	ܓܠܦܩ̈ܐ
tooth enamel	ܡܣܢܐ ܕܟܟܐ	eye brows	ܓܒ̈ܝܢܐ
throat, gullet	ܓܪܓܘܪܬܐ	pupil	ܒܒܐ ܕܥܝܢܐ
neck, vertebra	ܦܩܪܬܐ	eye ball	ܦܘܩܪܐ ܕܥܝܢܐ
beard	ܕܩܢܐ	nose	ܦܘܢܐ
lashes	ܓܠܦܩ̈ܐ	mustache	ܣܒܠܬܐ
face	ܐܦ̈ܐ	lips	ܣܦܘܬܐ

SECTION TWO

THE CHEST AND STOMACH ܨܕܪܵܐ ܘܟܲܪܣܵܐ

heart	ܠܸܒܵܐ	back	ܚܨܵܐ
blood	ܕܸܡܵܐ	spinal column, spinal cord	ܫܸܫܠܬܵܐ ܕܚܨܵܐ
artery	ܥܸܪܩܵܐ	side	ܕܸܦܢܵܐ
vein	ܘܪܝܼܕܵܐ	bone	ܓܲܪܡܵܐ
lung	ܣܡܘܣܡܬܵܐ (ܪܵܐܬܵܐ)	flesh, meat	ܒܸܣܪܵܐ
respiration	ܫܩܵܠܵܐ ܕܢܦܵܫܵܐ	arm	ܕܪܵܥܵܐ
small intestine	ܡܸܥܘܼܬܵܐ ܙܥܘܿܪܬܵܐ	elbow	ܟܘܼܥܫܵܐ
large intestine	ܡܸܥܘܼܬܵܐ ܪܲܒܹܐ	shoulder	ܪܘܼܥܵܐ
rectum	ܫܪܬܵܐ	hand	ܐܝܼܕܵܐ
stool	ܦܠܛܬܵܐ ܕܟܪܣܵܐ	forearm	ܙܢܕܵܐ
restroom	ܒܝܬܵܐ ܕܡܝܵܐ (ܟ̰ܟ̰ܡܵܐ)	palm of the hand	ܟܦܵܐ ܕܐܝܼܕܵܐ
kidney	ܟܘܼܠܝܼܬܵܐ	fist	ܕܟܘܼܪܬܵܐ
bladder	ܡܲܬܢܵܐ	finger	ܨܘܼܒܥܬܵܐ
urine	ܫܝܼܢܵܐ	nail	ܛܘܼܦܪܵܐ
gall bladder	ܡܲܪܪܬܵܐ	Rib	ܓܲܪܡܵܐ ܕܥܸܠܥܵܐ
liver	ܟܲܒܕܵܐ (ܟܘܼܡܬܵܐ)	breast	ܕܝܼܕܵܐ
Spleen	ܛܚܵܠܵܐ		
Rib cage	ܩܦܣܵܐ ܕܥܸܠܥܵܐ	Belly-button	ܫܘܼܪܬܵܐ

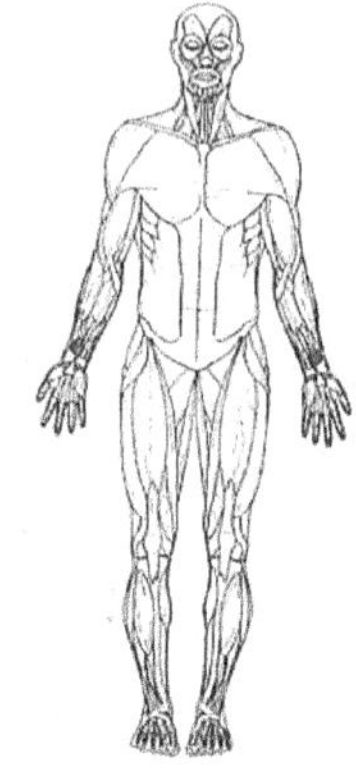

SECTION THREE

LEGS ܐ̈ܩܠܐ

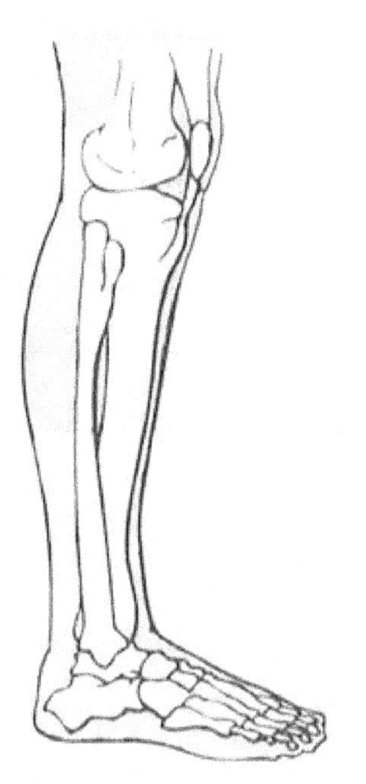

thigh	ܥܛܡܐ
hip	ܒܘܪܟܝܬܐ : ܩܘܦܬܐ
knee	ܒܘܪܟܐ
foot, leg	ܐܩܠܐ
metatarsus	ܡܫܪܬܐ ܕܐܩܠܐ
step, one foot	ܦܣܥܬܐ
toe	ܨܒܥܬܐ ܕܐܩܠܐ
hospital	ܒܫܡܟܢܐ
sickness	ܟܘܪܗܢܐ
sick	ܟܪܝܗܐ
doctor	ܚܟܝܡ : ܐܣܝܐ

❖ ❖ ❖ ❖ ❖ ❖ ❖ ❖ ❖

ܡܕܝܢܬܐ ܡܫܒܚܬܐ — ܢܝܢܘܐ ܕܡܠܟܐ ܐܬܘܪܝܐ (ܡܢܝܢ ܒ)

ܦܫܠܗ ܚܘܝܫܐ ܘܡܕܝܢܬܐ. ܒܫܢܬܐ ܡܚܠ ܬܠܬܐ ܒܢܝ ܢܝܢܘܐ. ܘܡܫܚܠܦܢܘܬ̈ܐ ܒܡܫܝܢܘܬܐ ܐܬܘܪܝܐ ܕܢܝܢܘܐ. ܘܒܬܪܗ ܝܡܡܐ ܡܢ ܛܘܪܐ. ܡܕܒܪܢܘܬܐ ܘܡܫܘܚܬܐ ܒܕܪܓܐ. ܘܡܫܠܛܢܘܬܐ ܡܠܟܘܬܐ ܒܡܕܝܢܬܐ. ܘܡܪܕܘܬܐ ܘܡܬܚܫܒܢܘܬܐ ܕܢܦܫܐ. ܘܡܠܟܘܬܐ ܘܫܘܠܛܢܘܬܐ ܒܐܬܘܪܝܐ. ܘܡܫܠܛܢܘܬܐ ܡܢܝܢ ܟܠܗ. ܠܗܘܐ ܡܫܝܚܐ ܕܠܗܘܢ ܫܢܐ ܐܬܘܪܝܐ ܡܢ ܗܕܝܡ. ܫܢܝܐ ܘܡܘܒܠܐ ܐܝܟ ܒܐܘܚܕܢܘܬܐ ܕܫܒܝܢܐ ܒܡܕܝܢܬܐ ܟܠܗ. ܘܡܢܝܢ ܗܘ ܕܒܝܢܐ ܒܘܫܟܐ ܡܢ ܥܡܪܐ. ܐܢ ܫܘܦܪܐ ܘܡܠܟܐ ܡܛܪܐ ܕܝܘܡܐ. ܟܠܗ ܘܡܢܢ ܡܢ ܕܦܢܐ. ܗܘܐ ܡܬܒܘܠܐ ܕܚܘܕܪܐ ܐܢ ܫܒܝܐ ܡܢ ܐܬܪܐ ܡܫܚܠܦܐ܀

ܡܬܪܐ ܘܫܒܝܬܐ. ܒܢܝ ܬܘܡܬܐ ܒܠܒܒ ܬܫܡܫܬܐ ܕܝܒܝܫܐ. ܘܫܒܝܬܐ ܡܢ ܐܬܪܐ. ܟܠ ܗܘ ܐܢܫܝܢܐ ܡܬܪܐ ܘܫܒܝܬܐ. ܠܟܢ ܗܘ ܡܫܢܝܢܘܬܐ ܘܡܪܕܝܢܘܬܐ. ܘܡܫܠܛܢܘܬܐ ܡܢܝܢ ܒܬܪܗ ܘܫܡܥܐ ܘܫܠܝܐ.

ܟܝܢܐ ܕܒܬܪܗ ܡܚܘܪܐ ܕܡܫܡܫܐ. ܗܘܐ ܒܦܢܝܐ ܒܠܚܘܕܝܐ ܕܫܡܫܐ. ܒܬܪܗ ܟܦܢܐ ܘܟܠܐ ܒܫܘܪܐ ܘܟܠ ܒܡܕܝܢܬܐ. ܘܟܠ ܒܡܕܝܢܬܐ ܡܢܗ ܟܦܢܐ. ܒܕܝܢܘܬܗ ܡܢ ܡܬܪܐ. ܠܟܢ ܒܬܪܗ ܐܘܝܪܐ ܘܡܘܢܐ. ܒܫܘܪܐ ܘܟܪ ܒܫܡܫܝ ܐܝܟܘ ܘܒܫܝܢܐ. ܘܡܕܝܢܘܬܗ ܡܢ ܫܒܝܬܐ܀

ܒܬܪܗ ܡܚܘܪܐ ܒܒܝܬܐ ܗܘܝ ܒܕܝܢܘܬܗ. ܗܘܐ ܡܬܪܐ ܡܢ ܫܒܝܬܐ. ܘܪܕܘܬܐ ܠܟܢܐ ܕܡܢܐ ܕܟܪ ܗܕܝܢܐ ܐܕܟܝܢ ܬܫܡܫܬܐ. ܘܒܬܪ ܒܒܝܬܐ ܐܝܟܐ ܫܢ ܐܬܪܐ. ܡܕܪܘܢܐ ܒܟܘܗ. ܘܒܘܒܠܐ ܫܒܝܬܐ ܡܘܕܥܐ. ܒܪܫܠܢܐ ܕܫܡܫܐ. ܒܒܠܝܬܐ ܕܐܕܟܝܢ ܬܫܡܫܬܐ. ܡܟܢܫܘܬܐ ܠܕܫܡܫܬܐ ܐܫܕܬܐ ܕܒܝܬܐ. ܕܕܘܐ ܠܐܦ ܕܫܡܫܬܐ ܡܦܩ. ܘܡܠܟܘܬܗ ܒܫܒܝܐ ܡܢ ܟܠܗ ܒܬܪܗ. ܘܡܦܩܝܢܐ ܕܘܚܕܐ ܗܐ ܡܢܝܢ. ܡܢ ܥܕܘܬܐ ܐܕܟܝܢܐ ܕܚܘܝܠܗ ܠܕܫܡܫܬܐ ܐܫܕܬܐ ܡܠܘܐ ܝܘܕܐ ܒܦܪܝ ܕܫܡܫܬܐ ܕܐܘܬܪܗ ܡܬܪܐ ܡܢ ܫܒܝܬܐ ܡܘܕܥܐ ܘܐܘܪܚܐ ܕܐܫܡܫܐ ܡܢ ܐܦ ܕܫܡܫܬܐ. ܘܟܠ ܠܥܕܘܬܐ. ܘܡܥܕܘܬܐ ܒܝܠܦܐ ܒܕܫܡܫܬܐ ܕܐܦܝ ܡܕܝܢܬܐ. ܘܡܫܡܫܐ ܕܡܫܢܝܢܘܬܗ ܕܫܡܫܬܐ ܡܕܡܝܬܐ. ܕܕܘܐ ܒܦܠܚܗ. ܗܦܟܠܝܐ ܘܡܫܡܫܐ ܘܫܚܘܪܐ ܘܦܪܕܐ ܕܕܝܢܐ ܡܢ ܕܒܝܬܐ. ܒܠܚ ܐܝ ܡܕܝܢܬܐ ܕܒܝܬܐ ܒܟܪܟܐ ܒܕܫܡܫܬܐ. ܘܟܝܢܐ ܕܒܬܪܗ ܒܫܒܝܐ ܡܫܝܢܐ ܦܠܚܐ ܒܥܘܦܝܐ ܘܝܘܦܝܐ ܘܥܘܠܐ ܕܫܡܫܝ ܬܫܡܫܬܐ܀

ܡܬܡ ܝܬܝܐ. ܐܝܟ ܕܒܝܬܐ ܐܝܬܘܗܝ ܕܝܠܗ. ܒܬܪܗ ܗܘܐ ܦܕܝܐ ܘܕܝܢܐ ܒܚܕܘܬܐ ܕܘܝܫܬܐ. ܡܢ ܒܝܬܐ ܐܦ ܒܕܫܡܫܐ. ܘܟܠ ܫܢܐ ܐܝܬܘܗܝ. ܡܢ ܒܬܪܗ ܡܢ ܫܒܝܬܐ. ܕܟܝܢܐ ܡܢ ܡܠܝܬܐ ܒܘܛܘܠ. ܐܘ ܦܠܚܐ ܕܒܘܛܘܠ ܡܢ ܕܘܟܝܬܐ. ܘܐܝܟ ܕܟܠܝܬܐ ܒܫܡܫܐ. ܘܦܝܫܐ ܕܝܠܗ ܡܫܡܫܐ ܟܠܗ ܕܫܒܝܐ. ܫܡܠܝܬܐ ܐܬܪܐ ܕܐܦ ܟܝܢܐ. ܡܫܡܫ ܕܐܬܪܐ

ܘܡܫܬܘܕܥܝܬܐ ܦܠܓܐ ܕܬܘܪܟܝܐ (ܕܒܠܝܗ ܩܝܡ). ܗܐ ܣܝܡܢܐ ܘܚܠܨ. ܘܗܐ ܐܢܝܐ ܕܐܪܥܐ ܘܟܘܪܐ ܘܩܪ̈ܝܐ ❖

ܓܢ̈ܢܐ ܕܡܬܬܠܝܢܐ ܕܒܒܠ. ܒܬܒܝܬܐ ܚܕ̈ܐ ܕܡܫܬܘܕܥܢܘܬܐ ܐܡܪܝ ܚܕ̈ܐ ܕܫܒܥ ܬܗܪ̈. ܘܚܠ ܘܟܕ ܡܢ ܢܩܦܐ ܕܥܡܡܐ. ܐܝܬܘܗܝ ܕܫܪܟܢܐ ܘܡܪܕܘܬܐ ܘܥܒܕܘܬܐ. ܕܡܬܝܕܥܐ ܫܒ̈ܥ ܬܗܪ̈ܐ. ܘܦܫܝܛܐ ܒܗ ܥܠܡܐ. ܘܡܫܬܘܕܥܢܘܬܐ ܒܡܥܒܕܐ ܒܝܕ ܐܢܫܐ. ܗܐ ܕܒܠܝܗ ܐܬܪܐ ܘܫܘܬܐ ܘܫܪ̈ܐ. ܘܐܝܬܝܗܝܢ ܗܐ ܝܬܝܗ ܡܕܝܢܬ ܒܒܠܬܐ. ܘܡܥܪܐ ܘܡܕܝܢ̈ܬܐ. ܘܡܫܬܪܝܢ ܒܥܠܡ̈ܐ ܕܟܬܒ̈ܐ ܓܢ̈ܢܐ ܡܠܟ̈ܐ ܕܒܒܠܐ ܡܬܩܠܝܢܐ. ܥܠ ܐܝܟ ܡܫܝܢܐ ܕܩܘܝܬܐ ܒܗ ܥܠܡܐ. ܘܐܝܟ ܒܫܢ̈ܐ ܦܫܝܛܐ ܕܠܗܐ ܣܠܝܩܐ. ܒܥܠܡܐ ܕܝܘܢܝܐ ܒܡܠܟܘܬܐ ܥܡܢܝܬܐ ܐܡܝܢ ❖

❖ ❖ ❖ ❖ ❖ ❖ ❖ ❖ ❖

At Babylon, Nebuchadnessar constructed vast city walls, on which four chariots could drive abreast. For himself, he built a palace, on top of which were the famous "hanging gardens" -- one of the seven wonders of the ancient world. 580 B.C.

The Hanging Garden of Babylon

VOCABULARY

English	Aramaic	English	Aramaic
licrice	ܡܗܣܐ	to dry out,	ܐܘܫܠܗ
effort, hard worve	ܝܗܘܐ	to solidify	
clean	ܢܕܝܦܐ	large wooden spoon	ܐܪܡܟܢܐ
to keep, to observe	ܢܛܝܪܗ	bottle	ܒܘܛܘܠ
to drip	ܢܛܝܦܠܗ	oil, grease, butter	ܕܗܢܐ
to forget	ܢܫܝܠܗ	water container	ܕܢܐ :ܐܢܬܐ
quince	ܣܦܪܓܠܐ	made of clay	
to press, to squeeze	ܥܨܝܪܗ	wedding	ܕܥܘܐ :
			ܫܠܘܟܐ
compress , to		strong, tight	ܫܘܒܩܐ
arak, anisette, ouzo	ܥܪܩ	sesame seeds	ܛܚܢܓܒ
one shot of alcohol	ܦܝܟ	mill worker	
to increase,	ܦܪܐܠܗ	numerous, much	ܟܒܝܪܐ
to multipl		small ceramic jar	ܟܕܘܢܬܐ
shell, skin	ܩܠܦܐ	sesame seeds	ܟܘܣܦܐ
reed, bamboo, tube	ܩܢܝܐ	thick oil	
lid, cover	ܩܦܟ	bride	ܟܠܘ
quarter of bottle	ܪܘܒܥܝܐ	strong taste	ܟܗܟܘܝ
to get drunk	ܪܘܝܠܗ	hen	ܟܬܝܬܐ
non concentrated	ܪܦܝܐ	to winnow	ܡܕܘܪܝܠܗ
liquor, weak		to insert, to stir	ܡܘܥܒܪܗ
movement, tradition	ܪܫܡܬܐ	to hit, to blow,	ܡܚܐܠܗ
work	ܥܘܒܕܐ	to attack	
to hang to dry	ܥܛܝܓܠܗ	to refine , to purified	ܡܨܘܪܪܗ
to spread out		to lock, to seal	ܡܠܘܚܟܠܗ

	kingdom ܡܲܠܟܘܼܬ݂ܵܐ

VOCABULARY

Cont.

English	Aramaic	English	Aramaic
vinegar	ܚܠܐ	sesame oil	ܫܝܪܓ
wine	ܚܡܪܐ	sesame seeds	ܫܫܡܐ
groom	ܚܬܢܐ	wooden or	ܒܕܘܡܐ: ܫܘܒܫܐ
to become dizzy	ܚܕܝܪܗ ܪܝܫܗ	metal tube	ܫܘܦܐ
to turn around, to spin		alcoholic	ܫܬܝܐ
hard work, effort	ܓܗܘܐ	steam, vapor	ܗܘܘܓܐ
sesame seed mill	ܓܪܕܐ	apple	ܚܒܘܫܐ
spread, diffused	ܦܫܝܠܗ	to mix, to stir	ܓܘܓܠܗ

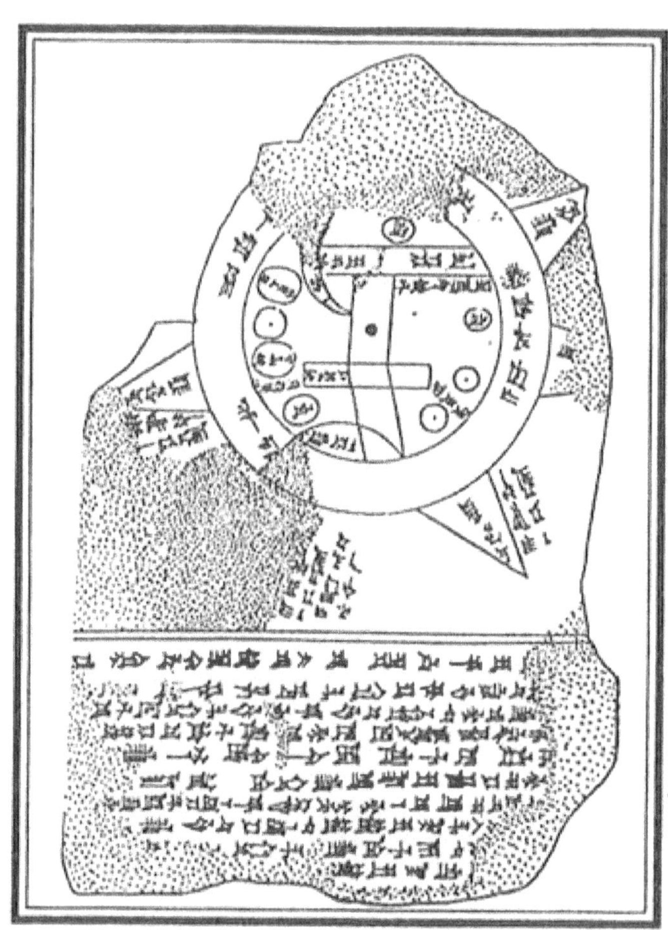

A Babylonian map of the world, about the sixth century B.C. The large circles indicate the seas surrounding the world, and the two vertical lines the Tigris and Euphrates.

English Index

D

I

J

K

L

M

N

O

P

Q

R

S

T

U

V

W

Y

Aramaic Index ܦܗܪܣܬ ܕܡܠܐ

ܠ

ܡ

ܦ

ܨ

ܪ

ܢ

ܣ

ܥ

ܦ

ܨ

ܩ

ܪ

ܫ

ܢ

TWENTY READINGS FROM *ARAMAIC II*

FIRST READING

TIMES AND SEASONS

The Chaldean patriarchs of the early centuries took care of (the problem of) the times and seasons. And they were those who established the beginnings of the knowledge of astronomy. And from the movements of the stars and the changes of the weather, they gave knowledge for the east and the west and the mountain (north) and the plain (south), for farmers and all workers of the fields, those who wait all year to plant and to harvest their crops and to bring their produce into the house. The year contains four designated seasons:

A. Spring
B. Summer
C. Autumn (Fall)
D. Winter

Each season has three months, and one year contains twelve months. Their names are these:

A. January
B. February
C. March
D. April
E. May
F. June
G. July
H. August
I. September
J. October
K. November
D. December

Every month contains four weeks, and every week has seven days. Their names are:

A. Sunday
B. Monday
C. Tuesday
D. Wednesday
E. Thursday
F. Friday
G. Saturday

SECOND READING

SIMON AND ANNE

From the roof of his house Simon called to his neighbor Ann and said to her: "Come, my neighbor, (I want) to speak to you about our lives when we were living in our villages. And I want for you to help me to begin to teach our children, now and in the future, to speak the Chaldean language, which is a branch of the Aramaic language—the language in which He spoke—Our Lord Jesus Christ—and His mother, the Lady Mary, and the holy apostles. And in it they spoke and they prayed. And our Chaldean patriarchs conversed (in it) from the time of Christ until the final centuries of the second millennium. Chaldeans (originally) spoke and wrote in the classical Aramaic language, but with time and from the mingling of the people of our nation with other people, foreign words entered into our Chaldean language. Chaldean Christians of Mesopotamia who live in the mountain (north) mixed with their language words of the language of the Kurds. And those who lived in the plain (south), the language of Arabs entered into theirs. And (for) those who live in Turkey, the Turkish language mixed with their language. And (for) those who resided in Iran, Persian words enter into their speech."And therefore the modern Chaldean Aramaic language is not pure Aramaic, like the classical language. And also it is not easy sometimes for Chaldeans from the mountain to understand Chaldeans of the plain." Ann heard Simon with joy, and she said to him: "With the help of God we will work together and with all Chaldeans—men and women, young men and maidens—to teach our modern Chaldean Aramaic language, consecrated by the mouth of Our Lord, for our children and our relatives and our friends."

THIRD READING

THE LIGURGICAL YEAR OF THE CHALDEAN CHURCH

All peoples of the world start the beginning of the New Year on the Feast of the Circumcision of Our Lord, on the first day of January. The churches of the east, and among them the Chaldean Church., start the liturgical year at the beginning of the month of December. Chaldean Christians pray every day just as Our Lord commanded: prayers of evening, and of night, and morning. Jesus said in the Gospel of Mark 13:35 "Watch, because you do not know at what time your Lord will come. Perhaps at evening or at the middle of the night or toward dawn." In the evening (prayer) service, believers thank God for his blessings to them on that day. And at night prayer they follow the words which the psalm said: "In the middle of the night I arose to give you thanks because of your ordinances, O Just One." And at Morning Prayer believers thank God who raised them from the sleep of night which is a symbol of death to the light of day. All the prayers of these three times of days and of Sundays and of feast days and of memorial days (remembrances of the death of saints or the killing of martyrs) these prayers are placed in three books called prayer books. The first prayer book has the prayers from the day of the Annunciation until the Great Fast (Lent). And in the second prayer book (there are) the prayers from the Great Fast until the end of the season of the Resurrection (Easter). And the third and final prayer book it contains the prayers from the feast of Pentecost (the descent of the Holy Spirit) until the final Sunday of the season of the Consecration of the Church. The prayers of the liturgy of the Chaldean Church are collected from (the writings of) the apostles and the disciples of Our Lord, and from the holy Bible— the Old Testament and the New Testament and from the writings of the holy Chaldean Fathers. And especially in the year of Our Lord four hundred and ten, at the synod (local council) of St. Isaac and St. Marotha, they collected the prayers of St. Adday and St. Mari and St. Simon the son of dyers and St. Jacob of Nisiwin and St. Ephrem the harp of the Spirit and other Chaldean teachers of the first four centuries of Christ. And they called them "the prayers of the liturgy from the customs and traditions of the church of the cities of Saliq and Qatisfon.

FOURTH READING
SEASONS OF THE LITURGICAL YEAR OF THE CHALDEAN CHURCH

The liturgical year of Chaldeans fills twelve months, and it has these seasons: A. Annunciation (Advent): it has four Sundays; B. Birth (Christmas): it has two Sundays; C. Epiphany: it has eight Sundays; D. Fast (Lent): it contains seven Sundays; E. Resurrection (Easter): it has seven Sundays; F. Apostles (Pentecost): it has seven Sundays; G. Summer: it has seven Sundays; H. Elijah: it contains seven Sundays; but the season of the Cross starts from the fourth Sunday of Elijah (four Sundays parallel with the last four Sundays of Elijah); I. Moses: it has four Sundays; J. the Consecration of the Church (the final season): it contains four Sundays. And at the end of the last week of this season the liturgical year ends. Every twelve months Chaldean believers meditate on the holy mysteries of the Christian religion—from the time that God sent his Son, Our Lord Jesus Christ, to the world. He was born and he was baptized. And he preached and he suffered. He was crucified and he died and he arose. And he sent the Holy Spirit upon the apostles. And they with the disciples and the early Christians spread the Catholic Christian religion through all creation. Many from the peoples and the nations repented and were baptized. And in the last seasons the prayers show us how at the end of the world the holy cross will be seen. And they will appear, Elijah the prophet, representing all the prophets, and Moses the prophet, the symbol of the Law and the commandments. The two of them confess that Jesus is the Messiah who came for the salvation of the world. And through him are fulfilled all the prophecies of the prophets of the Old Testament. And after him there is no prophet who will come. And in the Last Day, at the end of the world, Christ will come the second time to judge the living and the dead. And when he comes the holy Church will welcome him. And she will be dressed in the clothes of a bride. And she will greet him, with her children, with psalms and hymns. And they all will live with him in the kingdom of heaven forever.

FIFTH READING

CHALDEAN FARMERS AND SOWERS

In the month of December, rain and lightning and thunder are seen and heard everywhere. The cold air and long, dark nights make people go inside and keep themselves safe in their houses. Many of the farmers and sowers those who were not able sow in the summer waited until the moisture moistens (the ground enough), when the moisture from the surface of the ground reached the moisture of the soil of the bottom of the ground (i.e., the water table). And the sower is obliged to sow before the winter reaches him. The farmer in the villages of Nineveh wakes up before dawn. The woman of the house or mother or sister prepares hot food for him: rishta and (fried) rishta, lentils and shopateh. And she puts in his bag provisions for all his day: bread and cheese and onions or jagig and date syrup or grape syrup and dates or raisins. Before he starts eating, the sower puts out teednay and barley for his beasts ol burden, he takes out his equipment into the yard. He looks to the sky and he remembers the proverb of the fathers which says: "The red clouds in the evening twilight call the farmer to come and eat dinner. But the red clouds of the dawn send away the farmer from the yard." If from the early morning the clouds are not red, the sky will be serene. There is no danger of rain. After one heavy meal in the morning the farmer puts *charokheh* on his feet and he puts a thick khameyseye on his shoulders. He ties his trousers and he wraps his sosekydthd on his arms. He goes to the yard and he leads out his beasts of burden: donkeys and she donkeys or mules and she mules or workhorses and she workhorses. He saddles his animals and he puts the plow and the plowshare and the yoke onto one. And on another the rest of the farm equipment and thejuharat filled with hay. And on another he puts the seeds. And he takes with him a sower with his apron. And both the farmer and the sower and the beasts of burden go together before the sky lights up. And they turn their faces toward the field. And they are praying and putting their day in the hand of the Lord God.

SIXTH READING

THE MONTH OF DECEMBER IN THE VILLAGES OF THE CHALDEANS OF NINEVEH

This month in the liturgy of the church is a month of joyful annunciations. All the Catholic Chaldeans pray the *Tabrikat* in honor of the Lady Mary. Some who are able to go to church after vespers pray the *Tabrikat* together. And those who are not able to come to church gather at night after supper at the house of one of the relatives—at (the house of) the father and mother or of the brother or of the sister. Little ones and adults gather around the large *manqal* filled with wood or charcoal, which is filled with wood or charcoal brought by the charcoal trader from the mountain. After the *Tabrikat* prayer they tell stories and fables and parables. And they grill oak nuts, and they drink tea with cardamom or with cinnamon, which exude their aroma through all the house. From the early times until the beginning of the twentieth century people lit their houses with the light of a lamp of linseed oil or olive oil. But after the first quarter of the twentieth century they began using oil lamps and lanterns and they filled them with fuel and they lit them. In the beginning, for cooking in *paya* (small mud oven) they used to burn dry cow dung and dry sheep dung. And for the baking of bread in the *tanureh* (large oven for baking bread) they burn hay and straw. But from the second half of the twentieth century electricity entered into all homes and gave light and fire (heat) for cooking and heating and to make cold water. And it made the radio and the telephone and the computer work.

SEVENTH READING

SUNDAYS OF THE MONTH OF DECEMBER AND THE FEAST OF THE NATIVITY (CHRISTMAS)

Each Sunday of the month of December Catholic Chaldeans remember one of the four announcements of the gospel, the ones which were announced to them by the Angel Gabriel. In the first Sunday the Chaldean liturgical rite reminds (us) of the announcement of the joy which the angel gave to Zechariah and his wife, Elizabeth. He announced to them that they will have a son in their old age. And on the eighth day of this month occurs the feast of the Lady Mary, conceived immaculate (lit., "of unstained nature"). And in the second Sunday the Church remembers the announcement of Our Lady, the Virgin Mary, when the angel said to her: "You will be with child and will give birth to a Son and you will call his name Jesus." And in the third Sunday the Church remembers the joy of Zechariah and Elizabeth at the birth of John the Baptist. And in the fourth Sunday the liturgy speaks to us about St. Joseph the Righteous when the angel announced and said to him that the Lady Mary is a Virgin and she conceived by the power of the Holy Spirit. When the angel left Joseph, he took her to his house. And he allowed her to guard her virginity until his death. Also she kept her virginity and she knew no man until her Assumption from this earth to heaven in soul and body. In this month there are some Christians who fast from dairy products and meat tor twenty four days. And there are some who fast seven days, and there are some who (fast) three, and there are some (who keep a fast) of one day before the feast of Christmas. In the week before the feast of Christmas, Chaldeans make flatbread and *kuleche* and they sew or they buy new clothes and they prepare *charazeh* (roast mixed nuts) and oranges and sweet lemons. And in the evening of the small feast (i.e., Christmas, as opposed to the great feast of Easter) people hear (attend) the great vespers. And they wait until midnight Mass. The alleys of the town shake from the voice of the well-wishers who cry out in joy, and they said "The Lord is born," and the respondents say "Glory to his name." Before the beginning of the

Mass they burn torches in the yard of the church before the manger of the Baby Jesus. And after Mass they return in a hurry to the house and mom takes out from the *tanureh* the stewing jar of *kraeh* (i.e., beef tripe, barley, and sheep intestines filled with rice and ground beef). They sit down and eat happily after midnight and in the morning they distribute *charazeh* and oranges and money for small children. On the day after Christmas all the alleys of the town were filled with brides-those who slept during the feast day with their fathers (parents). And when they returned (to their husbands), while they were carrying their clothes bundles, they sang and said: "The feast is over and there is no *more mindaneh* (another word for *charazeh).* We are going to be stuck with the in-laws."

EIGHTH READING

THE MONTH OF JANUARY

IN TOWNS OF THE CHALDEANS OF NINEVEH

On the first day of the month of January the Christian New Year starts. And on this day Christian Chaldeans celebrate the feast of the Circumcision of Our Lord. Eight days after his birth it happened that Our Lord was named Jesus, whose translation means the Savior. Six days after the feast of the New Year, the feast of the Epiphany (i.e., the manifestation of Jesus to the world) occurs. When our Lord was age thirty years old he was baptized by the hand of St. John the Baptist in the river Jordan. And after this day Jesus started the three final years of his life, in preaching and teaching until the day he was crucified. And he died and he arose and he ascended into heaven. After the feast of Epiphany, on all the Fridays occur memorials of one or more of the martyrs and saints. The first Friday is dedicated to the memorial of the killing of St. John the Baptist. And on the second Friday occurs the memorial of the martyrdom of St.s Peter and Paul. And on the third Friday occurs the memorial of the four Evangelists. Their names are these: Matthew, Mark, Luke, and John. And the memorial of the martyrdom of St. Stephen occurs on the fourth Friday. And on the fifth Friday occurs the memorial of the Greek Teachers (Fathers): St. Basil.and St. Gregory and St. John and their friends. And on the sixth Friday the Chaldean Church remembers the memorial of the Syrian Fathers: St. Ephrem and St. Jacob of Nisiwin. And also on this Friday the Chaldean Church remembers the Roman teachers: St. Ambrose and St. Augustine and St. Jerome. And on the seventh Friday comes the memorial of the patron of all the Chaldean Church-that is, the memorial of one individual person. And on the last—the eighth Friday—the Chaldean Church remembers those who died—departed (or) dead ones. On this day Chaldeans eat turnovers of (i.e., filled with) either rice or dates, and after Mass the faithful go to the cemetery (lit., "home of tombs") to visit their dead and to pray memorial prayers for them.

NINTH READING

THE MONTH OF FEBRUARY AND THE FAST OF THE ATONEMENT

Winter in the villages of Nineveh starts in the month of October and November. But the beginning of winter really is on the twenty first day of December. From that time hard rains descend, and Chaldeans of these towns jump for joy. Their hearts are filled with happiness. Plants sprout, and ditches and swamps and reservoirs and wells are filled with water. And also people drank from them and also make their animals drink from them. And young men learned how to swim in them. But in the second quarter of the twentieth century clean water entered into the towns, and houses allowed pipes to be installed, and many of the wells were shut off. And the swamps were tilled with dirt. Since tne days running water entered into tne nouses, cleanness spread everywhere and people got rid of the dirt and especially were relieved (lit., "rested") of lice and fleas and glaucoma and various other sicknesses. On the second day of this month of February the Chaldean Church celebrates the feast of Old Simeon. On it the Church remembers Our Lord when he was forty days of age. Mary and Joseph presented him in the Temple in Jerusalem and Old Simeon carried him in his arms and blessed the Lord.

Twenty one days before the Great Fast, on the Monday which occurs after the fifth Sunday of Epiphany, the Chaldean Church holds three days of fasting of atonement, a time of asking forgiveness from God in penance and prayer. All Catholic Chaldeans fast three days from meat and dairy products. There are some who do not eat anything those three days. On the day of Thursday after the day of atonement (Chaldeans) eat the sweets of St. Elijah and also this day they call it the Thursday of Thanksgiving, the day of thanking God.

TENTH READING

THE MONTH OF MARCH AND THE GREAT FAST

In the month of March, the countryside clothed with a green suit, the plants sprout up and fields start blooming and all the parks and territory are filled with lilies and wild roses of all colors: red and blue and yellow, brown and black and white. The smell of greenery opens the heart, and all creation becomes one voice and cries out to God and says "How wonderful are the deeds of your hands, O Lord!" Families which have animals are glad in the young ones which are born. The cows give birth, and mares and she donkeys and ewes (female sheep). The nesting hen hatches her chicks, and also the baby birds (hatch). All these add beauty to creation and sweetness. Spring normally starts on the twenty first of this month, but in the villages of Nineveh spring starts at the end of February. At this time the seven weeks of the Great Fast of fifty days begin. Many Chaldean Christians do not eat meat all these days. Some fast the first week and the last week, and they don't eat breakfast until midday. The food for these days is *ta<u>h</u>ini* and *<u>h</u>alawah* and bread and green onion and lentils and chickpeas and *gurgur* or barley cooked with onion and widow's stew, which is crushed onion with sumac and from the field urtica, leg of rooster, and malva. From the second Sunday of Lent until Palm Sunday Chaldeans go out to festivals during the day after Mass. Each village has its own saints which are honored. Priests and deacons and people go out to hear the teaching of Christ and the preaching of the priest, and after this folk dancing and dancing. And sellers of nuts and *charaze* spread out. And many young men make races with stallions or mules or donkeys, and people walk from the village to the place of the shrine, and they are dressed in clothes of all kind of colors. Just like the river which runs, thus the people are coming and going. There are some who go walking, and there are some who ride animals. All of them happy, all of them laughing, all of them conversing, and small children play hide and seek between their families and strangers. People spend all day out doors. Mothers carry food with them, loaves of bread and *taẖini* or *kulaycheh.* And those who are engaged (i.e., those who have engaged sons) carry fiancee's food for the son's fiancee—that is, a pan of yellow barley (i.e., barley colored with saffron)—so they could eat together in the large yard of the shrine. And at sunset of the day, every one returns to his house, and his heart is open and joyful and filled with love and faith and from the air and the sweet aroma of spring.

ELEVENTH READING

THE MONTH OF APRIL AND THE FEAST OF EASTER

Chaldeans of the villages of Nineveh wait for the air of spring and wild roses. The Great Fast passes in a hurry, and people spend most of their days in the field. Some of them go to cut weeds, like thorn bushes and pod trees and darnel. And others search for the holes of mice, and they kill them with a pump (i.e., they smoke them out). And many small children go out and dig out truffles and *lagneh* and parsnip with a hoe. And with their hands, they cut mushrooms and rooster claw and *khnakhtasota* (a kind of green leaves) and malva and *gurgaymeh.* The least ot Easter occurs between the twenty second day of March and the twenty titth ot April, as was ordered by the Fathers of the council of

Nicaea in the year 325 of the Lord. On every Sunday of the Great Fast Chaldeans celebrate the feast of one of the saints, but on the seventh Sunday comes the Feast of Hosanna (i.e., Palm Sunday). On the Saturday of Hosanna (i.e., the day before), they prepared yellow loaves colored with saffron. All the little children went to the church, and there the priest divided them in groups, and some kids went with one of the priests or one of the deacons. They took one alley of the village alleys, and they sang the songs of Hosanna. One of them carried the cross and another carried the banner, and they took both the cross and the banner to every room in a house (i.e., to bless it). At the end of the blessing people used to hand to the priest or to the deacon and the little kids either money or *charazeh* or eggs. On Hosanna Sunday the priest blessed the olive branches. Everyone carried the branches and took them to their fields. And in every field they put one of the blessed olive branches. On Holy Thursday, all people went to confession and received Communion, and the priest washed the feet of the twelve disciples. All Fridays of the Great Fast people did the way of the cross after the prayer of vespers. But on the seventh Friday, the Passion Friday (i.e., Good Friday), people fasted until midday and then ate bitter herbs, like rooster claw and *khnakhtasota.* In the evening they attended the homily and then a procession with the cross and the tomb of Our Lord (i.e., a wooden box covered with black sheets, symbolizing the tomb of Christ). And many stayed awake all night in the Church. On the evening of the Saturday of Light (i.e., Holy Saturday) [so called because it was believed the Holy Spirit descended on the tomb while Christ was taking the dead to heaven], after the vespers prayer they prepared for midnight Mass. And many who came to the church brought with them hardboiled eggs, also colored eggs. When the priest began the announcement that Jesus is risen, after Mass all the people broke the eggs and ate. And they returned to their houses, their heart filled with joy, and well-wishing each other and saying "The Lord is risen." (The response is:) "Blessed is his name."

TWELFTH READING

THE MONTH OF MAY

TIME OF HARVEST AND *BUDRA*

Chaldeans of the villages of Nineveh, those who depend for their lives on the crops, wait all year for these days to harvest and bring theircrops into their homes. And to repay the debt that they incurred (lit., "that there was on them") in the days of winter. In the month of May the sky gets warm. People wait to take their bedding up to the roof. Little children run from roof to roof playing with each other. And relatives and older neighbors pass and cross over the barrier (between houses) to sit together and to drink and to tell stories and the daily news. In the night the supper is taken to the roof or balcony. And the people of the house gather around the *lagan* or *Sayniya* and the *Ṯabaq* (is) filled with bread, either flatbread or loaves, with cheese or blue cheese or olives or tahini or date syrup if there was no cooked meal prepared. The joy of the relatives together, and the good outdoor air, and sometimes the songs of some drunk people, or the drums or the horn of people who have at home an engagement or a wedding, and sometimes those who make the *chali* fly (those who make the *ch-ẖa-ly* fly tie a piece of cloth on his leg and they pour gas over it and they tie it with wire and all the children cry out "That is, that is *ch-ẖa-ly"* all these things make sleeping on the roofs a good time which is unforgettable. Many farmers harvest barley or lentils or fava beans and they collect cucumbers. The farmers and those who own fields hired workers who were standing in the market waiting. They took them to work in their fields. And all trails and roads and paths were filled during these days from those going and coming (lit., "goers and comers") to the work—especially, the *sawale.* And they conducted their animals carrying *shakhreh* filled with barley or lentils which were brought to the threshing *budratha.* And the *sawaleh* returned time after time until the sun set. And sometimes some people were seen riding on a wagon pulled by a donkey or mule. And they were singing or praying. With them the birds of the sky sing, because some of the heads of the grain which fell from the *shakhra* or from the *ashafeh,* which left much food for the birds. The name of the Lord God and prayers used to be in the mouth of everybody because the farmers are bringing their crops and workers are having their wages. Many prayed the rosary while they walked, and they sang religious poems, stories, and ballads—especially the story of the Virgin Mary (called) "In the name of the Father and the Son." On the fifteenth day of this month, Chaldeans celebrate the feast of the Virgin Mary the keeper of the fields. In these days, they request from the Mother of God, through her intercession toward Jesus her Son, that all the melon patches and the fields will be kept safe from all the *qopta,* and locust, and grasshoppers, and grain weevils, and worms, and scorching weather, and birds.

THIRTEENTH READING

THE MONTH OF JUNE

MELON PATCHES

Those who own melon patches wait for these days to pick cucumbers, melon, and squash. And they bring some of these to their homes, and some to be sold in the market or for the (neighboring) villages, and more for taking to the Gep in Mosul. They carry grain with the *shakhra,* or in wagons or in flatbed trucks to *budratha,* and they start crushing garbanzo beans, and they use the hay thresher for lentils, barley, and wheat. Every day at evening many prepare to go picking in the melon patch. They go in the early morning. They ride their animals, and they walk with the stars of the morning. And before the sun rise they reach the melon patch. And in that place there are already men sleeping at night on their *hushatha.* And in the evening those men broke white marble, and they made them (into) small pieces and put them by yellow and ripe melons. And before the dawn, and (with) darkness still on the ground, those men and those who came from the house start picking and cutting from the plants each melon which has by its side a (piece of) white marble. They bring melons to the market in the gunny sacks *(guniyeh)* or *zabul,* or they leave them so that a large flatbed truck comes and carries them.

Anybody who tilled the land or built a booth and guarded the melon patch or who slept in the melon patch never forgot those beautiful days as long as he lives. How beautiful it is when the owners of those patches gathered thistles and *kessuk* and *khata* and made a fire until they went to sleep, and each one leaves to the *hushe* of his own melon patch. In this month, the Chaldean church celebrates the month of the Sacred Heart of Jesus and the feast of Pentecost—the descent of the Holy Spirit on the apostles in the upper room in Jerusalem. In this month schools close and little children and young people help their families. Some gather crops and some till the land and some harvest. And some guide the *shakhra.* And others watch the melon patches or pick the melons or cucumber and carry them from the patch to the market or the house. Or they ride on the thresher. Work is available for boys and for girls and for men and for women—even for those who are in age. How beautiful it is, that the city become like ant colony, with people going and coming (lit., "goers and comers") from everywhere. This month of blessings renews life in all the people. And those who waited all winter and spring now receive money in their (money) bags. They pay their debt, and they save for the wedding of their children, or for building, or for buying animals or lands, or to travel to the far lands.

FOURTEENTH READING
THE MONTH OF JULY - HOT

In these days vegetable patches give all their blessings and slowly, slowly the roots start to dry out. There is nothing left from the cucumber except *shlanka* for the seeds of next year. There are some of the people who give their crops for the harvesters with the combine, and they collect the crop with gunny sacks, and they carry it to the house or to the market for sale. And there are others who give their crops for harvesters who use sickles, and they collect the it with hooks, and they bring it with *shakre* to threshing floor. And they crush it with *garigra* and they winnow it. The straw is carried to the house in the *khararat* for food for the animals and also for baking. Each home had its own threshing floor. No one was able to carry his crops to his house until after the appraisal of the tax collector, and he gave him a bill which obliged him to pay money to the government as soon as possible. With the appraiser and the tax collector come hundreds of poor people, whether from the village itself or from outside, and each one of them is carrying sacks and each owner of a threshing floor gives one or two handfuls of wheat or barley or lentils for those needy ones. In these days people would bring from mountain fruits, like grapes or figs, and trade them for wheat or barley. In this month carobs would dry out, and they became *bajinjeh.* And many small children would fill their bags with them. And they took them to the street of the village and sold them by the bowl. In this month there was nobody who was not working. And there was nobody who was not earning. And life was so sweet. And people forgot the heat and the hot wind of July.

FIFTEENTH READING

THE MONTH OF AUGUST

THE FEAST OF THE TRANSFIGURATION

On the sixth of this month the feast of the Transfiguration occurs. And on it people say the summer is going to end and the cool days are coming. On the fifteenth of this month the feast of the Assumption of the Lady Mary-soul and body to heaven-occurs. Some of the faithful fast nine days before the feast. They do not eat meat and dairy products. But into their bread they put suffra, which is made of roasted melon seeds and roasted garbanzo beans crushed together with sumac, mulberry, or sugar. People prepare for construction. Those who are stone cutters go out to work in their stone or marble quarries. From the stone quarry they cut huge pieces of rock with the pickaxe. Then they put a piece of iron (i.e., an iron wedge) in a small opening in the middle of the rock, and they split it. But when the rock resists then they blast (lit., "hit") with dynamite. They make a deep hole in the middle and they fill it with dynamite, and they place a fuse, and the dynamite shatters the rocks, and the stonecutters start to cut the rock into small pieces. And they would bring a donkey, and they put a rock carrier on his back. And they would stack the broken rocks on thc carrier. And they carried them to the village for construction. And from the limestone quarry they would break fardatba into small pieces and take them to a furnace to bake them. There were some clever people whose job was constructing furnaces. They would dig a wide ditch in the ground and build a small room on the ground out of bricks and cover the furnace from the top. They would leave some holes so that the smoke would escape through them. They stacked the small pieces of limestone around and on the top of the furnace. They would light the furnace and start to feed (the fire), throwing the straw of the grain, for a period of three days and three nights without stopping until all the limestone is baked. They waited two days until the furnace cools and became cold. After that they carried the baked pieces of limestone to the village. They put them over the stone mill, and then a mule goes around, pulling behind him a stone wheel which is a wheel of granite stone. After they crushed the limestone they took it to one side and then sifted it and took out of it the powder of the limestone for building. They put it in a *zabeera* (and carried it) to a *zabul*, and they brought it to the house (that is to be built). The people of the house who have prepared to build would bring the mason, and with him rock handler who gives him the rocks. With him also are mortar mixers. And the house owners would invite neighbors and friends to eat barley soup with meat, and they would ask them to help them free of charge, especially those who relay the mortar. People of villages would build rooms in the house, and a living room, and a porch. And they would open windows and holes in the room. And from inside they would build a loft, and in the back of the loft they would build a closet or a store room. Underneath the loft they would leave a basement for animals, and those who had money would put marble on the floor of the porch to make a court. And some rich people would have (separate) rooms for people and the crops and rooms for animals. But those who are poor people had one loft, and all the household would sleep up there, and from the same stairs which people use, animals also would enter to descend to the basement to be tied to their own manger. And between the door of the loft and the outer gate, or outer door, there was a courtyard. And in it there was a tanureh for making bread and a paya for baking.

SIXTEENTH READING

THE MONTH OF THE CROSS

In the beginning of the month of September the weather cools, and people come down from the roof, fearful of the rain showers. And the children prepared straw, candles, and *muchekiatha* (like a small *manq̱al)* and sticks for the campfire on the day of the Saturday of the Feast of the Cross. Every day they carried *a̱inabba* through the streets. Each one of the young boys carried with him a *taptapa.* They stacked cow chips over it, and they put straw or gas over that. And all the little kids of the area gathered, and then they lit the cow chips of the *a̱inabba.* The young man stood, and the people applauded, and they went around in the alleys until the fire of their *taptapa* is extinguished. And they will not be satisfied until they went to other kids who had a *a̱inabba.* When the Feast of the Cross approached, the roofs of the village would be so brightened with the fire of *muchekiatha,* the ones which were made of red mud, like small bowls filled with sheep droppings or burning wood.

All Chaldeans remember the Feast of the Cross, the fourteenth of September, the day in which St. Helena, the mother of King Constantine, in the year of the Our Lord 321, gave money to the workers. They dug around the mountain of Calvary in Jerusalem, and they discovered the living (true) Cross. On it Our Lord was crucified. Because of the joy of Christians, they lit a fire at that time. And the good news spread all over the eastern countries. And this custom was used in all Christian countries (in the Middle East) until today.

SEVENTEENTH READING

THE MONTH OF SEPTEMBER - SUPPLIES

In the month of September the Chaldeans of Nineveh prepare supplies for all year. Farmers have three seasons of planting. Some plant in summer, from the month of August until September. Others plant when the first rain comes in the Fall. And still others plant when the flow flows, from Christmas until the month of February. In these times people plant grain and barley. But they plant lentils and fava beans at the time of the flow. Garbanzo beans are planted in the month of April. Melon and cucumbers in March. People planted two kinds of barley: the white kind and the other, black. The black they have nicknamed "local." The *karoniya* grain—they make out of them yellow *gurgur.* The *khamrik* kind of grain (is used) for white *gurgur.* Italian grain (is used) only *for puqota* (pearled barley). Almania grain and *ketchla* (are used) for bread and noodles. Chaldeans of Nineveh are very skilled in making *gurgur.* The people of the house bring home the grains, and they pick the small rocks out of them, and they boil them in big pot, and they dry them on the roof. Then after that they take them to the stone mill to be hulled. After they finish hulling them, they carry them to the house. And they put them in a hand mill or machine (i.e., to crack the grain), and then they sift them, and they make out of the: (a) *gursa reshaya,* (b) *palgaya* (medium), (c) *qtaa-wublaa* ("cut and swallow"). And (concerning) those who prepare *puqota:* The people of the house bring grain, and they pick the rocks from them again. And they take them to the stone mill, and they remove the shell from them, and they put them in gunny sacks and bring them to the house by gunny sacks. And they take from them with a sifter: (a) *puqota,* (b) *mbarghal,* (c) *gursa* (the grade) below *puqota,* for *kubaibeh.* On these days all the members of the family work: ladies picking out (the rocks) and boiling (the grain), and with them (are) all the girls and small children; and the men: carrying (grain) with gunny sacks to the stone mill. And some of them sift, and others sift finely, and some others built a big pot from clay to put provisions in for all year. With the preparation of the provisions, people also stored salt and peppers, onions, olives, date syrup, and grape syrup for all year. Many of the Chaldeans from Nineveh not only prepare provisions for themselves but also for their relatives in Mosul, Baghdad, and other villages far away. And in the years of the last quarter of the twentieth century, people sold provisions to merchants, and they carried them to all the villages of Mesopotamia, and from there to other nearby countries, especially after they start hulling (in) the mill with electricity. In September schools begins (lit., enters), and little children in the first half of the twentieth century wore clothes: *shoqta* (a garment like a shirt reaching to the feet) and sweaters made at home on the loom, which the people of the house used to operate. But after that clothes started to be bought from the market. Ladies rested from spinning wool thread with the spindle, and also from spinning cotton thread in the spinning wheel, and from the weaving wheel to prepare the spool for weaving. And men forgot the subject of preparing thread for weaving in the yard. And they rested their legs and their hands and their ears from the noise of the beam, the shuttle, and the weaving with the loom.

EIGHTEENTH READING

OCTOBER

In these days the plain of the villages of Ninveh is filled with many kinds (lit., "from kinds and kinds") of birds: skylarks, finches, starlings, hedge sparrows, and then the mountain birds: quail, wild pigeons, and doves. Fowlers who wait for this time take their traps out of the crawlspace. And (for) the traps which are old and are useless, they throw them away, and they buy instead of those other, new (traps). Every fowler looks at the traps one by one. He puts them around the trap tester. And he prepares the wooden catch from strong wood, and the peg to be hit into the ground, and the thread of cotton, and then moist, new grain. And then he makes a hole in them, and he put the thread in those grains which are prepared for the trap. The fowler of the villages of Nineveh gets up from early morning, before the bird wakes. When he reaches the field, the hatchet with him, he makes a place for the trap and covers it, and he doesn't allow (anything) to be seen except for the grain. And then he smoothes it with dust around the grain. And he places three clods of dirt: one on the right side, another on the left, and the other on the head of the trap. Then the fowler waits for the light of the sky. When the flock of birds starts moving, he begins praying so maybe they will land on the ground where his traps are. And sometimes he himself chases them from neighboring places to move them toward his traps. There were some fowlers who used to trap between ten and fifty quails or wild pigeons or doves in one day. And some used to catch between one hundred to two hundred skylarks or finches or starlings. And some of the fowlers used to take with them skewers and barbecued in the field. In the evening when the fowlers returned, their own little children welcomed them to take from them starlings, and they held (the starlings) by their wings and made them sing. And when the fowler entered the house, all the people of the household came around him to pluck the birds and to barbecue or fry (them), and put the birds' heads over the charcoal in the *manqal* or in the hot dish with *gurgur* or pearled barley. They sold the feathers to people, and those (people) put them in their pillows. They cleaned skylarks, or the rest of the birds, and sold them in the morning in the market. Not only fowlers caught birds, but also some people who had hounds would go to the field searching for rabbits and deer for their meat, and foxes for their skin. And on foggy days (lit., "in the day of fog") some people searched around the telephone wires of the water, and they caught the birds with the broken wings. And there were some others who went catching fish in the places which have water, especially in the Tigris River or in the place called *bene dawaya* or in the One and Ten River or in the other rivers around the villages of the Chaldeans of Nineveh.

NINETEENTH READING

BLESSING IN THE HOUSE

There was no house in the villages of Nineveh in which they did not have either one cow or more. From the early morning they sent the cow to the cattle area. In the evening it came back, alone and loaded with milk. They milked it and warmed its milk, and when they poured the cooking pot, the small children they fought over the milk residue. They put yeast in the milk, and the next day it would become yogurt. Or they produced cheese from the milk. And the curds of the yogurt were kept only for the workers of the household (who were) greater in age. And they produced from the yogurt, after shaking it, butter for cooking and *mayana* (liquid) or *kishya* (thick) or *khamusa* (sour). The yogurt of autumn was more delicious than all year around because those who make yogurt in the summer produced *khamusa,* and in the winter they produced *mayana,* but in the fall the weather was not hot and not cold. The yogurt leavened well, and they said, "From the yogurt of the fall, a sister does not feed her sister with it" (i.e., because it is so good). Some people in the villages of Nineveh kept sheep, and from the milk of the sheep also they make yogurt or cheese. And many in these days kept cattle for slaughter-either lambs or calves-and they slaughtered them the week of Christmas or Easter. Before electricity entered the villages, some people slaughtered those kept animals: calves or bulls or lambs. They brought water, and they put in it salt, and to know that there is enough salt they floated an egg in the salt water. If it floated, they poured the salt water in the crock, and they put in it pieces of meat. And they covered the mouth of that crock or pot. And they buried it in a cold place in the basements. And they also did it this way when they wanted to keep cheese and olives for all year. From those they ate all winter.

TWENTIETH READING
NOVEMBER

Strong wind and cold strike from all sides in this month. The makers of tahini prepare their mills. They bought sesame from the mountain (north). They soak them, and then hull them in the stone wheel. They took off their shell with another tool called *makhidhranuneh.* And then they winnowed them and spread them out to dry. Then they fried them and threw them in the mill. And they made tahini from them. There was no area without one or two mills. Neighbors and strangers carried their own pans with them to buy *waqiyat* of tahini. Some also bought *kuspa* or *shireq* for cooking and frying instead of oil. Tahini and date syrup or grape syrup, these were the daily food for many poor people. Dates and raisins in these days were very available in the villages of Nineveh. Many people not only ate dates and raisins but also heated them and squeezed them and made *araq,* wine, and vinegar from them. The odor of pure *araq* with *mistakkeh* spread in the alleys of the village. Weak *araq* which does make people drunk and does not make the head dizzy-they made it out of dates. But the dry and strong *araq* which makes people dizzy and hot is delicious. They made it out of grapes. This is how they made distilled *araq* in the house: They brought dates or raisins and they put them in a large pot filled with water. They waited forty days, but every week one of the household came and stirred and mixed the moist raisins with a large wooden spoon. At the end of forty days they moved the raisins to the other large pot. They put a cover on this pot and sealed it with mud on all sides. And they left a place for a reed made into a long tube which goes to another pot. They burned fire under the pot which had moistened dates or raisins. And the vapor which came out from the first pot went through the tube and started to drip droplets in the second, cold pot. And before they put fire under the first pot they put in it *sparigleh* and *mistakkeh* and apples, and the meat of the rooster or the hen. All these things they moistened together in the pot and the good smell of *araq* made the workers forget their hard work and effort and the work of fifty days. A long time ago, when there was a wedding in the family, the *araq* was very abundant, and it was put in small, wide ceramic jars or water vases or in the pot. And everybody from the relatives or the friends was able to drink or to fill a bottle or have a bottle or a flask. And when they paraded in the village, and when the wedding party passed before the house of the friends, the people of that house stood before the door and they offered a flask, first for the groom and the bride and then the people of the parade, young and old. Chaldeans of the villages of Nineveh mixed a life of faith with every day life. In every time of the month of the year they had customs, feasts, and festivals, which made life so beautiful and a joy in this world, along with their faith in Christ the Son of God—who is the Way, the Truth, and the Life—and their honor to his mother the Virgin Mary and the martyrs and saints. They kept the teaching of the Chaldean fathers and teachers of the Catholic Church. All these made them enjoy this world while they were awaiting the joy which never ends in the world to come, in the heavenly kingdom. Amen.

THE END OF THE TWENTY READINGS

By Fr. Michael J. Bazzi and Jimmy Akin. 2003

A PROCESSION GREETING THE BABYLONIAN NEW YEAR ON THE FIRST OF APRIL
IN FRONT OF THE GATE OF ISHTAR – IN MESOPOTAMIA

Acknowledgments

This book has come about through the initiative of Cuyamaca College, in El Cajon, California and the generous assistance of my students and parishioners. I am very grateful to Cuyamaca College for offering a three semester Aramaic language course. Due to this initiative, this book is to be used in the second semester.
The Aramaic Language Chaldean Dialogue Read, writes, and speaks Modern Aramaic: Chaldean dialect to be used in the first semester. And my textbook dedicated to Classical Aramaic, for use in the third semester, Classical Aramaic Elementary book 1 by Michael J. Bazzi / Racco A. Errico, 1989.

Many Chaldean students from the first semester and various parishioners, working in teams, have made this book possible. The first semester is offered twice: three of my students who finished three semesters, and also being my parishioners, generously volunteered to type my hand written materials for the twenty lessons of this book in both Aramaic and English and in Arabic. The members of this team were: Mrs. Christine Alkass, Mrs. Adeeba Alnajar, and Mrs. Suham D. Shamoon. Working extremely hard for four hours per day from May 2001 to November 2001, these generous volunteers prepared the first draft of this book for editing.

The second team was composed of Deacons from St. Peter Chaldean Catholic Church in El Cajon, California, who were students of my weekly liturgical classes. This team contributed useful suggestions to the Aramaic text based on their extensive knowledge of the Aramaic language. I am very grateful to the members of this team for their valuable contribution; Mr. Maolood Yaldo, Mr. Louis Attiq, Mr. Karim Attiq and Mr. Salam Betty.

The third team working in parallel with the second team reviewed the English portions of this book. This team consisted of two young parishioners: Mr. Zane Tominna, an attorney by profession who was also one of my first semester students in Fall 2001, headed this team and was assisted by Mr. Tom Alsaigh, a senior high school student. Given their fluency in English, these young men helped to re-shape both the lessons and the English portions of the glossaries included in this book, dedicating a large part of their free time to this project.

The fourth team provided the crucial task of ensuring consistency between the Aramaic and English portions of this book. This team consisted of Mrs. Wasan Jarbo and the parish secretary Mrs. Christine Dawisha. Wasan generously gave her free time to review the lessons in great detail, ensuring that the vocabulary lists and glossaries were complete. Her proficiency with the program used to document the text and her knowledge of English and Aramaic was extremely helpful. Christine greatly assisted in the formatting and presentation of this book.

Great help was also provided from a dear friend, Msgr. John B. Dewane, Vicar for priests in Green Bay, Wisconsin. He very kindly reviewed the English portion of this book providing a purely American point of view, thus making this book more accessible to a broader audience.

For the second edition Editor, Format, Layout, Outline, and Review: Kheloud Issa Allos. Thanks to Mr. Garvin Garmo for his effort of converting the entire text from MLS application to Microsoft Office Word.

I am extremely grateful to all of volunteers who have given so generously of their time. Thanks to their efforts, this book was completed in just eight months. This book is a great resource for both students of the second semester of the Aramaic language course at Cuyamaca College and for those who wish to study, independently, the correct usage of the Modern Aramaic Chaldean dialect
May God bless all who have assisted in this project and all who will benefit from it.

Fr. Michael J. Bazzi

BIBLIOGRAPHY

1- Aprem, Dr. M.H.G., Teach yourself Aramaic, Kerala, India, Mar Narsai press, Trichur, India, 1981.

2- Arayathina;, Rev. Thomas, M.O.L. Aramaic Grammar. St. Joseph's, press, Mannanam, India, 1959.

3- Audo, Archbishop Thomas, Vernaculat Assyrian grammar, Assyrian language and culture classes incorporated, Chicago, 1911.

4- Bazzi, Fr. Michael, Beginner's Handbook of the Aramaic Chaldean Alphabet. St. Peter Chaldean Catholic Church, San Diego, 1992

5- Bazzi & Errico, Classical Aramaic elementary Book 1, Noohra Foundation, 1989.

6- Gabriel, Fr. of St. Joseph T.O.C.D. , Syro - Chaldaic grammar, St. Joseph's press , Mannanam, India, 1984.

7- Macdasaya, Abba Eramia, Grammar , Domenican press, Mosul, 1889.

8- Maclean, Artur John, Grammar of the Dialect of Vernacular Syriac, Phillo press, Amesterdam, 1971.

9- Noldeke, Theodore, Compendious Syriac grammar, William & Noragate, London, 1904.

10- Rhetore, P.J. , Grammaire de la langue soureth ou Chaldean vulgaire, Peres Domenicans, Mossoul, 1912.

How To Write The Aramaic Alphabet

The lines below show both the shape and thc size of the letters relative to each other. The two tables at the bottom of the page specify the levels to which the letters go above and below the base line (level zero). They group together letters of a given level. The first table groups together letters which do not go below the base line, the second table groups together those which do. The numbers in the far left column of the tables specify the levels of the letters relative to the base line.

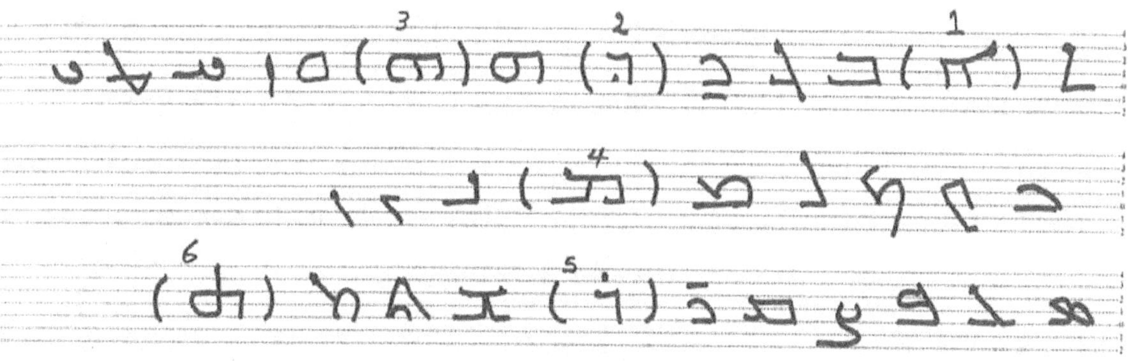

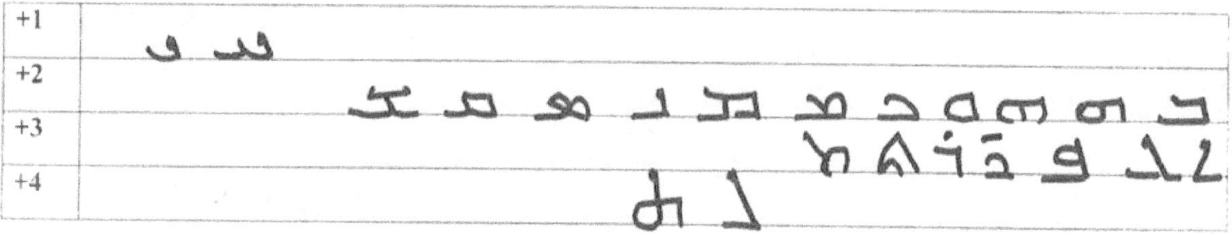

+2, -1	
+3, -1	
0, -2	
+1, -2	
+2, -2	
+3, -2	

THE LORD'S PRAYER IN SCHOLASTIC ARAMAIC

The Lord's Prayer in Estrangela Script in Scholastic Aramaic

ܨܠܘܬܐ ܡܪܢܝܬܐ

ܐܒܘܢ ܕܒܫܡܝܐ. ܢܬܩܕܫ ܫܡܟ. ܬܐܬܐ ܡܠܟܘܬܟ. ܢܗܘܐ ܨܒܝܢܟ.
ܐܝܟܢܐ ܕܒܫܡܝܐ ܐܦ ܒܐܪܥܐ. ܗܒ ܠܢ ܠܚܡܐ ܕܣܘܢܩܢܢ ܝܘܡܢܐ.
ܘܫܒܘܩ ܠܢ ܚܘܒܝܢ ܘܚܛܗܝܢ. ܐܝܟܢܐ ܕܐܦ ܚܢܢ ܫܒܩܢ ܠܚܝܒܝܢ.
ܘܠܐ ܬܥܠܢ ܠܢܣܝܘܢܐ. ܐܠܐ ܦܨܢ ܡܢ ܒܝܫܐ. ܡܛܠ ܕܕܝܠܟ ܗܝ
ܡܠܟܘܬܐ. ܘܚܝܠܐ ܘܬܫܒܘܚܬܐ ܠܥܠܡ ܥܠܡܝܢ ܐܡܝܢ.

The Lord's Prayer in Common writing in Scholastic Aramaic

ܨܠܘܬܐ ܡܪܢܝܬܐ

ܐܒܘܢ ܕܒܫܡܝܐ. ܢܬܩܕܫ ܫܡܟ. ܬܐܬܐ ܡܠܟܘܬܟ. ܢܗܘܐ ܨܒܝܢܟ. ܐܝܟܢܐ ܕܒܫܡܝܐ ܐܦ ܒܐܪܥܐ. ܗܒ ܠܢ ܠܚܡܐ ܕܣܘܢܩܢܢ ܝܘܡܢܐ ܘܫܒܘܩ ܠܢ ܚܘܒܝܢ ܘܚܛܗܝܢ. ܐܝܟܢܐ ܕܐܦ ܚܢܢ ܫܒܩܢ ܠܚܝܒܝܢ. ܘܠܐ ܬܥܠܢ ܠܢܣܝܘܢܐ. ܐܠܐ ܦܨܢ ܡܢ ܒܝܫܐ. ܡܛܠ ܕܕܝܠܟ ܗܝ ܡܠܟܘܬܐ. ܘܚܝܠܐ ܘܬܫܒܘܚܬܐ ܠܥܠܡ ܥܠܡܝܢ ܐܡܝܢ.

The Lord's Prayer in Common writing In Modern Aramaic – Chaldean

ܨܠܘܬܐ ܡܪܢܝܬܐ

ܒܒܢ ܕܐܝܬܠܟ ܒܫܡܝܐ. ܦܝܫ ܡܩܘܕܫܐ ܫܡܘܟ. ܐܬܝܐ ܡܠܟܘܬܘܟ. ܗܘܐ ܨܒܝܢܘܟ. ܕܐܟܡ ܕܐܝܬܠܟ ܒܫܡܝܐ ܗܕܟܡ ܒܐܪܥܐ. ܗܒ ܠܢ ܠܚܡܐ ܕܣܘܢܩܢܢ ܕܝܘܡܐ. ܘܫܒܘܩ ܠܢ ܚܘܒܝ ܘܚܛܗܝ. ܕܐܟܡ ܕܐܘܦ ܐܚܢܢ ܫܒܩܠܢ ܠܐܢܝ ܕܚܛܝܠܗܘܢ ܠܢ. ܘܠܐ ܡܥܒܪܬܠܢ ܒܢܣܝܘܢܐ ܐܠܐ ܡܦܠܛܠܢ ܡܢ ܒܝܫܐ. ܡܛܠ ܕܝܠܘܟ ܝܠܗ ܡܠܟܘܬܐ. ܘܚܝܠܐ ܘܬܫܒܘܚܬܐ ܠܥܠܡ ܥܠܡܝܢ ܐܡܝܢ.

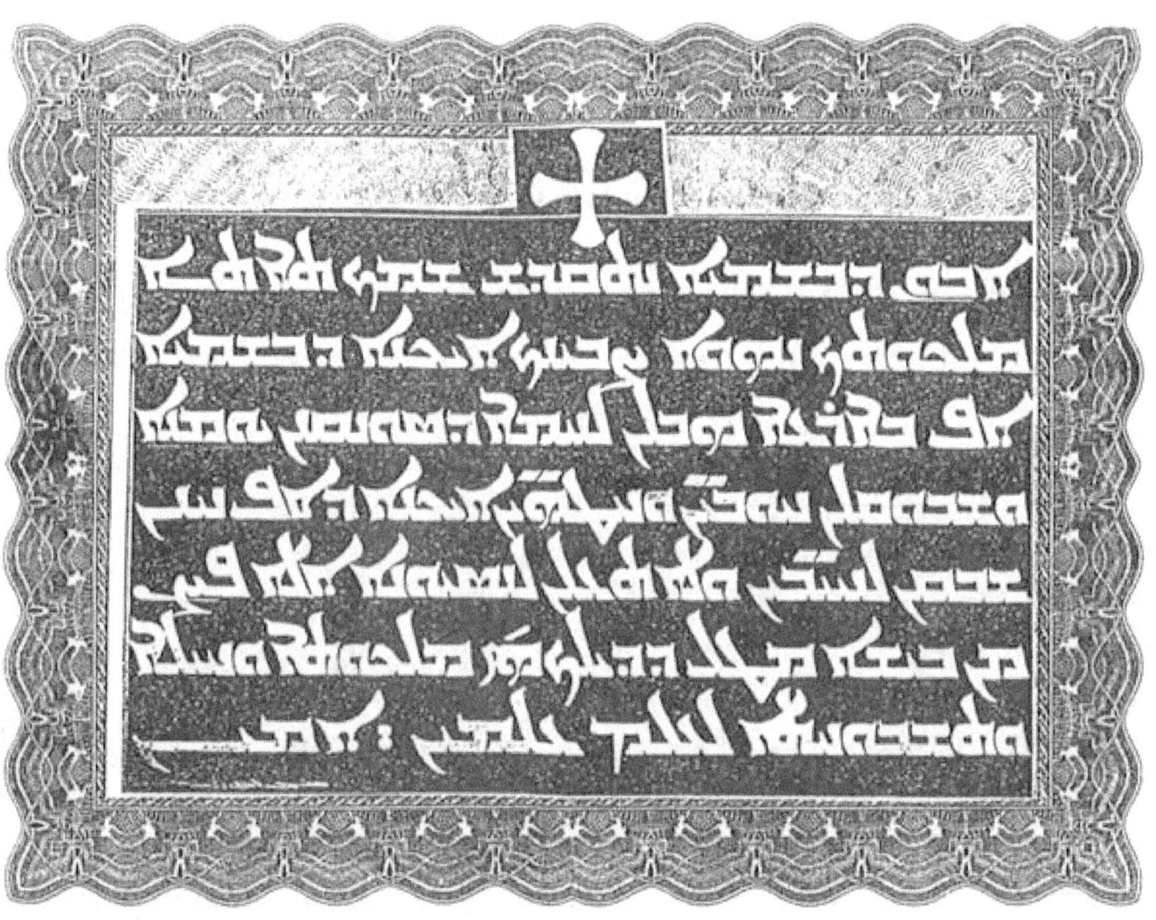

THE HAIL MARY IN CLASSICAL ARAMAIC

ܫܠܡܠܟܝ ܡܪܝܡ

ܫܠܡ ܠܟܝ ܡܪܝܡ ܡܠܝܬ ܛܝܒܘܬܐ. ܡܪܢ ܥܡܟܝ ܒܪܝܟܬܝ ܒܢܫ̈ܐ ܘܡܒܪܟ ܗܘ ܦܐܪܐ ܕܒܟܪܣܟܝ ܝܫܘܥ. ܡܪܬܝ ܡܪܝܡ ܝܠܕܬ ܐܠܗܐ ܨܠܝ ܚܠܦܝܢ ܚܛܝ̈ܐ. ܗܫܐ ܘܒܫܥܬ ܡܘܬܢ ܐܡܝܢ.

THE HAIL MARY IN MODERN ARAMAIC

ܫܠܡܐ ܐܠܟܝ ܡܪܝܡ ܡܠܝܬܐ ܛܝܒܘܬܐ. ܡܪܢ ܐܝܡܟܝ ܡܒܘܪܟܬܐ ܝܘܬ ܒܝܢܬ ܢܫ̈ܐ. ܘܡܒܘܪܟܐ ܝܠܗ ܦܐܪܐ ܕܟܪܣܟܝ ܝܫܘܥ. ܡܪܬܝ ܡܪܝܡ ܝܡܐ ܕܐܠܗܐ ܡܨܠܝܐ ܡܚܠܦܢ ܐܢܚ ܚܛܝ̈ܐ. ܕܗܐ ܘܒܫܥܬܐ ܕܡܘܬܢ ܐܡܝܢ.

ܝܐ ܩܠܐ ܚܕܬܐ ܕܐܬܬܘܣܦ ܕܠܫܢܐ ܐܪܡܝܐ

11 صوتا زيادة على حروف اللغة الآرامية

THE 11ADDITIONAL SOUNDS OF THE ARAMAIC LANGUAGE

ENGLISH	ROMANIZATION	ARABIC	ESTRNGELA	SMALL LETTER	11 SOUNDS
w	WEH	و		ܒ݂	ܒ݂ܶ
gh	GHEH	غ		ܓ݂	ܓ݂ܶ
gdth	DTHEH	ذ	ܕ݂	ܕ݂	ܕ݂ܶ
dkh	KHEH	خ		ܟ݂ ܟ݂	ܟ݂ܶ
hw	WEH	و		ܘ݂	ܘ݂ܶ
wth	THEH	ث	ܬ݂	ܬ݂	ܬ݂ܶ

ENGLISH	ROMANIZATION	ARABIC	ESTRNGELA	SMALL LETTER	11 SOUNDS
f	FEH	ف		ܦ	ܦܶ
ch	CHEH	چ		ܟ̰ ܟ̰	ܟ̰ܶ
tdh	TDHEH	ض		ܨ݂	ܨ݂ܶ
j	JEH	ج		ܓ̰	ܓ̰ܶ
v	VEH	ف		ܦ̮	ܦ̮ܶ

ܐܬܘܬܐ ܕܠܫܢܐ ܐܪܡܝܐ ܥܬܝܩܐ ܘܚܕܬܐ

حروف اللغة الآرامية القديمة والحديثة { الكلدانية - سورث}

THE CLASSICAL – MODERN ARAMAIC ALPHABET

ENGLISH	ROMANIZATION	NUMBER	ARABIC	ESTRNANGELA	SMALL LETTER	22 LETTERS
a	ALAP	1	ا	ܐ	ܐ	ܐܠܦ
b	BETH	2	ب		ܒ	ܒܝܬ
g	GAMAL	3	گ		ܓ	ܓܡܠ
d	DALATH	4	د	ܕ	ܕ	ܕܠܬ
h	HE	5	ه	ܗ	ܗ	ܗܐ
w	WOW	6	و		ܘ	ܘܐܘ
z	ZAYN	7	ز		ܙ	ܙܝܢ
h	HETH	8	ح		ܚ	ܚܝܬ
t	TETH	9	ط		ܛ	ܛܝܬ
y	YOD	10	ى		ܝ	ܝܘܕ
k	KAP W KAP	20	ك		ܟ ܟ	ܟܦ ܘܟܦ
l	LAMADH	30	ل		ܠ	ܠܡܕ
m	MEEM W MEEM	40	م	ܡ ܡ	ܡ ܡ	ܡܝܡ ܘܡܝܡ
n	NOON W NOON	50	ن		ܢ ܢ	ܢܘܢ ܘܢܘܢ
s	SIMKATH	60	س		ܣ	ܣܡܟܬ
a	AE	70	ع		ܥ	ܥܐ
p	PEH	80	پ		ܦ	ܦܐ
s	SADE	90	ص		ܨ	ܨܕܐ
q	KQOP	100	ق		ܩ	ܩܘܦ
r	RESH	200	ر	ܪ	ܪ	ܪܝܫ
sh	SHEEN	300	ش		ܫ	ܫܝܢ
t	TAW W TAW	400	ت	ܬ	ܬ	ܬܘ ܘܬܘ

SEMITIC LANGUAGES

	ARABIC	ARAMAIC SQUARE CHARACTERS (HEBREW)	SYRIAC SMALL LETTERS	MODERN ARAMAIC (CHALDEAN)		
				ESTRANGELA	CHALDEAN SMALL LETTERS	
	ا	א	ܐ	ܐ	ܐ	1
	ب	ב	ܒ	ܒ	ܒ	2
	ك	ג	ܓ	ܓ	ܓ	3
	د	ד	ܕ	ܕ	ܕ	4
	ه	ה	ܗ	ܗ	ܗ	5
	و	ו	ܘ	ܘ	ܘ	6
	ز	ז	ܙ	ܙ	ܙ	7
	ح	ח	ܚ	ܚ	ܚ	8
	ط	ט	ܛ	ܛ	ܛ	9
	ى	י	ܝ	ܝ	ܝ	10
	ك	כ ך	ܟ	ܟ ܟ	ܟ ܟ	20
	ل	ך	ܠ	ܠ	ܠ	30
	م	ל מ	ܡ	ܡ	ܡ	40
	ن	ם	ܢ	ܢ	ܢ	50
	س	נ	ܣ	ܣ	ܣ	60
	ع	ף ן	ܥ	ܥ	ܥ	70
ث	پ	צ	ܦ	ܦ	ܦ	80
خ	ص	ץ	ܨ	ܨ	ܨ	90
ذ	ق	ק	ܩ	ܩ	ܩ	100
غ	ر	ר	ܪ	ܪ	ܪ	200
ض	ش	ש	ܫ	ܫ	ܫ	300
ظ	ت	ת	ܬ	ܬ	ܬ	400

About the Author

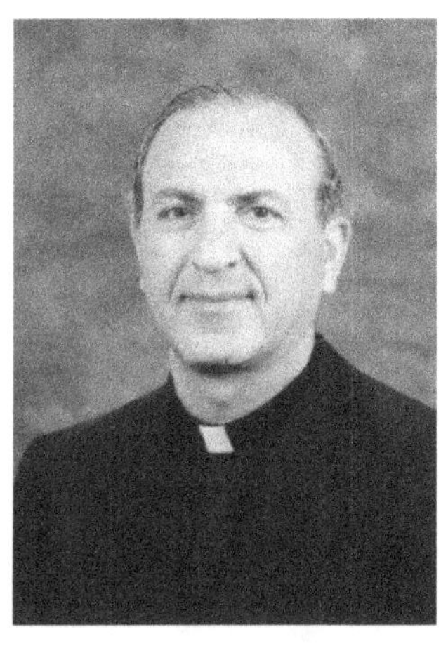

Fr. Michael J. Bazzi, Pastor - Fr. Michael J. Bazzi, born in Tilkepe, Iraq in 1938 and ordained a Chaldean Catholic priest in Baghdad 1964. From 1964 to 1972, he served in Tilkepe as an assistant pastor and youth director. In 1969 he published a book in Arabic titled *Tilkepe: Present and Past.* In 1972, he received a scholarship for further study in Rome. He studied for two years in the Lateran University and received a master's degree in pastoral theology and two diplomas, one in mass media and the other in group dynamics.

Arriving in the United States on June 20, 1974, he taught Scripture for five years in Oshkosh, Wisconsin and throughout Green bay Diocese. He published there two books in English, *The Pentateuch* (1976) and *Matthew's Good News* (1978). From Wisconsin he moved to Michigan, where in 1979 he established Mar Addai Chaldean Catholic Church in Oak Park. Then, in 1981, he established St. Joseph parish in Troy, Michigan. In 1983 he moved to Los Angeles, where he served as pastor of St. Paul parish in Montrose. On Sept. 1, 1985, he moved to San Diego and became assistant pastor at St. Peter parish. He became its pastor after the death of Fr. Kattoula in 1987.

He has taught the Aramaic language at Cuyamaca College since 1989. During this time he published several introductory textbooks on modern and classical Aramaic. He also published a guidebook, *Chaldeans: Present and Past,* and an edition of the Divine Liturgy with parallel Aramaic, Arabic, and English columns. He also has established youth and adult Bible study groups and directed Saturday catechism classes for more than 600 students a year. In Oct. 2012 he published "Know your faith in the year of faith" in Arabic and English.

This book is an addition to four other publications about the Aramaic-Chaldean dialect:

- Classical Aramaic Elementary Book 1 by Michael J, Bazzi/Racco A. Errico, 1989
- The Beginner's Handbook of the Aramaic Alphabet, Volume I, 1992
- The Advanced Handbook of the Modern Aramaic, Volume II, 2002
- Beginner Chaldean Dialogue Book, 2012

❖❖❖❖❖❖❖❖❖❖❖

www.ingramcontent.com/pod-product-compliance
Lightning Source LLC
Chambersburg PA
CBHW080806300426
44114CB00020B/2853
9781941464007